FRANCE TODAY

eighth edition

EDITED BY J. E. FLOWER

Hodder & Stoughton

A MEMBER OF THE HODDER HEADLINE GROUP

ACKNOWLEDGEMENTS

The authors and publishers would like to thank the following copyright holders for their permission to reproduce illustrative material in this book:

Le Monde Dossiers et Documents (map, p. 3); Topham Picturepoint (photo, p. 57 P. Dejong/Associated Press; photo, p. 117 Associated Press; photo, p. 142 © Chapman Parry; photo, p. 195); Plantu (cartoons, pp. 63, 108, 109 and 180); Steve Mccurry/National Geographic Society (photo, p. 129); Serguei (cartoon, p. 174); Arte (photo, p. 231); La Cinquième/DDB Les Arts/Patrick Jacob (advert, p. 231); Presses Universitaires du Septentrion (Table 6.1, p. 144, and Table 6.2, p. 145); Organisation for Economic Cooperation and Development (Table 6.3, p. 148); Ministère de l'Education nationale, de l'Enseignement supérieur et de la Recherche (Table 6.4, p. 155).

Every effort has been made to obtain necessary permission with reference to copyright material. The publishers apologise if inadvertently any sources remain unacknowledged and will be glad to make suitable arrangements at the earliest opportunity.

British Library Cataloguing in Publication Data
A catalogue record for this title is available from The British Library

ISBN 0 340 63093 0

First published 1997
Impression number   10   9   8   7   6   5   4   3   2   1
Year   2002   2001   2000   1999   1998   1997

Selection and Editorial Material Copyright © 1997 by Professor J. E. Flower
Individual Contributions Copyright © 1997 the Contributors

Typeset by Wearset, Boldon, Tyne and Wear.
Printed in Great Britain for Hodder & Stoughton Educational, a division of Hodder Headline Plc, 338 Euston Road, London NW1 3BH by Scotprint Ltd, Musselburgh, Scotland.

CONTENTS

CONTRIBUTORS

ALAN CLARK, B.A., Ph.D., Senior Lecturer in French, University of Canterbury, Christchurch, New Zealand. Main interests: French intellectual, social and political history of the twentieth century; ideas and policy of Mitterrand and the French left; French foreign policy; the political history of New Caledonia. Publications include *La France dans l'histoire selon Bernanos* (Lettres Modernes), an edition of Valéry Giscard d'Estaing's *Démocratie française* (Methuen/ Routledge), an *Anthologie Mitterrand* (Methuen/Routledge), and numerous articles on French foreign and Pacific policy.

RAY DAVISON, B.A., M.Phil., Lecturer in French Studies at the University of Exeter. Main interests: modern French literature and thought. Publications include critical editions of Camus's *L'Etranger* (Methuen/Routledge), Simone de Beauvoir's *Une Mort très douce* (Methuen/Routledge), a contribution to *The Second World War in Fiction* (Macmillan) and a chapter on the French press in *France Today* (previous editions). He has also written on Camus, Dostoevsky and Sartre and made a number of tapes for Drake Educational Tapes on Sartre, Gide and Camus. His full-length study on Camus and Dostoevsky will shortly be published by the University of Exeter Press.

ROGER DUCLAUD-WILLIAMS, B.A., Ph.D., Lecturer in the Department of Politics and International Studies at the University of Warwick. Publications include *Politics of Housing in Britain and France* (Heinemann), and more recently articles on various aspects of French educational policy-making in *The British Journal of Political Science*, *Western European Politics* and *The European Journal of Political Research*.

BRIAN FITZPATRICK, M.A., Ph.D., Senior Lecturer in Modern European History in the University of Ulster at Jordanstown. Main interests: nineteenth-century conservative and counter-revolutionary groups in France and Spain. Publications include *Catholic Royalism in the Department of the Gard, 1814–1852* (Cambridge), 'L'Ultra-realisme francès del Midi i les seves contradiccions internes' in J. M. Fradera and R. Garrabou, eds, *Carlisme i Moviments absolutistes* (Estudis Universitaris, Vic, Catalunya), 'Ultraroyalism and Legitimism in the French Midi' in J. Agirreazkuenaga and J. R. Urquijo Goitia, eds, *150 Años del Convenio de Bergara y de La Ley del 25-X-1839* (Parlamento Vasco, Vitoria), 'The emergence of Catholic politics in the Midi, 1830–1870' in F. Tallett and N. Atkin, eds, *Religion, Society and Politics in France since 1789* (The Hambledon Press).

JOHN FLOWER, M.A., Ph.D., Chevalier des Palmes académiques, Professor of French, University of Kent at Canterbury. Main interests: French literature, culture and history of ideas from the late nineteenth century to the present. Publications include *Literature and the Left in France since the Late Nineteenth Century* (Macmillan and Methuen), *Provence* and *Lombardy and the Italian Lakes* (George Philip), *François Mauriac: Visions and Reappraisals* (with B. C. Swift) (Berg), *Pierre Courtade: The Making of a Party Scribe* (Berg) and *François Mauriac: Psycholectures/Psychoreadings* (Presses Universitaires d'Exeter et de Bordeaux).

GEOFFREY HARE, B.A., Ph.D., Chevalier des Palmes académiques, Senior Lecturer in French Studies, University of Newcastle-upon-Tyne. Main interests: French broadcasting, political communications and methodology of language teaching. Publications include: *Alphonse Daudet: a Critical Bibliography* (Grant & Cutler), *Parlons Sciences Po* and *Parlons Sciences Po '89* (British Institute in Paris), *Media Studies in France: a Guide to Sources of Information* (with A. Chauveau) (Kingston Polytechnic), *Communicative Approaches in French in Higher Education* (with M. Bate) (AFLS), and *Le français en faculté* (with nine others) (Hodder & Stoughton); contributions to journals *Francophonie*, *French Cultural Studies* and *Modern and Contemporary France*.

RICHARD McALLISTER, M.A., Senior Lecturer in Politics, University of Edinburgh. Main interests: the politics and policies of the European Community/Union: politics of certain west European states, notably France and Germany. Publications include *From EC to EU* (Routledge); the regular Annual Review of the Activities of the EC for *Journal of Common Market Studies* from 1986 to 1993; contributions to several other books including R. Davidson & P. White (eds) *Information and Government* (Edinburgh University Press); articles in *Common Market Law Review*, *Futures*, and *The New Atlantis*.

ANDREE SHEPHERD, Agrégée d'Anglais, Docteur d'Etat ès Lettres et Sciences Sociales, Professor of English, University of Grenoble 3. Main interests: twentieth-century French and English sociology and politics. Publications include a study of the occupation of French factories in May 1968, *Imagination in Power* (Spokesman Books), a translation of Serge Mallet's book *The New Working Class* (Spokesman Books), and contributions to the *Encyclopédie de civilisation britannique* (Larousse), *Littérature anglaise* (Bordas) and

Les enquêtes sociales en Grande Bretagne (L'Harmattan). Currently working on a book on the New Left in Britain and a translation of Karl Polanyi's *The Livelihood of Man*. Also working in *animation culturelle* in the Grenoble area, in connection with the *Maison de la poésie Rhône-Alpes*.

MALCOLM SLATER, M.A., B.Sc. (Econ.), LL.B., Lecturer in French, University of Bradford. Main interests: French foreign policy, European Community politics. Publications include *Contemporary French Politics* (Macmillan), and contributions to *Cahiers de droit européen* and *Revue des Pays de l'est*.

FOREWORD TO THE EIGHTH EDITION

With the end of François Mitterrand's second mandate as President in 1995 a significant era in the history of modern France also came to an end. Although in the election campaign for his successor Lionel Jospin briefly – and surprisingly – threatened to carry the Socialist banner to the Elysée palace once again, the victory ultimately belonged to Jacques Chirac, who thereby satisfied a lifelong ambition. (Whether the result would have been any different had Jacques Delors stood, remains a matter for interesting speculation.) With its landslide victories in the general election in 1993 and now with a President who had unashamedly appealed to the widespread desire for a return to the values exemplified and expressed by de Gaulle, the right found itself in an impregnable position. Faced with this and beset by internal wrangling, the left began to fragment. Successful opposition in the National Assembly to proposals by the new government under Alain Juppé was virtually impossible though, faced by a series of strikes and demonstrations in December 1995, the prime minister was obliged to change his cabinet and to modify some of his strategies. Essentially, however, a policy of austerity drives government planning forward with cuts in the budgets of most major public sector areas and with increased privatization. There have at the same time been moves to remind the rest of the world of France's power and stature, for example nuclear tests in the Pacific which were only curtailed after prolonged international protests or Chirac's efforts to take a leading role in Europe, albeit in the face of his fellow countrymen's increasing uncertainty about the whole venture.

Slightly nearer home and more immediate are problems which had already been emerging over the previous decade. In Corsica, nationalist groups have pursued a policy of terrorism with the aim of obtaining what they consider to be their island's right to greater recognition and eventual independence. In Algeria, Islamic fundamentalism has resulted in violent confrontation and multiple killings, and there is a constant threat, as the Moslem population of France increases, that similar violence will spread to the mainland. Jean-Marie Le Pen's extreme right-wing party, the *Front national*, for which support continues to grow, has made considerable inroads, and its anti-liberal policies have led to a number of demonstrations, notably in Toulon in February 1997. In the same months the government's proposals for immigration control promulgated in the *loi Debré* resulted in a massive show of public disapproval in Paris, involving in particular many of France's leading intellectuals and provoking from some quarters a call openly to defy authority. Conscious of some of these problems, perhaps, and very aware of those concerning European integration, Chirac has called a surprise general election. His timing appears astute and a victory for the right seems likely, albeit with a much reduced majority, and whether or not Juppé will survive as Prime Minister must be in doubt.

As in the past, the chapters of this new edition of *France Today* chart these events and speculate in an informed way on the future of key national issues as the end of the century approaches. Each has been fully revised and, as always, is as up-to-date as printing schedules permit. Readers of earlier editions will notice a change in format and a greater use of illustrative material. Once again I am grateful to contributors for respecting deadlines and to our publishers for their continuing interest and support.

John Flower
Canterbury, May 1997

1

SOCIAL STRUCTURES

Andrée Shepherd

Introduction

French society today can no longer be neatly divided into the traditional units of ruling class, middle class, working class and peasantry. During the last hundred years in particular, wars and social unrest, demographic change and developments in industry, science and technology have all helped to create a kind of uniformity and standardization which makes any clear-cut divisions of that nature difficult. This trend has also been emphasized by the evolution of the more traditional institutions of society – the Church, the family, the educational system and even military service. French society has changed, and is still changing, a fact which has been recognized in social legislation and in a number of important administrative reforms, such as the breakdown of excessive centralization and the creation of 22 regions as increasingly autonomous units, each with an appointed head (the *préfet*), an elected regional assembly (the *Conseil régional*) and its own budget. Essential social and cultural services are now administered on a regional level. Much remains to be done, however, and the economic crisis still weighs on the future.

POPULATION

Today, France has 58 million inhabitants including nearly 4 million foreigners (although with legal immigration now at a standstill and the rise in the number of naturalizations, the number of foreigners is decreasing). This, combined with low birth and death rates, explains the slower rate of increase of the population. During the last fifty years French governments have been in favour of larger families – the *Code de la famille* was first drafted in 1939 though not put into effect until after the Second World War and, more recently, there have been campaigns to encourage couples to have three rather than two children. However, in spite of government incentives (in the form of tax rebates from the first child and increased benefits and allowances for families with three or more children), the birth rate has fallen to 1.6 (which is below replacement level), and family-forming habits seem to have settled into a stable pattern: people marry later, divorce more (one in five marriages ends in divorce) but tend to remarry and have two rather than three children, or even fewer (44 per cent of all couples are childless). Except perhaps in working-class and immigrant groups, large families are very much a thing of the past (9 per cent of all couples have three children and only 3.6 per cent have four children or more). With increasing numbers of women at work (often in low-paid, insecure and part-time jobs), there seems to be little chance of a reversal of recent trends, and the present balance between the 25.1 million economically active (out of which, in 1990, 2.2 million were unemployed, with numbers rising to 3.4 million in 1995, decreasing to 3 million in 1996) and the thirty or so million dependent members of the population is unlikely to improve. The unemployed represent an average of 12.5 per cent of the active population, but a shocking 25 per cent of the under-25s. Almost one in every four people is still under twenty and one in five over 60, but by 2010 the two groups are expected to be equal in number: with more time spent in education, earlier retirement and steadily increasing unemployment, there is bound to be a mounting burden on health, social and educational services.

A large proportion of the population lives in towns – 75 per cent in towns of over 2,000 people compared with 40 per cent in 1900 – and the migration from countryside to town continues at a faster rate than ever before. But even more significant is the fact that the population has become tripartite: 16 million in towns proper, 26 million in suburbs and *grandes banlieues*, and the remaining 16 million spread over a countryside of about 500,000 sq km. This growing suburbia has created new challenges and new problems. The architectural horror of Sarcelles, north of Paris, for example, brought with it fresh social problems. The very existence of this kind of dormitory suburb, catering for vast numbers of industrial and office workers, has had unexpected consequences, one of which is the introduction of the continuous working day, which was anathema to French workers used to one- or two-hour lunch breaks. A solution may be to develop these distant suburbs into viable economic units. From 1956 to 1965, Sarcelles grew from 8,400 to 30,000 inhabitants, a *grand ensemble* with no life of its own. Socio-cultural facilities have gradually changed it into a proper town. Sarcelles in the 1990s, with its population of some 56,000 inhabitants, regional commercial centre, industrial development zone and municipal bus service, no longer relies on Paris, although Paris is only nine miles away. A few miles to the west the 'new town' of Cergy Pontoise is still expanding around new factories, office blocks, schools and colleges in an attempt to avoid previous mistakes, but so far, with only limited results. Together with the other eight 'new towns' in France – five of them in the Paris area – Cergy Pontoise still suffers from the rapidity of its growth rate and its close proximity to the capital. Another problem is the change in the overall plan, especially in the development of the Paris area: originally the five 'new towns' (Marne-la-Vallée, Melun-Sénart, Saint-Quentin-en-Yvelines, Evry and Cergy Pontoise) were supposed to be large autonomous units, close to, but not dependent on, Paris. Together, they now have 600,000 inhabitants and are seen as an integral part of a restructured greater Paris with its fast suburban RER network. By the year 2000, the capital will be a megalopolis of 14 million inhabitants.

Concentration of population in France, 1994
Source: *Le Monde Dossiers et Documents*, no. 224, September 1994

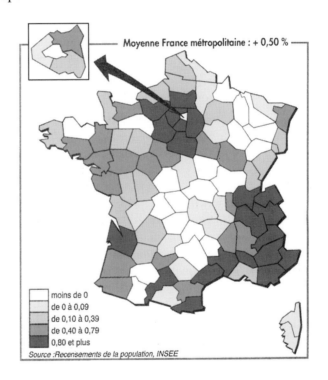

Moyenne France métropolitaine : + 0,50 %

moins de 0
de 0 à 0,09
de 0,10 à 0,39
de 0,40 à 0,79
0,80 et plus

Source : Recensements de la population, INSEE

The massive exodus of French people from the land towards the expanding towns has meant a radical change in the distribution of the population between agricultural and other activities: over the last fifty years, the number of people employed in agriculture has decreased from 25 per cent to just over 5 per cent of the active population, while the professionals and *cadres* have grown from 9 per cent to 20 per cent. This points to a large-scale reorganization of the socio-economic structure. A direct comparison between agriculture and industry (still strong, with 25 per cent of the population in blue-collar jobs in 1992) leaves aside the most important sector of activity, known as the tertiary sector – transport, distribution and services. Today, this 'non-productive' sector (which accounts for almost two-thirds of the active population) is still growing apace: most of the new jobs are in non-manual occupations and are filled by an increasing proportion of women. Industrial growth is still greatly impaired by the effect of successive economic crises, with large-scale redundancies resulting from restructuring in all the major industries. A further factor is the regional imbalance between the hard-hit areas in the North and in Lorraine and the still-developing regions – the Ile-de-France around Paris, the Rhône-Alpes area and the southern regions of Provence-Alpes-Côte d'Azur. A continuation of these trends because of further technological change and rationalization is leading to a society in which only a minority will be directly involved in production, with the majority occupied in administrative and servicing activities. The division between manual and non-manual workers has become more marked, leading to a greater proletarianization of a smaller manual working class, the increasing marginalization of the unemployed (many of them young people) and growing social unrest. With a large number of people facing redundancy, and in spite of retraining facilities, the wealth created by automation will only heighten the problem of inequality and a new class of 'unemployables' will emerge. The expression 'fourth world' (*le quart-monde*) has been coined to refer to the growing social group living mostly in twilight zones surrounding the large conurbations. Around Paris, Lyon and Marseille, for example, the combination of suburban dilapidation with large-scale youth unemployment has meant that rioting has become so frequent an occurrence that there is now a junior minister in charge of urban development and the 'integration' of ethnic minorities attached to the Minister of Town and Country Planning. Such administrative changes point to an assumption that the pressures of urban living are heightened by the presence of immigrant minorities which are often too readily accused of being the cause of the outbursts of violence. However, the immigrant community proper does not represent a higher percentage of the total French population than it did ten years ago: many of the young *Beurs* are French-born and educated. Even though they remain identifiable as belonging to a racial minority, their integration into a youth culture which cuts across racial barriers is undeniable. The Saturday night 'rodeos' with 'borrowed' cars, and the looting incidents in suburban hypermarkets and shopping precincts in the spring of 1991 which led to violent clashes with gun-carrying guards and to police intervention, caused a number of casualties and aroused public concern. Since then, the *banlieues* (France's inner-cities) have become an obsessive focus for the media which repeatedly report acts of delinquency, looting incidents, the development of no-go areas and the banning of beggars from the streets of provincial cities in the summer. Some, like the Plan d'Aou in North Marseille, the Tarterets housing estate in Corbeil Essonnes (south of Paris), Vaulx-en-Velin and the Quartier des Minguettes in Vénissieux (east of Lyon) or the Cité Mistral in Grenoble, have become notorious for endemic violence, and occasionally serve as recruiting grounds for muslim fundamentalists. Terrorist attacks (summer 1995) have led to both the reinforcement of policing and the drafting of a 'Marshall plan for the *banlieues*', involving special programmes of urban regeneration and employment schemes in an attempt to prevent further disintegration and alienation of the long-term unemployed – most of them unqualified, ethnic minority school leavers. This involves the creation of Free Zones (*zones franches*) where new firms are to be given extensive tax exemptions (until 2002) in exchange for job creation aimed at the local young unemployed, where civil servants (including teachers) get special housing benefit and extra pay – all financed by state and regional subsidies. Although this *'Plan de relance pour la ville'* has come under criticism because of both insufficient financial provision and 'unfair' selection procedures, it is beginning to have an impact on some of the poorest French 'inner-city' areas. Local volunteer groups and associations working to fight deprivation and develop cultural and leisure activities for the young unemployed and ethnic minority populations are also beginning to revive hope in those suburban areas rife with drug and delinquency problems.

COUNTRY V. TOWN

Where have all the peasants gone?

France can no longer be described as a nation of small farmers, as the widely used phrase 'the death of the peasantry' indicates. The French farmers' lobby still carries weight in Brussels even though there are fewer farmers – 750,000 in 1995 with an expected decrease to 400,000 in ten years' time. This does not mean that the countryside has become a desert: moving away from agriculture has not necessarily meant moving out of the countryside. Many former farmers have only moved a short distance away to the nearest market town in search of a job, or even continue to live in their village and commute to work. Many families are now earning only part of their income from the land. The husband may, for example, remain a farmer but a supplementary (and regular) income is provided by his wife who has become a shop assistant, or by his sons and daughters who work as nurses, secretaries or in factories. This may not be by choice, but rather out of necessity, since small family farms are no longer viable economic units. Many small farmers and agricultural workers are among the poorest in the French community, while the regrouping of land, modernization of farming methods and judicious reconversion to intensive fruit, cereal or meat production has enabled the few (who may also draw high profits from the common market) to become very wealthy indeed. A reversal of the trend will be helped by the 1995 *Loi de modernisation agricole*, which includes legal, financial and tax measures aimed at relieving the tax burden on young farmers and giving them priority access to farm land becoming vacant through the early retirement of older farmers.

Whether or not they are still deriving their income from the land, villagers can no longer be sharply distinguished from the rest of the population in their way of life. In the 1960s they became bitterly aware of the fact that, far from being protected by the welfare state, they had not joined the consumer society and were not receiving their fair share of the national income in spite of the fact that they were doing more than their fair share: harder work, longer hours, lack of cultural facilities and modern conveniences were their lot. This is no longer the case and, increasingly, village-, suburb- and town-dwellers alike watch television, own a car and do their Saturday shopping in a neighbouring hypermarket. They may not all yet have a bathroom or an indoor toilet, but they have a deep-freeze (well-stocked with home-produced as well as pre-packed food) and a washing machine. They often have new, multi-purpose village halls where they can watch newly released films, local cabaret and small-scale theatre productions, and organize local music and theatre festivals and exhibitions in the summer. These serve both local population and tourists accommodated in renovated farms and barns turned into bed-and-breakfasts (*gîtes à la ferme, accueil paysan*). In the last twenty years, country life has in fact become an attraction for former town-dwellers who are no longer weekend migrants, but have turned what was originally a 'weekend cottage' (a *résidence secondaire*) into their permanent home and commute daily into the towns from their rural home. Thus, over 10,000 people (known as 'les navetteurs' or 'TGVistes') have moved out of Paris with their families to a home over 100 km away and use the TGV daily to get to work. The farming community has become a minority on its home ground, and village life has been transformed out of recognition by these 'neo-villagers' who have sometimes captured key positions on local councils. The rural community has become aware of its new role besides agricultural production proper: it is now entrusted with the preservation of the local heritage and environment, with the creation of a fund for the management of rural space (*Fonds de gestion de l'espace rural*) – a provision of the 1995 Pasqua law on town and country planning.

Generalizations are, of course, dangerous: historians and sociologists have repeatedly demonstrated through case studies that the contrast between town and countryside within a given area is less striking than the extreme regional differences. The great plains of the Paris basin with their rich crops of wheat and intensive farming, the mixed-crop farming of Brittany and the Rhône valley, the wine-growing areas and the mountain deserts of central France present widely differing problems and prospects. The healthy areas seem to be of two kinds: the capitalist type of intensive farming, and the more traditional type of mixed farming, which by increasingly involving co-operative enterprise, fulfils the need for skilful crop rotation and the division of labour. The extension of the common market to include vegetable and fruit-producing Mediterranean countries has made the situation of some French farmers more difficult because of new competition. Future prospects are certainly favourable given certain conditions: namely, larger farms; concentration on products which are in high demand such as good quality wine; sufficient organization (co-operatives); and well-planned marketing. In some favoured areas like the Côte d'Or, the agricultural labour force (vineyard labour) earns salaries comparable to those of the Dijon factories nearby. In less prosperous areas, like Brittany, however, some poultry farmers are worse off than industrial labourers. A large firm may deliver day-old chicks and chicken food and impose precise planning. After nine weeks the chickens are collected for slaughtering. The farmer is a home-labourer paid to work according to conditions laid down by the firm. He may own his poultry farm, but this is probably a liability as he is usually tied down by debt and is entirely dependent on the firm employing him. Some poultry farmers have managed to organize themselves into co-operatives, but these are exceptions. For the majority of the smaller farmers, proletarianization has reached the countryside in a brutal form, and even in the richer Rhône valley there are increasing tendencies for the farmers to contract with freezing and canning firms like the American firm, Libby's. All too often, the farmers' share of the profits is a minor one, and agricultural incomes vary even more than industrial ones. Over the last decade, agronomic and genetic research together with competition within the European Community/Union and Community regulations have been influential in making French agriculture evolve and become a prosperous export industry deriving just under half its income from cattle and poultry farms and dairy product with the rest coming from the production of cereals, fruit and vegetable and industrial crops. France exports more than it imports. While three-quarters of the exports are directed at EU countries, exports further afield are growing apace: breeds of cattle from the Limousin and the Nivernais are exported to Africa and America; chicken farmers from Brittany have conquered new markets in the Gulf countries; and the port of Rouen prides itself on being the world leader for wheat exports. The average agricultural income, however, points to continuing regional inequalities – top of the league are the Champagne-Ardennes area, the Ile-de-France and Burgundy areas, which fare twice as well as Brittany, the Franche-Comté and the Rhône-Alpes areas, and four times as well as the poorer Massif Central and Corsica.

In the last forty years or so, a certain amount of government planning has been introduced to improve the lot of rural communities, very often in answer to growing unrest and insistent demands by younger farmers who first began to organize themselves in the early 1950s around a Catholic youth organization, the JAC (*Jeunesse agricole chrétienne*). From Bible meetings and socials to study groups on accountancy and farming techniques, they developed a growing awareness of their lack of formal schooling and absence of cultural facilities. They soon openly entered the trade union arena, led by Michel Debatisse, who had coined the phrase 'the silent revolution of the peasants' to describe their aim. The main farmers' union, the FNSEA (*Fédération nationale des syndicats d'exploitants agricoles*) was controlled by the older, richer, conservative farmers. But its moribund youth section, the CNJA (*Centre national des jeunes agriculteurs*) could be revived. They took it over and gradually captured key posts in the farmers' trade union movement, while using their position as a platform to advocate new policies. They claim peasant unity is a myth, that there are rich and poor farmers whose interests are different. They admit that the rural exodus is normal – most of the small family farms are not economically viable – but they want it to be 'humanized' by the provision of proper training facilities. They insist on the importance of maintaining prices and act as a powerful pressure group to influence EU negotiations, but they also wish to give greater importance to structural reforms (land and marketing). Finally, they question the sacred principle of property ownership and individualism: 'The fishermen do not own the sea. Why do we need to own the land?' They have started implementing their own proposals by renting rather than owning their farms, by establishing group enterprises for marketing and shared production, by introducing computerized farm management, by supporting the government agency set up for buying land and letting it in order to prevent speculation and by encouraging the regrouping of land (parcelled as a result of equal inheritance laws dating back to Napoleon). The movement has not always been peaceful, however. There were riots in Brittany in 1961, for example, when ballot boxes were burned, and there are still frequent demonstrations by farmers and vine-growers disrupting car traffic on roads and motorways. Constant petitioning of the government has been effective; greater concentration and special-ization has also had some benefit; agricultural schools and training have been developed, with the added concern of environmental pro-tection in recent years, regional investments are co-ordinated and government and regional grants are given to young farmers willing to settle in depopulated areas or take over from a retiring farmer. Loans for equipment are now easier to obtain and the old-style co-opera-tives have federated into larger units and modernized their methods. This was given a boost by the charter signed by the Prime Minister Alain Juppé and the President of the CNJA, Christiane Lambert, in 1996. The *Charte nationale pour l'installation des jeunes en agri-culture* will provide increased grants for young farmers, and a national fund has been set up to guarantee complementary loans. Thus, the CNJA hopes to reverse the trend (43,600 farmers retired in 1992 while only 8,000 young farmers took over), with the aim of get-ting a replacement for all those who retire by the year 2000. The new intake of farmers will have to include 20 to 30 per cent of young peo-ple from other socio-economic categories attracted to farming after an initial move to town or suburbia. This is already the case in the Isère, for example – a mountainous *département* around Grenoble with mixed cattle and dairy farming, cereal, vegetable and fruit pro-duction. The Isère has lost over half its farmers in the last twenty years and the average age of the 6,900 remaining farmers now is 55. Of the 74 new farmers in 1994, 17 had no family connection with the land, and nearly all have post-school qualifications. This, together with other disadvantaged rural areas (*zones rurales fragiles*), is part of a programme of state-financed job creation aimed at *'zones de revi-talisation rurale'* which shows the government's concern for help-ing both rural and urban depressed areas.

There are also industries contracting out work over large areas of the countryside. This *saupoudrage industriel*, as it is called, pro-vides regular work for women at home or winter occupations for the whole family, but it has tended to decrease in recent years as industrial restructuring affected the industries concerned: watch-making in the Jura, textiles in the Loire, footwear around Cholet and cutlery in the Lozère. Another drawback is that it frequently leads to the exploitation of cheap labour.

Finally, the extension of tourism has brought a new lease of life to areas which are often beautiful but deserted (mountainous areas in particular), helped by the development of summer festivals and the organization of activities such as rambling, horse-riding, absail-ing, canoeing, bunjee-jumping, hang-gliding, etc. But the develop-ment of the tourist potential must provide new jobs if the local youth is to stay in the village and earn a proper and a regular wage, and in the coastal areas those responsible for development must beware of ecological – and architectural – disasters. The growth of the tourist industry, if properly controlled by local communities rather than by capitalist sharks, may help provide extra income and facilities for country people while answering the need of town-dwellers for open-air leisure activities and rest – thus further bridging the gap between the 'two nations'.

Paris and the French desert

And yet, it remains traditional to underline both the contrast between town and country and the divorce between Paris and the provinces – a metropolis in 'the French desert'. Taine put it in a nut-shell as long ago as 1863:

> There are two peoples in France, the provinces and Paris: the former dines, sleeps, yawns, listens; the latter thinks, dares, wakes and talks; the one dragged by the other like a snail by a butterfly, now amused, now worried by the capriciousness and audacity of its leader.

As the focus of national life in France, Paris is unrivalled and the Parisian has a somewhat haughty attitude towards anybody who does not belong there. This is somehow surprising to outside observers who happen to know that while one in five Frenchmen lives in Paris or the Paris region, relatively few have been established in the capital for more than a generation, and one if five Parisians is a foreigner. In spite of the pressure of life in the capital, the constant rush and noise (one million commuters spend two or more hours travelling to and from work every day), the still desperate housing situation, the high levels of pollution and the very high cost of living, the prestige and desirability of life there were unaltered until recently. Stifled by cars which encroach even on the pavements, much of the old Paris is being demolished and replaced by tall tower blocks, or tastefully renovated at high cost, thus driving the original slum inhabitants into the distant suburbs. With the extension of the underground outwards and the creation of fast RER lines, there has been a definite move to the outskirts of the city – a phenomenon which is true of all large towns – and since 1968 the number of provincials moving into the capital has consistently been smaller than the number of Parisians moving away.

Just as it is a social centre, so, too, is Paris an intellectual one: with its *grandes écoles*, its thirteen university campuses and its flood of students it contrasts sharply with quieter provincial university towns. But is prestige matched by excellence? Certainly it appears to be so. In a centralized and fiercely competitive system, a Paris appointment is often seen as a promotion for teachers, as indeed for most civil servants; and students compete for places in the *grandes écoles* which are still more often to be found in the Paris conurbation than outside (despite the attempt at moving some of them to the provinces, like the prestigious *Ecole nationale d'administration* to Strasbourg). Paris used also to be considered the world's cultural capital. It is still a very lively but expensive centre. Many of the new films are now released in provincial towns at the same time as on the Champs-Elysées or the Boulevards (and often at cheaper prices). The decentralization policy for the arts has enabled provincial theatre companies to survive and the increasing number of summer festivals, such as the one in Aix or Avignon, has made culture available to more provincials than ever before, though often at such a high price that many lower-paid people are effectively debarred from enjoying it. In 1995, the television magazine *Télérama* listed 150 festivals and exhibitions in the provinces, from theatre, ballet and classical music to jazz and rock concerts.

With industry the situation is similar and, in spite of efforts to decentralize, the city of Paris is bursting at the seams. Tax rebates are awarded to industries moving outside the Paris area. Thus, between 1968 and 1975, half a million new jobs were created in provincial cities, and government incentives are still helping to create jobs in manufacturing, especially in small and medium-sized firms (PME). Just as Paris, with its 2.2 million inhabitants, has lost out to its satellite towns, so have larger provincial cities like Lyon or Lille served as poles of attraction and developed faster-growing suburban towns like Villeurbanne (117,000 inhabitants in 1990) or Villeneuve-d'Asq (now over 65,000). Thus Marseille (1.1 million) moves from second to third place after the Lyon complex (with almost 1.3 million, when the conurbation is taken into account), but neither can compare with the 9.3 million of the metropolis and the 10.8 million of the Ile-de-France (with its 19 towns of between 63,000 and 110,000 inhabitants). With only three other cities numbering over 500,000 (Lille, Bordeaux, Toulouse) and another eleven over 300,000, this shows a lack of balance greater than in most neighbouring European countries.

Efforts to fight the growing suffocation of Paris have been extended by a policy of regionalism – a positive effort to adapt to the requirements of contemporary life and needs. It has involved the formation of viable and autonomous economic units: the *régions*, rather than being a negative rejection of the arbitrary division into *départements*, have thus been singled out as *métropoles d'équilibre*, and the first regional councils were elected in 1986. The regions are now asserting themselves politically and administratively, and are beginning to develop their own economic policy with their advisory economic and social council. But the economic imbalance remains great, and real industrial decentralization is proving difficult. Too many Paris-based firms are setting up one or even several factories in the provinces while retaining their headquarters in Paris. As a result, decisions are often taken in Paris without enough direct knowledge of local conditions. Regional development is bound to improve as the regions develop their own identity and even establish links with other regions in the EU, helped by better road and rail communications between towns with the extension of the 'bullet-train' links (like the Lille–Paris–Lyon–Marseille TGV and the *TGV Atlantique*), and by greater specialization of each industrial centre to avoid costly competition within one region. However, the *question régionale* still remains, with its political, economic and cultural undertones, because of the enormous differences in size and wealth between the richest (Ile-de-France and Rhône-Alpes) and the much poorer Limousin and Corsica. Regional cultures and languages, which the introduction of compulsory schooling and the imposition of the French language had helped to destroy, are being revived, for example in the south and Brittany. Nationalist, political or religious minorities act as pressure groups, attempting to restructure local communities. This quest for local, regional roots may be part of a search for identity in a mass society in which so many local and traditional features have been ironed out.

Thirteen years after the first decentralization laws on the devolution of state power to the 22 regional councils now in charge of regional economic development and planning, grammar schools, transport, museums and protection of the environment, new legislation was passed in February 1995 (*Loi d'orientation pour l'aménagement et le développement du territoire*) to try to eradicate persistent regional inequalities and give all citizens equal chances wherever they live. The new framework (*schéma national d'aménagement*) is to be presented to parliament in 1996, after widespread regional consultation under the responsibility of a National Development Council co-ordinating the work of five sectorial commissions (on universities and research centres, transport, telecommunications, cultural and health infrastructure), with an emphasis on 'zones for rural revitalization' and 'zones for urban re-dynamization'. This complex process, which must respect the power of the regional councils, is proving difficult to achieve. Yet on it depends the chance to bridge the gap between the rich and the underprivileged – the *fracture sociale* denounced by Jacques Chirac in his presidential campaign. The regrouping of small villages into a *Syndicat intercommunal* and of networking neighbouring towns (*réseaux de villes*, like the Poitiers–Niort–La Rochelle and Angoulême network in Western

France) are already a reality, but the definition of wider geographical sectors (under the name of *pays*) across the borders of *départements* and regions appears to some as yet another structure escaping the control of elected local and regional representatives.

YOUNG AND OLD, MEN AND WOMEN

In the early 1960s, the cult of youth invaded advertising, fashion and the entertainment and holiday industries. And *les jeunes* were the basis of France's faith in its political and economic future. This faith was shaken by the explosion of May 1968 when young workers and students were suddenly seen as a threat to the establishment. Until then, rebellious minorities had largely been ignored by the wider public. Even pop culture was tame. It was the reign of *'les copains* walking hand in hand' and listening to Françoise Hardy and Johnny Halliday on their transistor radios – nothing resembling the wild American or English crowds. They were on the whole conforming to accepted patterns of behaviour. The more culturally aware formed the audience for Georges Brassens, Juliette Gréco and other upholders of the poetical or the political tradition of the *chansons*; the more politically minded were militant in innocuous-looking *groupuscules* torn by infighting.

Rebellious youth was brought to the fore in May 1968 – untamed university and secondary-school students, unorganized union militants all defying the establishment. They questioned authority in all its manifestations and won some concessions. Student unrest of that magnitude has receded, but protest has continued to simmer under the surface as the 1986 widespread demonstrations indicated; this remained the case and will continue to do so as long as educational reforms remain inadequate. In a labour market dominated by unemployment, which necessarily hits hard the least-qualified youngsters, there will be youth revolts due to the crisis, especially among the suburban poor.

Today, in spite of the successive youth employment schemes, 40 per cent of the unemployed, among whom two-thirds are women, are under 25. Worse still, according to the *Agence nationale pour l'emploi* (ANPE), 35 per cent are still unemployed after six months (a phenomenon which is increasingly affecting university graduates). The jobs they find are often temporary (*emplois intérimaires*), and unqualified school-leavers only represent a small proportion of those who gain admission to one of the government schemes – a situation which the government is still trying to remedy by reviving special training schemes and offering firms rebate for each young trainee they take on. However, a hard core of unqualified young unemployed is emerging and it is hardly surprising that suicide and crime rates are increasing. But accusations of apathy, rejection of adult values or downright laziness are misguided. These accusations both ignore educational and social disparities (a university graduate still has three times more chance than an unqualified school-leaver of finding a first job) and fail to acknowledge the fact that most young people still share the same values as their elders. Recent opinion polls and government reports alike paint a more positive picture: most young people do not reject their own family and wish to have one of their own; they want to work and are worried about their prospects in a society which only offers them insecure and uninteresting jobs with no prospects of obtaining further qualifications. Work, therefore, is no longer the central value in their life since it will bring them neither satisfaction nor social recognition: their questioning of traditional hierarchical models, of repetitive fragmented tasks, their demand for greater autonomy and a sense of purpose are aspirations they share with many adult workers. They did not invent the consumer society, they were born with it and want to join it – though it may be true to say that they prefer spending their money on going to concerts or buying stereo equipment than buying a colour television or a new settee. And their life styles often imply different values, rather than a rejection of all values: cohabitation before marriage is widespread and may be read as the sign for a search for marital harmony and true respect for marriage itself.

There is a widening gap between young and old, partly based on the degradation of the situation of the under 30s by contrast with the improvement of that of the young retired (*troisième âge*). Another reason for the tension between the two groups may be that adults fear the approach of old age. While earlier retirement (at 60) is welcomed by those for whom work has been synonymous with physical strain, repetitive tasks, noise and long hours, those who find fulfilment in their job are often loath to retire. Nevertheless, there are already signs that retirement no longer means relinquishing an active social life: pensioners have their own clubs (*clubs du troisième âge*), travel, take up university courses and enjoy leisure activities – all the more so when they receive a decent pension and have not been worn out by a life of toil. Moreover, the pensioners of today are the last pre-war generation of workers; the grandparents of tomorrow will have spent their active life in the prosperous 1950s and 1960s, and will probably not have the same value systems. With its ageing population, French society must adapt to the new distinction between the 'younger pensioners' and the 'very old' (*le quatrième âge*) for whom isolation and health will remain the main problems.

Women, both young and old, are claiming their place in French society. Relatively recent legislation granted them formal equality with men: joint choice of the matrimonial home (1965), freedom to work, open a bank account and own property without the husband's consent (1965), equal pay (1972), protection from sex discrimination (1975), birth control (contraception and abortion acts of 1974 and 1975), divorce reform (1975). Yet French women, who now represent over 43 per cent of the workforce, constitute a majority of unskilled industrial workers, while in white-collar occupations (where they are mostly concentrated) they still rarely rise to a position commanding responsibility and initiative. As a result, they remain lower-paid (in the proportion of two to one for the lowest wages and of one to seven for the highest), and are twice as likely to become unemployed. Such inequalities were officially recognized in 1981 with the appointment of a Minister for Women's Rights who in the early 1990s campaigned for better protection against violence and improved living conditions. However, the Minister for Women's Rights disappeared with the return of a right-wing government, and eight of the twelve women appointed as junior ministers in the first Juppé cabinet fell victim to the November 1995 reshuffle.

Some observers are quick to point out that, paradoxically, women may have lost more than they gained by leaving their home for the world of work: the subordinates of men at work, they have also lost 'control' over the home since the domestic tasks are often shared – though often unequally – and they may well have the worst of both worlds. Yet most women, except perhaps the unskilled labourers, claim that having a job has meant an overall improvement in their lives, and many young mothers choose to continue working after the birth of their first child, helped by much better nursery provisions than in Britain. Thereafter, however, economic and practical difficulties may force a choice between outside employment and the birth of a second or third baby. But for over 3 million of the 9 million women at work, there is little freedom of choice: they are the single wage-earners, many of them with dependent children. Though still a minority in militant trade unions, political or cultural organizations, they are beginning to assert themselves. Opinion is divided as to the social consequences of these continuing trends.

SOCIAL CLASSES

The general improvement in the standard of living, the development of hire-purchase and changing patterns of consumption in the (relatively) affluent society have caused a blurring of former class distinctions. The family car and the television set and video have entered working-class homes, holidays are no longer the privilege of the rich and even home ownership is spreading (55 per cent of the population), though it is still less common than in Britain. Could this mean a destruction of class barriers and the end of the struggle for control and power which were the hallmark of pre-war French society, with its powerful working class and strong Communist Party? The language of the class struggle may have changed; but it does not necessarily mean that a classless society is emerging.

Wealth and income

Between 1950 and 1980, the purchasing power of the average annual wage has more than trebled, but progression in the 1980s has been very slow. The introduction, in 1968, of the index-linked minimum wage – the SMIC (*Salaire minimum interprofessionnel de croissance*) – helped at the time to reduce the gap between high salaries and low wages: a gap which is still greater in France than in any other European country except Italy. But since the austerity policy was first introduced in 1983, with increased insurance contributions proportionately heavier for low wages, greater flexibility in wage policy and contraction of the labour force, a comparison between the top and bottom 10 per cent of the salaried workers shows that the gap is widening. Even more serious is the fact that, since 1976, the growth of wages has hardly kept pace with the cost of living; in 1989, the improvement in the purchasing power of salaried workers was 0.1 per cent only. And for the period 1986–89, an official report recorded a stagnation for salaried workers, while the incomes derived from private enterprise and investment continued to grow (by 6.1 per cent and 7.7 per cent respectively for the year 1989). Low-paid workers are among the new poor and below them, excluded from the consumer society, we find the 'submerged' – the unemployed, the old, the immigrants and the handicapped who barely survive on social security.

This phenomenon, described as 'exclusion', has gained such importance that it was at the heart of the 1995 presidential campaign. A report commissioned by the Economic and Social Council (*Conseil économique et social*), published in 1995, warned that public policies aimed at relieving extreme poverty had failed to help those in greatest need – 60 per cent of the people interviewed had a monthly income below 2,800 francs (£300), 56 per cent were in temporary accommodation or homeless and 31 per cent in poor health. It denounced the specific policies which result in 'selecting, stigmatizing and excluding' and lead to a two-tier society (*société duale*). In 1994, 5 million people were found to be living below the poverty line and some 12 million more in a precarious situation, while 1.4 million were described as 'drifting' (*population à la dérive*) – among them 150,000 of those who receive the RMI (*Revenu minimum d'insertion*), 250,000 on a temporary part-time contract (*Emploi-solidarité*), 120,000 on 'remploy' schemes (*stages d'insertion*), 300,000 young adults under 25 (one-third of whom cannot claim any benefit), 250,000 homeless (*SDF – Sans domicile fixe*) and 300,000 long-term unemployed fast becoming unemployable. Critics of existing policies point to the failure of the 'social contract' rather than a series of individual failures. Indeed, increasing numbers of people are trapped in their situation and are gradually losing their rights and status as citizens. To fight this, the voluntary sector is developing, with some 30 large associations and a myriad of smaller ones fighting homelessness (*Droit au logement*), poverty and other forms of deprivation (*Compagnons d'Emmaüs, ATD quart-monde, Restos du cœur*) or promoting job creation (*Autonomie-solidarité, Association pour l'insertion des jeunes*) – but all are starved of funds and conscious that their action is limited to stop-gap measures to relieve the most dramatic situations. The present government is facing a multiple challenge: unemployment relief and employment schemes, regeneration of the *banlieues*, fighting multiple deprivation, including the impact of drug dependence, AIDS and illiteracy. With the departure of the two women ministers in charge of 'Solidarity between the generations' and the inner-city areas (*quartiers en difficulté*), the task is now left to the minister in charge of *Aménagement du territoire, ville et intégration*, helped by one junior minister of 'urban integration', and to a minister without portfolio advising the Prime Minister on 'emergency humanitarian action' – a change from the initial post-election emphasis which appears ominous to many observers.

At the other end of the social scale, the wealthy *grande bourgeoisie* still possesses considerable power and influence, particularly in the *Chambre des députés* (the legislative assembly) and in the civil service, especially, for example, in the Foreign Office. The economic rule of this class remains undisputed, though the frequency of mergers and takeovers by foreign firms (American and Japanese in particular) has caused signs of strain to appear. In the educational, social and cultural spheres, its influence is less marked. State education which is fairly democratic (but perhaps more formally than truly democratic) has almost completely escaped its grasp; but it still controls élite recruitment through private education and the prestigious *grandes écoles*. Bridging the ever-widening gap between the very rich and the very poor appears to be a formidable task.

The working class

The traditional condition of the working class has changed considerably in the last fifty years. The growth of unionization, the system of social security and the increasing mechanization of industry, leading to an overall higher level of training and skill, have certainly improved the lot of the workers. However, some problems remain and still more are heightened. There is a particular sense of insecurity at a time when many industries are under threat: mining and steel industries, as in Britain, are declining; the car industry is shaken by regular crises; bankruptcies have caused regional disasters; even in more advanced sectors like the aircraft industry, rationalization has led to large-scale redundancies, causing a phenomenon which has been described as 'the disappearing working class'.

Class consciousness seems to have remained somewhat sharper than in Britain, in spite of the electoral decline of the Communist Party which lost half of its voters in five years and now polls less than 10 per cent of the vote. A certain language or jargon and an analysis based on the class struggle are being kept alive by the labour movement, although the staunch unionists form a minority of the workers, and the commitment of workers to their unions seems to be changing: the very militant are probably becoming more politically conscious and active, while those on the fringe of union activity only snatch a limited amount of time and energy from their main commitment to a better standard of living. The search for security is a key word for the working class, who now prefer the monthly paid status to the hourly paid insecurity of the past. For many of them, more secure employment can no longer guarantee the maintenance of a newly acquired standard of living now under threat. As the shorter working week spreads, those with safe jobs will be able to satisfy their new cultural and leisure requirements, though time thus gained is too often wasted commuting to distant suburbs. For those out of work, the solution can only come from sustained efforts to couple the reduction of working time with job creation, work-sharing and the development of a rich programme of lifelong education.

The new middle classes

The new, extended middle classes are not a purely French phenomenon. But there are some specific French characteristics, the main one being the number of minor civil servants (*petits fonctionnaires*) who often earn less than manual workers, do a repetitive and often tiring type of office work, and yet consider their position as promotion, mainly on account of the 'image' (that of a white-collar worker) and the security (no fear of redundancy and a guaranteed retirement pension) which such posts offer.

It must be remembered that the French civil service represents one-third of the active population and includes, besides administrative workers, other sections of the working population such as teachers, post-office workers and those working in local government and hospitals. The social status of teachers is certainly higher than in Britain, though large numbers of supply teachers (a quarter of the total number) have low pay and no security of employment. Teachers are generally held to belong to the very French category of *cadres*, which forms a new middle class largely corresponding to the growth of the service sector. The *cadres* are distinguished from managers because they are salaried workers, not employers. They may be responsible for a large section of a factory or administration (*cadres supérieurs*) or only smaller groups of workers (*cadres moyens*). In some industries, they represent 3 per cent of the salaried workers (mining), in others 12 per cent (mechanical and chemical industries), and in others even 18 per cent (power) or 19 per cent (oil). They enjoy a high standard of living, due to the relative security of their jobs, but they too are increasingly suffering from unemployment. Their number has been estimated at around 1.5 million and is still rising. They mainly enjoy a better education, are more numerous in large towns and differ from the traditional bourgeoisie by their more reckless way of life with a tendency not to save but rather to consume.

Social mobility: a myth or a reality?

It is generally acknowledged that it takes three generations for the gradual change from the worker/peasant class to postgraduate or professional status to be achieved. But formal education, which plays such an important role in this, is not always attainable: scholarships and grants are scarce and in most cases insufficient to ensure reasonable chances of success. Of course, the unification of syllabuses, the *tronc commun* for all children aged between eleven and fifteen, and centrally organized examinations, though criticized for being overdone, are to some extent helping to standardize things. But inequalities remain, between those who are deemed capable of following the three-year *lycée* course leading to the *baccalauréat (cycle long)* and the others, who join technical schools for shorter courses of study, enter apprenticeships or drift out of school with no qualifications at all only to join the dole queue. Although all the *lycées*, in theory, cater for anybody according to ability, they do in fact have different clienteles. The best *lycées classiques* are still largely a preserve of the bourgeoisie, while the others, because of geographical distribution and lack of prestige, get more working-class and fewer brighter children. Access to the very top of the social structure remains the privilege of the very few: recruitment to the administrative élite (executive class of the French civil service) may be considered to be predominantly incestuous. However, there is considerable mobility around the middle of the occupational scale: investigation into the family background of the *cadres moyens* shows their extremely varied social origins, but this is also the case for the manual workers and the unemployed – social mobility is not always upwards.

INSTITUTIONS: STABILITY AND CHANGE

In May 1968, after ten years of stable Gaullist rule, France woke up in turmoil. The country came to a standstill, the regime itself was threatened. Everything seemed to be called into question: parliament and political parties, trade union bureaucracies, the educational system, the mass media, bourgeois culture. With the breakdown of normal communications – press, radio and television – came a general release: everybody talked to everybody else in university lecture theatres and cafés and on the streets (this was of course more true of large towns than villages, of Paris rather than the provinces, of young people than of old). For a short while, there was an impression of liberation from the constraints of normal life, an awakening, for people normally held down by routine; theatre companies, journalists, writers, television personalities who visited the occupied factories and universities were struck by the overwhelming response of their audiences. People became aware of the censorship of the government-controlled radio and television, of the cultural desert in which they were kept. But romanticizing is of no avail: the wave of excitement was followed by a Gaullist landslide victory. The staying power of institutions proved stronger than the wind of change.

The stability of the basic institutions of the state was not at stake. And, in 1981, the electoral victory of the socialists did not mean a radical departure from the past. The government did not attempt to change the Gaullist constitution of the Fifth Republic and was content to introduce reforms within the existing framework. Nor did it lead a frontal attack against the Church in the form of a straightforward nationalization of the private schools, which are often Catholic, nor an attack against the army by abolishing conscription or altering defence policy. The institutions closer to economic and social life were, of course, modified, but not out of recognition. Nationalization itself was not new – cars (Renault), banks (Crédit Lyonnais), railways and cigarettes were already nationalized. The reform of the judiciary and the symbolic transfer of the guillotine to a Paris museum have not meant a radical transformation of the system: the Home Secretary, when faced with the continuing problem of terrorist bomb attacks and insecurity, repeatedly asserted confidence and pride in his police force. Social and education policy tried to reduce inequalities, but the school and the university system were not lastingly modified, and the survival of the family as a basic element in the social fabric continued to be encouraged by government incentives. The return of a right-wing government did not mean a total reversal of previous policies (except for privatizations) but rather a tightening of policing and greater control over public expenditure on social policy.

And yet, consumer groups and lobbies of all kinds are sprouting everywhere, organizing protests, putting pressure on civil service and local authorities, on trade union and political bureaucracies. Over the last twenty years, a new consciousness seems to have developed, however diffuse. It is revealed through many initiatives and practices which are growing at local level, close to the grassroots, with the expansion of a rich voluntary sector; just as if the French, realizing the rigidity of their institutions, were constantly trying to find ways of bypassing bureaucracies in a battle against an abstract enemy – the 'administration'. Thus, unofficial strikes and claims for workers' control (*autogestion*) have at times been given equal weight with traditional wage claims, all the more so in a trade union like the CFDT (*Confédération française et démocratique du travail*) which is less centralized than the vertically structured CGT (*Confédération générale du travail*). Grassroot militancy has also developed within political parties: the socialists are often faced with minor revolts from their rank and file, while both the left- and right-wing parties hold regular summer schools hoping to develop a new image among the young by extending the activities of their local branches outside election periods. Christian associations openly debate problems of doctrine, young magistrates and judges criticize the judicial system, conscripts demand new rights of association, and discipline has been transformed beyond the wishes of many teachers and administrators in the *lycées*. More say in decision-making is the order of the day, even though 'participation' tends to be quickly formalized and therefore anaesthetized in the process.

This may be painting too bland (or too fractious?) a picture: activists will remain a minority in a population which is above all trying to survive economically and snatch as many crumbs as possible from the cake of affluence. The fabric of society is being changed, but this does not necessarily mean a lack of continuity.

The best example is perhaps the family: its death has been prophesied. Some people deplore the loss of many of the family's former functions while others attack it for curbing the development of its individual members. And yet the French family is going strong. When asked about ideal family size many people say they would like to have three or more children, and yet they only have one or two. This contradiction may be partly explained by factors like poor housing and economic difficulties which bring them down to earth. Young parents are not willing to have larger families at the expense of a standard of living which has been painfully attained through the added source of income of the increasingly numerous working wives and mothers. Indeed, as a result of the number of working mothers, there are twice as many places in crèches for young children in France as in England. Young people seem to favour 'juvenile cohabitation' rather than marriage and a large-scale survey carried out by the INED (*Institut national d'Etudes démographiques*) showed that 44 per cent of the couples who married in 1976–77 had lived together before marriage compared to 17 per cent in 1967–69. In 1990, one in every eight couples was unmarried. At the same time, their decision to have children is often linked with the decision to legalize the union. But 39 per cent of the 2 million cohabiting couples have a child under 25, compared to 24 per cent in 1984, and today illegitimate births make up one-third of all births.

Close ties still exist everywhere between the small family unit (parents and children), and the extended family (grandparents, uncles, cousins, etc.) – ties which have survived the move of the children to the city. Parental authority, respect and politeness are on the whole more sternly enforced than in Britain, though how far this is due to a common Roman Catholic tradition is difficult to ascertain. Kinship links remain important in all social groups: they are useful when you look for a job, or a home; grandparents look after children after school and during the holidays; and with the widespread search for cultural roots, they recover a role lost in most western societies – transmitting to the younger generations the traditions and language of their own family's past, thus helping to bridge the gap between young and old, between peasant origins and urban living.

Another unifying element between social groups, conscription, is due to disappear by 2002 in its present form (ten months of military service for all young men aged eighteen). By then, volunteers only, from both sexes, will have three options to choose from: serving in the armed forces, engaging in civilian forms of national service in France (*action sociale*) or engaging in civilian service abroad – mostly in former colonial countries (*coopération*). A six-year transition period (1996–2002) will enable the evolution to a much smaller, professional French army. This corresponds to a major, and still controversial, change. Until the Second World War, this period *sous les drapeaux* used to create a real melting-pot, some kind of initiation rite in which young men from varying backgrounds shared. It still remains a meeting ground, but offers less social mixing. Great numbers of students used to obtain several years' delay and tended to serve their time as teachers in ex-colonial countries or, if they served in the armed forces, very often did so as NCOs, and in any case did not mix well because of their age and different interests. Besides, by 1996, 6 per cent of all conscripts – some of them conscientious objectors – were engaged in a civilian form of national service, representing five times the number for 1984 – and many of them were students. The rift between the educated and the uneducated was no longer bridged as it once was by a common experience of army life, which indeed was one reason for the change.

The reform passed by the *Assemblée nationale* on 2 February 1997 (but still open to amendments in the *Sénat* in March) replaces military service for young men by the registration of all young men and women at the age of eighteen and a five-day period for all called the *Rendez-vous citoyen* (RVC), to develop civic awareness and encourage some to volunteer for a twelve-month period in the armed forces. The length of the RVC and of the now voluntary period of military service are still the object of debate, but conscription has definitely come to an end.

These recent changes to French institutions must not be minimized. The most momentous is probably 'decentralization' (the Act came into force in 1982), hailed by the socialists as 'a quiet revolution' (*une révolution tranquille*), an attempt to bring decision-making closer to the people affected by these decisions – hence greater democracy. Inevitably it was denounced by their opponents as a divisive measure and a wasteful manipulation of committees and personnel, since the local and regional assemblies would need brains, trusts and advisers to help them perform their new functions. The *préfet* was the eye of the Home Secretary in each *département*; he is now the local representative of the executive, and the elected presidents of each regional council also carry a lot of weight. Time, and decisions over financing, will decide where power lies. The whole regional policy is under review in an attempt to reduce regional imbalance.

Decentralization may help defuse the Corsican time-bomb and may bring a new lease of life to regions like Brittany, the Jura, the Auvergne or the Dordogne, for which the distance from Paris ministries meant files sometimes 'got lost' on their way through the red-tape of administration and, in any case, suffered long delays. The results are already visible in the regional initiatives in cultural policy – a departure from the long tradition of Jacobin centralization.

LEISURE AND CULTURE

For three years (1981–84) there were in France two ministries in charge of leisure and cultural activities. The *Ministère de la Culture* was responsible for the development of libraries and museums, music, theatre and the cinema. The *Ministère du Temps Libre* dealt with problems connected with leisure: the timing of holidays to avoid the August mass migration and its consequences for both the tourist industry and the economy; the development of the tourist potential of the country areas to counterbalance the dominant choices of seaside or mountain holidays; the diversification of state subsidies to enable the less affluent members of the community to enjoy a holiday away from their urban or village homes; the balancing of work and leisure (*aménagement du temps de travail*). The reversal to a single *Ministère de la Culture* in 1984 implied a change of emphasis and perhaps a recognition that, for the unemployed and those on early retirement schemes, 'enforced leisure' was a burden rather than a conquest. But the concern with holidays and leisure still remains a leading issue in French society today. The pressure of urban living, longer life expectancy and earlier retirement, rising unemployment (hence the slogan *'travailler moins pour travailler tous'* – shorter hours mean jobs for all) combined with the return of a socialist government committed to fulfilling the task started by the Popular Front in 1936 which was for a shorter working week (40 hours, now reduced to 39 with the aim being a 35-hour week) and an annual paid holiday for all (increased from four to five weeks).

Holidays

The French seem obsessively to live for *les vacances* – eleven months of noise, work and stress, of scrimping and saving for an annual spending spree. Two-thirds of the population regularly migrate south and west in the summer. Farmers account for nearly half of those who remain behind. Half the holidaymakers rush to the seaside and the sun. The spectacular success of such institutions as the *Club Méditerranée*, with its thatched-hut villages built around the Mediterranean as well as in more exotic places like Tahiti, Mexico or China, is a witness to this trend. But the majority of holiday-makers either stay with friends or relatives (35 per cent), go camping (23 per cent) or rent a flat or a cottage (*gîtes ruraux*). An interesting new trend seems to be emerging: according to an INSEE survey in 1995, among the 42 per cent of people who did not leave their homes in summer 1994, an increasing minority declared they preferred enjoying their homes, gardens and deserted cities in the summer to joining the great migration on the roads. Among the less affluent, schoolchildren often go away without their parents, staying with grandparents or in *colonies de vacances* (holiday camps) – the social security system partly footing the bill. Underprivileged children from the towns and suburbs frequently have only the streets and some adventure playgrounds for their holidays, and confrontation with the police for their excitement – a problem which, after the long hot summer of 1981 (with all the headlines reporting 'rodeos' being carried out with stolen cars in a Lyon suburb), the government tried to tackle by providing special holiday camps and day outings. The CRS (*Compagnie républicaine de sécurité* – the riot police) are now drafted in as youth and sports leaders in the summer, which is going some way to improve the image of the police in the *banlieues*.

When they can afford it, families go away together with organizations like *Villages-Vacances-Familles*, *Les Maisons familiales*, *Vacances-Loisirs-Familles* and so on, which offer family accommodation, communal catering and leisure activities for all ages. A more recent trend is the distribution of holidays over a (longer) summer period and a (shorter) winter period. Even skiing holidays, still a preserve of the urban upper-middle class (only 8 per cent of the population can afford them), are in a minor way open to the underprivileged. This is through the system of *classes de neige* whereby primary schools from town areas can in turn send one or more classes to the mountains for a fortnight, complete with teacher and skiing equipment, to combine normal teaching in the morning with outdoor activity in the afternoon. This is still far too sporadic to be effective in a general way, and too expensive for all children concerned to be able to go, but it does point to a future when what used to be the privilege of the better off may be available to many more.

Pastimes and leisure

Besides holidays proper, leisure activities of many kinds develop in all social groups – the advent of a 'civilization of leisure' has even been prophesied. People often say they would prefer a longer weekend to a bigger pay packet: time is too often 'wasted' in the mad rush to earn a living (*'on perd sa vie à la gagner'*) and increasingly, those in regular employment insist on choosing how to divide their life between work-oriented and leisure activities (*le temps choisi*), or increasing the amount of time to be devoted to leisure (*le temps libéré*).

Pastimes vary greatly depending on social class and education. Gardening has become a national pastime for rich and poor alike; one Frenchman in three now mows his lawn, grows vegetables or flowers, and may even decorate his garden with plastic gnomes or reproduction nymphs. Radio, television and newspapers are part of most people's daily lives, though they were only mentioned by a tiny minority as being among their 'favourite pastimes' in a recent IFOP (*Institut français d'opinion publique*) survey, while reading and sports vied for the lead followed by music, needlework, do-it-yourself (*bricolage*) and gardening. 'Sports', of course, holds a different meaning for teenagers and adults, for workers and professionals.

Football and cycling are the most popular sports and are more often watched than actively practised, with the ritual Tour de France taking over from cup matches on television in July. Elite sports like tennis, golf, horse-riding, sailing and wind-surfing are becoming accessible to increasing numbers of young people through the multiplication of municipal clubs and investments. However, cultural activities outside the home remain largely the preserve of the middle and upper classes: few people frequently attend concerts (7 per cent) or go to the theatre (12 per cent), though one in five still goes out to the cinema at least once a week – the highest percentages being among the *cadres* and Parisians. More films are watched on the family television than on the screen, however, and the number of films hired from video clubs doubled between 1983 and 1985 and is still growing apace.

There is certainly greater demand for cultural activities now than ten or twenty years ago, as the success of classes for classical or modern ballet dancing, learning languages, pottery, playing the guitar and other instruments has demonstrated. However, the dream of a popular culture bridging class differences remains, at present, a pious one. The gap between the cultured and the deprived (rural communities, the working class, the 'submerged' poor) seems likely to continue for quite a long time. Formal education is still insufficient, and adult education sadly underdeveloped. Industrial workers may be alienated for a number of reasons: working with machines, closed community living, lack of time and facilities, or the poor quality of the mass media, for example. This alienation causes a reversion to what one such worker calls 'illiteracy' when he compares the reading and writing abilities of adult factory workers to that of their children still in junior schools. But the role of 'associations' of all kinds in developing an awareness of cultural needs has led to initiatives – both private and public – for extending cultural activities to an ever-growing audience, and the dominance of Paris is beginning to be challenged by provincial initiatives.

Decentralization of culture

Besides the fifteen *Maisons de la culture* (arts centres), there are 1,200 *Maisons des jeunes* (youth centres) in France, with some 600,000 members (half workers, half schoolchildren and students). They are subsidized partly by the state, partly by local and regional councils, and each centre is administered by a permanent head (who nearly always has experience outside the educational profession) and by a house council elected by the young members themselves. Very often, the centre is used for amateur dramatics, film shows, lectures, concerts, dances, and other indoor leisure activities. It also serves as a base from which to organize outings, holidays and so on. A high proportion of the worker members of the *Maisons des jeunes* are active trade unionists, and their members are in general among the most literate young people apart from students. Over the last ten years, they have been under attack for being hotbeds of politicization of youth, and for wasting public money through bad administration. Not surprisingly both charges have been denied, but action has been taken against them. Under the pretext of decentralization, state subsidies have been reduced by 13 per cent, and more financial responsibility has been placed on local councils who thus became direct employers of the staff. The consequences of this are tighter control over cultural policy by local councils (generally right of centre) and the tendency to demand that what is supposed to be a public service should also be economically viable. A new source of finance are the regional councils which sometimes seek to develop cultural activities in order to boost the reputation of their region. But budgets are too limited for this to mean a large-scale extension of activities.

The *Maisons de la culture* were created by André Malraux. The idea was to give a single home to all the arts, where culture would be represented with many of its facets, and where various types of audience could meet under one roof. The fifteen *Maisons de la culture* created since 1961 in provincial cities (except for Créteil and Nanterre near Paris) have helped the development of a variety of cultural projects and practices. They have three principal aims. The first is creativity (*création*), the presentation of new high-quality productions often undertaken by permanent theatre or ballet companies (Grenoble and La Rochelle), by teams of film makers (Le Havre) or musicians (Amiens) and sometimes with the collaboration of specially invited and well-known artists. The second is cultural dissemination (*diffusion*) and outside companies, itinerant exhibitions and orchestras are welcomed. The third is cultural animation, an encouragement for all forms of cultural activity, especially those which favour confrontations and exchanges between actors, designers, painters and their public, thereby encouraging cross-fertilization and experiment. Although the *Maisons de la culture* have developed into lively arts centres transforming life in their city, they are plagued by a shortage of funds and often have to curtail their own most adventurous projects and instead invite in well-known companies on tour to boost their bookings. Unfortunately the development of a real cultural policy is bound to be inhibited by the need to make a profit. The decentralization policy may be a source of new subsidies because of the competition between regions for artistic as well as economic dominance over other regions (regional councils have their cultural department and budget and control cultural policy in their area). The impact so far has been the opening of provincial museums to contemporary art (in Lyon, Marseille, Bordeaux) or even the creation of new museums of modern art (Saint-Etienne) or additional buildings (Strasbourg, Grenoble), as well as the renovation and extension of many provincial museums. The regional collections of contemporary art (FRAC: *Fonds régionaux d'art contemporain*) are funded by equal state and regional subsidies.

The *Maisons de la culture* regularly welcome the regional theatre companies, themselves formed as a result of the decentralization policy for the arts and also fighting for survival. When Jean Vilar's *Théâtre National Populaire* (TNP) in Paris (founded in 1951) was forced to close down through lack of government subsidy in 1972, Roger Planchon (who had gathered his company in Lyon during the early 1950s) inherited the title of national theatre for his *Théâtre de Villeurbanne*. This may have been a victory for decentralization but it also meant the disappearance of the stronghold of popular theatre in élitist Paris. In the provinces, nineteen *Centres dramatiques* sprang up, with financial support from both government and local councils: the *Comédie de l'Est* (Strasbourg), *Comédie de l'Ouest* (Rennes), *Comédie du Centre* (Bourges) and so on. Their policy is to serve both the town where they are based and the surrounding local community by regular tours, and their 'consecration' comes when they are invited to Paris for a season. Their aim is obviously to reach out to a working-class audience and they partly succeed: some 30 per cent of the audience of Planchon's TNP in Villeurbanne is *populaire*. But the limited working-class public reached is mainly skilled workers, foremen and the like – perhaps because the ordinary workers have fewer contacts with the union bureaucracy that handles the bookings, and because the price of season tickets remains high for working-class budgets. There is now an increasing realization that the theatre and the arts must go out to people in their normal surroundings; the general difficulties then are how to combine artistic quality with mobility, and to ascertain what degree of effort can be demanded of the audience. Much more specific is the financial problem. It is much easier to organize a summer festival every year to catch the tourist audiences than to create a base for regular artistic life in the regions and support permanent structures. Thus lively areas in the tourist season become cultural deserts through the winter months.

In 1995, 1 per cent of the national budget went to support the arts, double the figure for 1981. In 1977, state help to the *Centres dramatiques* increased only by 7 per cent, even though a 25 per cent increase had been written into the contracts. The same year, the prestigious *Centre Beaubourg* opened, absorbing in running costs almost half the state budget allotted to the arts. Mitterrand's choice of a well-known personality of the arts, Jack Lang, as his Minister of Culture, and his government's commitment to a larger share of the national budget undoubtedly helped make culture available to all. Subsidies were distributed very widely, even though the money available was never enough and the *Conseils régionaux* were increasingly asked to supplement state grants.

Debates on what exactly is meant by 'the explosion of culture' have been revived in the wake of the spectacular success of the *Centre Beaubourg* whose (now ageing) futuristic and metal architecture in the historic heart of the city attracts millions of visitors from all countries and backgrounds (8 million visitors a year). Provincials and foreigners view Paris from the top of the escalators encased in glass across the west façade; Parisians, young and old, visit the Public Information Library, the *Cinémathèque*, the Museum of Modern Art's permanent collection or one of the many temporary exhibitions, and the Centre of Industrial Creation or the Experimental Music Department (IRCAM) directed by Pierre Boulez. Everything cultural is under one roof, with permanent fairground activities outside. Is it culture made available to the masses, a catalyst for artistic development, or a kind of supermarket of culture? In any case the *Centre Beaubourg* has become a leading landmark on the tourist route from the Eiffel Tower to Notre-Dame.

The *Centre Beaubourg* remains attached to the name of President Pompidou to whom it is dedicated. The Mitterrand era will be remembered by such architectural landmarks as the new Museum of Science and Technology at La Villette in northern Paris, with its futuristic, many faceted *géode*, the renovation of the Louvre museum preparing for the twenty-first century with the glass pyramid designed by the Japanese architect Pei, the prestigious arch built at La Défense and the new French National Library built on the banks of the Seine – all reflecting the Paris sky with their glass structures. They will remain a lasting testimony to an audacious policy for the arts which also included the large-scale development of theatre and music festivals in the provinces, and the controversial new *Opéra Bastille* which has already attracted motley crowds of spectators. The festival marking the 200th anniversary of the French Revolution which attracted millions of visitors and viewers was the most publicized – and costly – of Jack Lang's initiatives. Less publicized developments, like the opening to the public of the reconstructed Lascaux prehistoric caves, the renovation of the Lyon Opera, the building of multi-purpose centres for the arts in major provincial cities and the renovation of many old city centres with new pedestrian precincts also testify to the determination of successive national and local administrations to preserve the country's historical heritage.

BIBLIOGRAPHY

Alternatives économiques, no. 130, September–October 1995. Contains a collection of articles on inequalities, *'La France inégale'*. See also a special issue, *'Les riches'*, Autumn term 1995.

Barou, J., and Prado, P., *Les Anglais dans nos campagnes*. Paris, L'Harmattan, 1995. An examination of the phenomenon denounced by the press as the 'purchase of the French countryside' – by foreigners – a property boom which has developed since 1989, with interviews with these new inhabitants of rural France in Brittany, Normandy, the Périgord and the Ardèche.

Bauer, G., and Roux, J. M., *La Rurbanisation ou la ville éparpillée*. Paris, Seuil, 1976. On the invasion of rural areas by the urban overspill which thus creates the new 'rurban' phenomenon.

Biraben, J. N., and Dupaquier, J., *Les Berceaux vides de Marianne*. Paris, Le Seuil, 1981. Analyses the failure of the government incentives to increase the French birth rate.

Bourdieu, P., *La Misère du monde*. Paris, Le Seuil, 1993. A series of sociological enquiries with many life stories. Makes gripping reading.

Braudel, F., *L'Identité de la France*. Paris, Arthaud-Flammarion, 1986. The three-volume history by France's greatest historian is a major reference book. The first volume, *'Espace et histoire'*, presents a 'retrospective geography' of modern France. The second and third volumes, *'Les Hommes et les choses'* (vol. 2: *Le nombre et les fluctuations longues*; vol. 3: *Une 'économie paysanne' jusqu'au xxème siècle*) concentrate on the evolution of the population and economic development, showing the passage from a predominantly rural to an urban reality, and put the demographic and immigration problems in their historical context.

Chenu, A., *L'Archipel des employés*. Paris, INSEE (Institut national de la Statistique et des Etudes économiques), 1990. On white-collar workers and civil servants.

Cordero, C., *La Famille*. Paris, Le Monde-Editions, 1995. The main trends in the evolution of family-forming habits.

de Montricher, N., *L'Aménagement du territorire*. Paris, La Découverte, 1995. On regional policy.

Decugis, J.-M., and Zemouri, A., *Paroles de banlieues*. Paris, Plon, 1995. Interviews from inner-city areas, with introductions on the various aspects considered.

Données sociales, INSEE (Institut national de la Statistique et des Etudes économiques). Paris, 1986. Statistical information on all aspects of social life, with an analysis of the main trends and reports on social surveys and consumer studies.

Dossiers et documents. Paris, *Le Monde*, ten issues a year. A supplement to the well-known daily newspaper, gathering recent articles concerning social, political and economic problems. A very useful tool for the student who wants to keep up to date with the evolution of French society. Relevant issues include 'Logement: parfum de crise' (no. 196, February 1992), 'Les Agriculteurs français' (no. 197, March 1992), 'La Population française' (no. 224, September 1994), 'L'Exclusion sans réponse' and 'L'Avenir des régions' (no. 227, December 1994), 'Les Délocalisations: danger pour l'emploi?' (no. 228, January 1995), 'Consommation-épargne: la vertu change de camp' and 'Les Mutations de la famille' (no. 229, February 1995), 'L'Emploi en crise' (no. 235, September 1995), 'La Société française des années 90' (no. 238, December 1995), 'Le Galop ralenti des mégalopoles' and 'L'Inévitable réforme du système de santé' (no. 240, February 1996), 'Le Dernier Etat de la France' (no. 243, May 1996).

Guillaume, P., *Initiation à l'histoire sociale contemporaine*. Paris, Nathan/Université, 1992.

Jazouli, A., *Une saison en banlieue*. Paris, Plon, 1995.

Le Temps des exclusions. Paris, *Le Monde*, Collection Manière de Voir, no. 20. In the same collection, see also *Le modèle français en question*, no. 23.

L'Etat de la France 95–96. Paris, La Découverte, 1996. A mine of information on all aspects of social life and public policy, with an analysis of the main trends, reports on social surveys, maps and statistics. A yearly publication.

Le Roy Ladurie, E., and Vigne, D., *Inventaire des campagnes*. Paris, J. C. Lattès, 1980. The first part traces the history of the 'peasantry', the second presents the *paysans* in a series of live interviews. Both informative and enjoyable reading.

Les femmes – Portrait social. Paris: INSEE (Institut national de la Statistique et des Etudes économiques), Collection Contour et Caractères, 1995. An analysis and a concrete vision of the life of French women in contemporary France – a reference book.

Mallet, S., *La Nouvelle classe ouvrière*. Paris, Seuil, 1963 and Nottingham, Spokesman Books, 1976. A classic on the changes in working-class life and consciousness.

Manière de voir, no. 20, November 1993. Published by *Le Monde diplomatique*, this issue is devoted to 'Le temps des exclusions'.

Mendras, H. et al., *La Sagesse et le désordre: France 1980*. Paris, Gallimard, 1980. An excellent collection of articles including social and institutional aspects of contemporary France.

Minc, A., *La France de l'an 2000*. Paris, Editions Odile Jacob/La Documentation française, 1994. The text of the report of the commission which Alain Minc co-ordinated at the request of the Prime Minister.

Mouvement ATD quart-monde, *Une politique à partir des plus pauvres*. Paris, 1993. One of the voluntary associations presenting its ideas on a policy in favour of the most deprived.

Neyrand, G., and M'Sili, M., *Mariages mixtes et nationalité française*. Paris, L'Harmattan, 1995. On mixed marriages and national identity, from a historical and sociological perspective.

Nicolas, J. P., *La Pauvreté intolérable*. Paris, Erès, 1985. The life of a family on public assistance.

Politis, June/July/August 1995. Includes a remarkable collection of articles on the theme *'Vivre banlieue'* (pp. 17-72).

Projet, no. 243, Autumn 1995. This issue of the quarterly journal is devoted to 'urban civilization today'.

Reynaud, J. D., and Grafmeyer, Y. (eds), *Français, qui êtes-vous?* Paris, La Documentation française, 1981. A collection of articles on social classes, the industrial world, the institutions and intellectual life, with useful statistics. Most informative.

Rochefort, M., *Dynamique de l'espace français et aménagement du territoire.* Paris, L'Harmattan, 1995. An analysis of the economic, social and demographic changes over the last twenty years, and their consequences on planning policies – including industrial change, the modernization of French agriculture and the rise of the tertiary sector. A comprehensive survey.

Roudy, Y., *A cause d'elles*. Paris, Albin Michel, 1985. The socialist Minister for Women's Rights presenting her work.

SOFRES, *Opinion publique 1986*. Paris, Gallimard, 1986.

Sue, R., *Vers une société du temps libre*. Paris, PUF, 1982. The changing patterns of leisure.

Syndicat de la magistrature, *Justice sous influence*. Paris, Maspero, 1981. An examination of the judicial system by judges who analyse its evolution and discuss the balance between social control and individual liberty.

Télérama/Hors série, T 2096, 1996. On 'La culture pour s'en sortir': this special edition of the weekly magazine *Télérama* presents a variety of experiments in the field of culture, and gives details of associations and cultural groups which work among the poor and ethnic minority groups.

Vaughan, M., Kolinsky, M., and Sherif, P., *Social Change in France*. London, Martin Robertson, 1978.

Verret, M., *L'espace ouvrier*. Paris, L'Harmattan, 1995. On the conquest of a living space by workers, and the threat to their life style in an age of growing unemployment and accompanying 're-exclusion'.

Weil, P., *La France et ses étrangers*. Paris, Gallimard, Collection Folio/Actuel, 1991.

A very comprehensive collection of government reports was published in 1982, the result of surveys carried out by commissions appointed to study the state of the country at the time of the socialist return to power in 1981. Well-informed, comprehensive, programmatic as well as analytical, they are all published by La Documentation française, together with many other books and reviews, among which are *Les Cahiers français*. There are five issues per year, each devoted to a particular subject: for example 'La Fonction publique' (nos 194 and 197), 'Le Monde urbain' (no. 203), 'La Décentralisation', (no. 204), 'La France et sa population' (no. 259). These publications are available from La Documentation française, 29-31 Quai Voltaire, Paris, which also houses a well-stocked library.

2

POLITICAL PARTIES

Malcolm Slater

Introduction

The basic outline of political parties in France is, from left to right on the political spectrum:[1]

PCF	PS	UDF	RPR	FN

PCF – *Parti communiste français*
    (communists)
PS – *Parti socialiste*
    (socialists)
UDF – *Union pour la Démocratie française*[2]
RPR – *Rassemblement pour la République*
    (Gaullists)
FN – *Front national*
    (extreme right)

The background to this outline is that in 1981 the socialists captured the Presidency of the Fifth Republic when François Mitterrand narrowly beat Valéry Giscard d'Estaing in the second round run-off; a few weeks later the nation confirmed this choice by electing a new National Assembly with a socialist majority which for five years supported the policies and guaranteed the survival of governments consisting overwhelmingly of socialists.

Although Mitterrand had a seven-year term of office (*un septennat*), the end of the five-year parliament in 1986 led to the replace-

---

1 The main ecologist party, *Les Verts*, rejects the left-right configuration and regards itself as being located 'elsewhere' (*ailleurs*).
2 From its foundation in 1978 until 1996, it was convenient to refer to the UDF as 'the Giscardians' since Valéry Giscard d'Estaing was its inspiration and for most of the time its President. In April 1996, he was replaced as President of the party by François Léotard, whose immediate task was to reform what had always been a confederation, consisting in the mid-1990s of five elements: *Parti républicain, Force démocrate* (until 1995 called *Centre des démocrates sociaux*), the small *Parti radical*, the even smaller *Parti populaire pour la démocratie française*, and its own 'direct members' (*adhérents directs*).

ment of the socialist majority in the National Assembly by a right-wing majority supporting a new government under Jacques Chirac which had to 'cohabit' with President Mitterrand. Mitterrand was re-elected President in 1988, beating Jacques Chirac, the Gaullist RPR leader, in the second round run-off; as in 1981, he dissolved the right-wing-dominated National Assembly, and enough socialists and supporters were then elected to support a minority left-wing government which was never in danger of being overthrown because communists and right-wing opposition never united to pass a vote of no confidence.

In March 1993, legislative elections returned a massive right-wing (RPR and UDF) majority to the National Assembly, and the government, under Edouard Balladur, began a second period of 'cohabitation' with President Mitterrand. At the end of Mitterrand's second *septennat* in 1995, Jacques Chirac was elected President of the Republic, beating the Socialist Party's Lionel Jospin in the second round. Balladur, a Gaullist challenger to Chirac in the first round, was replaced by Alain Juppé as Prime Minister of a government supported by the huge right-wing National Assembly majority.

POLICY PROGRAMMES

What policies did the parties put to the electorate in March 1993, after five years of socialist government and twelve years of a Mitterrand presidency? Clearly, it is at election times that the parties are at their most salient, and the average voter has the best chance to be aware of the difference, not just between right and left, but also between individual parties, large and small. Electoral choice is a complex process, often with a high degree of irrationality and volatility, but obviously the established parties play an important part in this process, by dominating the institution which makes the choice necessary (parliament), by having a virtual monopoly of candidate selection (at a time when political office has become a form of employment), and by indulging in political marketing.

In 1993, the RPR and the UDF (together comprising the 'parliamentary right' or the 'traditional right', to distinguish it from the more recently established *Front national*) campaigned under the umbrella title of the UPF (*Union pour la France*). The main ecology groups also combined temporarily to campaign as the *Entente des écologistes*.

French political parties in the March 1993 campaign for elections to the National Assembly tried to differentiate themselves from their rivals in the major policy spheres:

Economy and employment

UPF – introduce more privatization; public spending cuts; a more flexible employment regime with lower 'social costs' for employers; more effective job centres.

PS – develop a mixed economy; a European employment initiative; encourage job sharing; more job flexibility through negotiation in each industrial branch.

PCF – prioritize domestic demand and production; tax financial speculators; introduce a 35-hour week without loss of pay or more part-time employment.

FN – protection of domestic markets; public spending cuts; gradual abolition of income tax; help for low incomes and savers; jobs 'priority' for French nationals.

Ecologists – encourage the 'non-market' economy; boost job-sharing by 35-hour week without loss of pay for low incomes; priority for local employment policies.

Education

UPF – parental choice of schools; local authority funding of both state and private schools; private universities and colleges; allow opting-out (*autonomie*) of schools.

PS – more flexible school management and curricula; state nursery provision for two-year-olds; expand vocational qualifications and practical training.

PCF – urgent school building and repair programme; all children eventually educated to *baccalauréat* level; increase status of teaching profession.

FN – freedom of choice in schooling; private universities and colleges; opting-out of schools; reintroduction of education for citizenship (*instruction civique*).

Ecologists – more decentralization of education; a personal achievement record for each child; reduce isolation of higher education.

Environment and planning

UPF – a new offence of environmental damage; more powers and funding for regions and *départements*; rural renewal areas; partnership revitalization of run-down suburbs.

PS – more urban public transport and social housing; equitable central funding for local government; tax polluters; create EU-wide environment volunteer corps.

PCF – more social housing and housing renovation; halt rural decline; increase safety of nuclear energy and disposal of pollution and waste.

FN – hold local referenda on environmental issues; tax and fine polluters;

boost medium-sized towns; encourage organic agriculture and provision of public transport.

Ecologists – job creation outside urban areas; develop renewable energy; eventually scrap nuclear energy; reduce road-building programme; modernize railways.

Europe

UPF – political initiative with Germany on currency matters; defend principle of subsidiarity; improve EU institutions to boost 'European construction'.

PS – defend French interests by use of veto; increase powers of European Parliament; work with European trade unions and left-wing parties on common objectives.

PCF – ensure EU legislation protects employees' rights; close watch by parliament on government application of EU laws; more European Parliament power over EU Commission.

FN – abrogate Treaty of Maastricht; abolish the EU Commission; create a 'Confederation of the Nations of Europe'; protect the European market.

Ecologists – press on with a political Europe; make EU institutions more democratic; develop 'social' Europe and 'environmental' Europe, and a Europe of the regions.

Law and order, justice, immigration

UPF – more effective police and judicial system; abolish many recent PS reforms in criminal procedure; crack down on employment of illegal immigrants; expulsion easier.

PS – develop crime prevention and conciliation; work with Europe on frontier controls; crack down on entry of and jobs for illegal immigrants; preserve ancient right of asylum.

PCF – defend basic freedoms and trade union rights; make police and immigration policy more democratic; oppose stricter nationality laws; enforce anti-racist laws.

FN – more police powers and identity checks; bring back death penalty; nationality only by naturalization; reduce political influence of Islam; end all immigration.

Ecologists – ensure everybody's basic rights; a stronger and independent judiciary; equal housing and education rights for immigrants; oppose stricter nationality laws.

Defence and foreign policy

UPF – develop European defence within the Atlantic Alliance; establish a European arms agency; retain French nuclear deterrent; improve co-operation with Africa.

PS – strengthen moves to nuclear disarmament; level of defence spending on basis of need; a Development Bank to help African states; an International Human Rights Court.

PCF – stop nuclear tests; efforts to eliminate all nuclear weapons; no integrated European defence pact; strengthen United Nations; cancel Third World debt.

FN – a European military alliance; a French intervention force; professional armed forces; a volunteer National Guard; resist Japanese economic pressure.

Ecologists – stop nuclear tests; cut defence spending; stress European 'joint security'; increase Third World aid; end the arms trade; talks on nuclear disarmament.

The 1993 legislative (National Assembly) elections were characterized by a lack-lustre campaign, a highly predictable outcome (resignation of the electorate to a right-wing victory and a second two-year period of *cohabitation*) and the unpopularity of politicians for their inability to tackle economic recession and unemployment.

The electoral campaign of the *Parti socialiste* was considerably weakened by political scandals and internal disputes, creating the image of an unstable, untrustworthy party. In particular, friction between Michel Rocard (Prime Minister, 1988–91) and Laurent Fabius (Prime Minister, 1984–86, then Party leader) had been causing problems for party unity since the acrimonious 1990 party conference in Rennes. The *Parti socialiste* was weary after ten years in government (1981–86 and 1988–93) and the electorate had seen little progress on the economic front, with unemployment still at 3 million at the beginning of 1993.

Electoral support for the Ecologists had grown in the late 1980s and early 1990s, but peaked at 19 per cent in January 1993 and fell to less than 8 per cent at the March elections. This was due to a combination of factors:

- increasing volatility of the electorate;
- inconsistent statements by leaders ('*Mais que veulent les Ecolos?*' asked the cover story of the weekly magazine *Le Point*, 27 February 1993);
- ecology parties were still regarded as single-issue movements;
- the call by Michel Rocard (PS) for a broad left movement of socialists, ecologists, centrists, dissident communists, and human rights and trade union activists.

In the end, the main question posed by the massive right-wing victory (four-fifths of National Assembly seats) was whether the 1993 results, like similar outcomes in 1958 and 1968, would affect long-term electoral behaviour; or whether electoral volatility would maintain the pendulum effect of the 1980s, leading in 1998 to a third period of *cohabitation*, this time potentially of four years and therefore more prone to crisis.

PROLIFERATION OF PARTIES

The scheme of political parties in France is complicated by the existence of many minor parties. The 1988 law on state financial aid to political parties introduced the concept of an official list of parties which qualified for such aid by having at least one parliamentarian (*député* in the National Assembly, or senator) as a member. This was widely abused and had the odd effect of giving official status to what was in effect a party of non-party members (the *Union des Sénateurs non-inscrits*). More importantly it was another cause of party proliferation – 29 parties were registered in 1990, though fourteen of these, many from the overseas territories and *départements*, had only one parliamentarian member.

The one-off experiment of a single-round proportional system in the 1986 election did not reduce the incidence of minor parties which are usually eliminated on the first round of a two-round system. It simply meant that they were presented to the electorate either as no-hope lists, sometimes of minor parties in combination, or as adjuncts of the major parties trying to extend the range of their appeal.

In the March 1993 legislative elections, there was an average of over nine first-round candidates in each of the 577 constituencies, since the 46 parties involved needed to field 50 or more candidates in metropolitan France (or just one candidate in overseas *départements* and territories) in order to qualify for state aid – proportionate to the number of votes received – for the duration of the new parliament (1993–98); an overseas ecologist 'party' received 783 francs a year on this basis.

Excluding regionalist groups, the list of party labels in 1993 was:

Association des démocrates; Alliance des Français pour le progrès; Alternative (pour la) démocratie (et le) socialisme; Alliance populaire; Alliance rouge et verte; Centre national des indépendants; Chasse, Pêche, Nature et Tradition; Démocratie chrétienne française; Entente des écologistes; Front national; France Plus; France unie; Génération écologie; Ligue communiste révolutionnaire; Lutte ouvrière; Mouvement des démocrates; Mouvement des citoyens; Mouvement des réformateurs; Mouvement des radicaux de gauche; Nouvelle Action royaliste; Nouveaux écologistes; Nouvelle solidarité; Parti communiste; Parti des forces nouvelles; Parti humaniste; Parti de la loi naturelle; Parti ouvrier européen; Parti socialiste; Parti des travailleurs; Rassemblement des démoc-

rates et républicains de progrès; *Ras le bol*; *Rassemblement pour la République*; *Solidarité écologie gauche alternative*; *Union pour la Démocratie française* (as well as all its component parties); *Union pour la France*; *Verts*.

Of course, the name of what may generically be called a 'party' is not always helpful in definitional terms. Of the five main parties in the mid-1990s only two were called *'parti'*. Sometimes this appellation is avoided in favour of a word with more rousing connotations, like '*Front* national', 'Nouvelle *Action* royaliste', '*Lutte* ouvrière', or '*Initiative* 86'. Similarly, the Gaullist party in its various guises has always been a *'union'* or a *'rassemblement'*. Use of the term *'mouvement'* may foster the impression that there is a wider basis of sympathy for political aims waiting to be mobilized, as in *'Mouvement des radicaux de gauche'*, *'Mouvement pour l'autodétermination'*, the extreme right-wing *'Mouvement nationaliste révolutionnaire'*, or the Trotskyist *'Mouvement pour un parti des travailleurs'* (though this was the *Parti communiste internationaliste* from 1981 to 1985, and became the *Parti des travailleurs* in 1991). Yet *'parti'* can refer to what are clearly groups limited in membership, in appeal (*Parti humaniste*), or in territorial concern (the former *Parti pour l'organisation d'une Bretagne libre*).

Moreover parties, pseudo-parties and political 'clubs' can often spring up at the whim of a single person. Many of these have more impact in a media context than in terms of lasting organization. Examples have been:

1990   *Génération écologie* (Brice Lalonde, Environment Minister at the time)
1990   *Démocratie 2000* (Jacques Delors, preparing as European Commission President for a possible attempt at the French presidency – which he eventually decided against)
1990   *Nouvelle Démocratie* (Michel Noir, on resignation from the RPR)
1991   *Société civile* (Bernard Kouchner)
1991   *Union des indépendants* (Général Lacaze, after his resignation from the *Centre national des indépendants*)
1992   *Combat pour les valeurs*, changing its name to *Combat pour la France* in 1993 (Philippe de Villiers)
1992   *Mouvement des citoyens* (Jean-Pierre Chevènement)
1994   *Mouvement écologiste indépendant* (Antoine Waechter)
1994   *Mouvement pour la France* (Philippe de Villiers again, as a vehicle for his 1995 presidential bid)
1995   *Convergences écologie solidarité* (Noël Mamère)
1995   *Alliance populaire* (Jean-François Touzé)
1995   *Forum alternatives européennes* (Charles Fiterman, after he left the Communist Party)

1995 *Association pour le renouveau socialiste* (Michel Rocard, reluctant to retire from politics)

1995 *Parti populaire pour la démocratie française* (Hervé de Charette, Chirac's Foreign Minister)

Returns in November 1994 for the obligatory register of income (in the interests of *transparence*) identified some 140 parties, clubs and movements across the whole political spectrum; the reference book *Quid* (1995 edition) gives 148 entries under 'Partis, clubs et mouvements actuels' (pp. 767-77), but some are in fact no longer in existence.

Small groups often disappear by amalgamation. In 1990, the declining *Parti socialiste unifié* (PSU), which was Michel Rocard's political home between 1960 and 1974, and the even smaller *Nouvelle gauche* dissolved themselves and threw in their lot with the Greens under the banner of *Alliance rouge et verte*. Parties can also disappear on being dissolved by the authorities, often because of implication in acts of violence – Corsican movements are particularly susceptible to dissolution.

PARTY IDENTITY

Even if the plethora of minor groups is ignored, the student of French politics will encounter an abundance of initials because of two common phenomena of French political parties; firstly their tendency to change their names much more frequently than is the case in Britain or the USA, usually to emphasize to the public that they have a new image. The Socialist Party was called *Section française de l'internationale ouvrière* (SFIO) from 1905 to 1969 and the *Parti socialiste* (PS) from 1971. During the 1969-71 hiatus, it was referred to as *'le nouveau parti socialiste'* which was a description rather than a title. The PCF was originally (1920-36) called *Section française de l'internationale communiste*. The Gaullist party has assumed various titles:

1946 *Union gaulliste*
1947–53 *Rassemblement du peuple français* (RPF) (between 1953 and 1958 Gaullists in parliament after the dissolution of the RPF called themselves *Républicains sociaux*)
1958 *Union pour la nouvelle république* (UNR)
1967 *Union des démocrates pour la Cinquième République* (UDV^c)
1968 *Union pour la défense de la République*, then *Union des démocrates pour la République* (UDR)
1976 *Rassemblement pour la République* (RPR)

Secondly, parties and groups frequently co-operate just for election periods under umbrella titles established only weeks before. Examples have been in the elections of:

1993   *Union pour la France* (a flimsy electoral umbrella over the RPR and UDF, despite having been mooted earlier as a step towards a single party)

1993   *Entente de écologistes* (a successful attempt by *Les Verts* and *Génération écologie* to avoid duplication of candidates)

1993   *Solidarité écologie gauche alternative* (combining the two small groups *Alliance rouge et verte* and *Alternative pour la démocratie et le socialisme*)

1988   *Union du rassemblement et du centre* (co-ordinating the RPR and UDF)

1986   *Alternative 86* (comprising the *Parti socialiste unifié*, *Ligue communiste révolutionnaire*, *Parti pour une alternative communiste*, *Fédération de la gauche alternative*, and assorted ecologists, regionalists and trade unionists)

1981   *Union pour la nouvelle majorité* (linking the RPR and UDF)

1978   *Union pour la Démocratie française* (UDF) (mainly comprising the *Parti républicain* (PR), the *Centre des démocrates sociaux* (CDS), and the *Parti radical*. This co-operative venture of course survived the election for which it was originally intended)

1973   *Union de la gauche socialiste et démocrate* (linking the PS and *Mouvement des radicaux de gauche* (MRG); these two parties co-operated closely in all subsequent elections)

DEVELOPMENT OF PARTIES AND POLITICAL GROUPS

It must not be forgotten that parties in the sense of permanent and centralized organizations did not appear on the French political scene until the beginning of the twentieth century, whereas a durable parliamentary republic was established in 1875 and universal masculine suffrage in 1848. But a very limited suffrage before then meant that 'parties' (in the sense of loose groups) in parliament had no incentive to organize or appeal to the electorate, as was the case in Britain, and political activity outside the *pays légal*, as Guizot called it, was restricted to clubs, often existing clandestinely. This fact, together with the massacre or exile of thousands of insurgents who had taken part in the Paris Commune of 1870–71, meant that even after the establishment of the Third Republic in the 1870s, socialists in France were divided over aims and methods, and a socialist party (the SFIO) was not founded until 1905.

In other parts of the political spectrum, parliamentary politics was traditionally organized through loose groups of local worthies (*notables*) whose electoral clientelism was limited to their own constituency and who felt little need of a national party organization, with the constraints which this implied. Thus it was not until 1901 that the radicals created a *Parti républicain radical et radical-socialiste*; it survived in the 1990s as a shadow of its former self, always referred to simply as the *Parti radical*. It was furious when the *Mouvement des radicaux de gauche*, itself an offshoot from the main body in 1972, changed its name in November 1994 to the single word *Radical*; court proceedings were instituted to end the alleged confusion.

The phenomenon of a loosely organized group with minimal parliamentary discipline and electoral co-ordination was still evident until the 1960s. In 1962, Valéry Giscard d'Estaing formed a pro-de Gaulle group of *députés* of the *Centre national des indépendants et paysans* (CNIP) into the *Républicains indépendants* (RI), but it was not until 1966 that he decided to organize it as a party in the sense of a nationwide organization dedicated to disseminating a doctrine, recruiting members and maximizing electoral support. It became the *Parti républicain* (PR) in May 1977.

In fact, as late as the 1960s, the French political party scene reflected almost perfectly Maurice Duverger's analysis of the distinction between the old, established *parti de cadres*, like the ones just described, and the newer phenomenon of the *parti de masse* such as the SFIO and PCF, more suited to parliamentary democracy in the second half of the twentieth century because of their higher membership, tighter organization, clear policy alternatives based on a distinct doctrine, and high level of political activity outside election periods. But this analysis needed to be refined in the light of the emergence of a Gaullist party in the 1960s and a new *Parti socialiste* in the 1970s which perceived its functions in a different light and could best be called a *parti d'électeurs*, that is, a party which tried to appeal to the widest possible electorate. The consequences of this development were, firstly, a more even geographical spread of the electoral support for a specific party (though sometimes 'bastions' survive) and, secondly, a reduction in the extent to which party programmes were inspired by ideologies, which were reduced to a source of slogans used to mobilize support, justify allegiance and attack adversaries. However, commentators in the 1990s still suggest that the purely local concerns of *notables* distort the role of parties in the democratic process.

PARTY APPEAL

All parties now have to appeal to a wider circle than their 'natural' or traditional supporters. Aware of its waning support from the

1970s onwards, the PCF adopted less ideologically specific slogans, and instead called for an *'Union du peuple de France'* (at its 22nd Congress in 1976) and a *'Rassemblement populaire majoritaire'* (at its 25th Congress in 1985). In 1994 (28th Congress) it finally dropped the doctrine of democratic centralism, when Robert Hue, the new leader, said *'Le PCF a définitivement rompu avec le stalinisme'*. Emphasis was to be on *'le progrès social à la française'*; much of its rulebook was rewritten, though factions (*tendances* or *courants*) within its ranks were still not permitted.

Conscious of the mobilizing force of the word 'socialism', the RPR–UDF was led in the mid-1980s to use 'liberalism' as a counter, even though this created problems of interpretation in such a wide-based coalition before the March 1986 elections and into the 1990s. Moreover, the distinction must be made between the anti-interventionist emphasis of continental 'liberal' tradition, dating from the nineteenth century, and the preference for state-sponsored social reform characteristic of British liberalism.

In the 1990s, the ideological basis of parties had weakened to the extent that the Socialist Party had moved very close to a free-market position to broaden its appeal, and the right had to some extent embraced the concept of solidarity in the fight against social exclusion – a strong theme of Chirac's 1995 presidential campaign, though less in evidence after his victory.

In more concrete terms, political parties in France can hope to enlarge their appeal through the press and television, but they have also exploited the relatively high propensity of French people to buy paperbacks, by publishing political manifestos and sometimes 'blue-prints for society' (*projets de société*) in this easily digested format. Early examples were the Radical Party's *Ciel et terre* in 1970 (the most comprehensive electoral promise of all time?), and *Changer la vie* (PS, 1972). In the mid-1980s appeared *Réflexions pour demain* (Raymond Barre, 1984) and *Pour la France* (FN, 1985). By the end of the 1980s, however, the paperback book format tended to give way, on the grounds of cost, to mere booklets such as *La France citoyenne* (*Parti radical*, 1987), *Propositions pour la France* (PS, 1988), *Justice, liberté, paix* (PCF, 1988) and *Le Pacte UDF pour la France* (UDF, 1988). In the 1990s, examples of publications outlining political programmes have been *La France en mouvement – rassembler pour changer* (RPR, 1991), *La Réforme, maintenant!* (RPR, 1992, in anticipation of the 1993 elections), *Projet socialiste pour l'an 2000* (PS, 1991); and the list-making *20 réformes pour changer la France* (RPR, 1993) and *40 priorités pour l'alternance* (UDF, 1993). In 1995, the *Parti radical* issued the very solid *Humaniste, laïc, social, européen – le manifeste des radicaux*. 1995 presidential candidates published manifesto paperbacks:

Mon ambition pour la France (Philippe de Villiers), *La France pour tous* (Jacques Chirac) and *Inventer ensemble un autre avenir* (Robert Hue, the communist candidate).

Opinion polls confirm the suspicion that television is the main influence on electoral behaviour, followed by newspapers, radio, magazines, and meetings, leaflets and posters. But 'conversations' and opinion polls themselves, over which the parties have in law no control, also figure on the list.

PARTY ORGANIZATION

The major political parties in France tend to have remarkably similar organizational structure. The basic geographical framework of party organization, as in so many aspects of French administrative life, is at the level of the *département*, and usually called a *fédération*; these normally have at least some full-time staff and co-ordinate groups at the local level, whether *comités de base* (Rad.) or *cellules* (PCF) grouped into *sections* (PCF and most other parties). The focus of membership activity in organizational terms is the national delegate conference held typically every two years, and called *congrès* (PCF, CDS, UDF, Rad., FN), *congrès national* (PS, *Fédération anarchiste*), *assemblée générale* (Les Verts), or *assises nationales* (RPR, *Génération écologie*). Parties can of course call special conferences when necessary, and the parties sometimes hold mini-conferences on matters of the moment in the intervals between full party conferences.

The conference elects (or rubberstamps the appointment of) a consultative body, sometimes referred to in the press as the 'parliament' of a party, called *conseil national* (RPR, PR, UDF, *Génération écologie*), *comité national* (PCF), *comité directeur* (PS, CNI, MRG), or *conseil national interrégional* (Les Verts), above which is the central policy-making group, the 'government' of the party: *bureau national* (PCF, PSD, MRG, CDS, *Génération écologie*), *bureau politique* (Rad., PR, UDF, RPR, UPF, FN), *commission exécutive* (CNI), *bureau exécutif* (PS) or *collège exécutif* (Les Verts), sometimes with a smaller core of leaders, a *secrétariat national* (PS, PCF, PR) or *commission exécutive* (RPR). The party leader, with whom of course the party will be associated in the minds of the public, is a *président* (RPR, UDF, CDS, Rad.), or *premier secrétaire* (PS), or *secrétaire national* (PCF, since 1994, when Robert Hue replaced the long-serving Georges Marchais).

PARTY MEMBERSHIP

Membership of French political parties is always difficult to assess with accuracy, since parties tend to inflate figures to prove their own popularity. In 1996 party claims were: CNI (*Centre national des indépendants*) 25,000 ['members and sympathizers'], *Mouvement des citoyens* 5,800, *Génération écologie* 2,500, *Les Verts* 3,500, PCF 450,000, PS nearly 140,000, *Parti radical* 5,000, *Radical* (the former MRG) 25,000, CDS (since November 1995, *Force démocrate*) 52,000, PR 20,000, UDF 'direct members' 15,000, FN 60,000 (the secret service appears to put the real count at half this figure); the RPR claimed 99,161 members in August 1996 in a memorandum leaked (probably deliberately) to the right-wing newspaper *Le Figaro*. The sum of these figures, which in the 1990s is shrinking every year, is at odds with the more objective estimate of academic commentators who put the total membership of French political parties at not much more than half a million.

A major problem is to determine what constitutes membership, and to take account of the rapid turnover of members. Parties which emphasize the possession of a membership card tend to ignore the concomitant requirement of a valid contribution payment record throughout the year, and their claims may rely too much on the number of cards sold, or given away, at mobilizing events such as the long-established *Fête de l'Humanité* (PCF, annually on the second weekend in September), the more recent *Fête de la Rose* (PS), *Fête des bleus-blancs-rouges* (FN), or *Fête de Lutte ouvrière* (since 1969). In fact, even among French people who identify positively with one particular party, that is, whose interest goes potentially beyond merely voting reasonably consistently for a party, the desire to join or financially support that party is not strong.

Mobilization of party activists at another level can take the form of periodic meetings of the leaders of the *fédération* in each of the 96 *départements* in metropolitan France (though not all parties have an organization in every *département*), of parliamentarians in *'journées parlementaires'* before the October and April National Assembly sessions (since 1995, the National Assembly meets in a single session from October to the following summer), and of sitting members and candidates, actual or potential, in an *'université de printemps'* or *'université d'été'*; these tend to be held in a salubrious part of southern France, though in the 1990s, the *Front national* was denied a meeting-place by the mayors of many places until it won control of three towns in the 1995 municipal elections.

PARLIAMENTARY CANDIDATURE

Candidature in parliamentary elections is open to every citizen fulfilling certain legal conditions, but was progressively monopolized by political parties between 1958 and 1981, and after 1988, that is, when the electoral system was based on single-member constituencies; moreover, this tendency was compounded in 1986 by the system of proportional representation requiring a list of at least four people in a *département* (it depended on population size), which presupposed some coincidence of viewpoint and led to a reduction in the number of candidates not readily identifiable by party.

The typical candidate will emerge directly from the party, regarding candidature as a further step in commitment or in a political career. This is particularly so on the left, where PS candidates must have three years' party membership behind them, and about one-third of PCF candidates will be full-time party members – which explains why the proportion of 'new' candidates tends to be smaller for the PCF than for any other party.

But a strongly entrenched 'independent' local politician is sometimes able (frequently on the right, very occasionally on the left) to negotiate, or tactically oblige, endorsement by a party with which he or she has the closest political affinities. In the 1990s, regional elections by direct suffrage (held every six years from 1986) provided many cases of dissident local candidates asserting themselves successfully over party machines.

Nevertheless, party central leaderships in Paris have played an increasingly important part in the Fifth Republic in approving candidatures arising at local constituency (or, in 1986, *département*) level, sometimes by mediating between rival personalities and their supporters, for example between a local contender and a total outsider indulging in what is called *'parachutage'*.

FINANCIAL AID

The question of the financial support which parties need for their activities, particularly at election times, traditionally caused considerable problems. Since 1995, if a parliamentary election candidate receives 5 per cent of votes cast, the state repays half of all campaign costs, provided the total is below the legal maximum, and accounts are approved. As well as this change, the state (to ensure equality) has always paid for the propaganda sheets which are posted with ballot papers to each elector, the ballot papers themselves (these are candidate-specific), and the posters put on official hoardings outside polling stations. The money involved is not insignificant, but proposals to give state financial aid to the parties themselves to cover adequately the whole range of their activities always ran into difficulties. Giscard in his reforming mood raised the question in 1974 and again in 1978, but recognized the problems. For example, which 'parties' would qualify? Would there have to be a stricter legal framework, including the difficult task of actually defining a political party? On what basis would money be distributed – should it be the percentage of votes received at parliamentary elections? The parties themselves, as one would expect, were generally in favour of official funding, but doubts about the destination of money given to the PCF used to be a problem; and sceptics pointed to the Italian and German examples, where a system of state financial aid did not put a stop to secret funding.

Laws in 1988, 1990 and 1995 established (in defiance of public opinion) and progressively refined a system of state finance for parties. The total sum (526 million francs in 1995) is distributed annually under two heads:

■ • half to parties as a proportion of total votes they received in the first round of the previous National Assembly election (proviso: a candidate in at least 50 constituencies; but no threshold percentage of votes received, hence the proliferation of parties in the 1993 election);

■ • half to parties qualifying under the first head, according to the number of their *députés* and senators.

The law has also tried to solve the problem of the openness (*transparence*) of political party accounts by bringing them into the public domain. Thus PS total receipts for 1993 consisted of 167 million francs state grant, 32 million in dues from ordinary members and 26.5 million from elected members at all levels, and 63 million in donations and fund-raising channelled through national and local party organizations – the legal upper limit for donations was 500,000 for companies (*personnes morales*) until this became illegal in 1995, and 50,000 francs for individuals.

For the RPR, receipts in 1993 included 134.8 million state grant, 29 million in dues, 47 million in donations from businesses (871 in all), and 51 million from individuals, for example through mailshots and subscription dinners.

In 1995, the main parties received from the state (in millions of francs): RPR 160.7, UDF 156, PS and *Radical* 90.5, FN 36.6, PCF 36.1, *Les Verts* 11.6, *Génération écologie* 10.3.

The recent spate of legislation has attempted to eliminate shady financial practices in political parties. However, the finances of the *Parti républicain* were scrutinized by a judge in 1994 (a PR government minister resigned), and the *Front national*, which is funded largely from the personal fortunes of its leaders, collections at meetings, local councillors' allowances, and donations from nobility and former members of the armed forces, has given explicit hints on evading legal constraints on political funding in its *Guide du candidat du Front national*.

INTRA-PARTY RELATIONS

The organizational structure of parties can reveal significant variations in the degree of internal democracy. The constitution (*statuts*) of the new PS in 1971 was based on a determined effort to move away from the 1945–69 period which allowed domination of the former SFIO by a small group under the leadership of Guy Mollet. The composition of the *comité directeur* is a direct reflection of the proportion of support at the party conference for general policy motions proposed by different factions (*courants*) within the party.

The PS in power after 1981 tried to minimize the centrifugal tendencies of factions in an effort to present a united front. Factions continued to put forward their own motions on party strategy and self-image to party conferences, but composite motions (*motions de synthèse*) were hammered out and usually carried overwhelmingly, though difficulties did occur occasionally, such as at the Rennes conference in March 1990. *Parti socialiste* election performance has sometimes been hampered by disputes between a party leader wanting the campaign to be narrowly party-led (Jospin in 1986; Fabius in 1993) and a socialist Prime Minister wanting a broader campaign based on the existing wider 'majority' (Fabius in 1986; Bérégovoy in 1993). In 1993, moreover, both personalities were tainted by scandal – Bérégovoy for a private interest-free 1 million franc loan in 1986, Fabius for continuing to allow contaminated blood to be given to haemophiliacs in 1983–85.

An examination of individual French political parties shows they are not monolithic blocs, any more than parties in other countries, and the extent of intra-party strife is quite significant. Even the Gaullist party (RPR) officially recognized factions in 1988 and institutionalized them in 1989, in an effort to contain a revolt of younger *rénovateurs* against the Chirac-led old guard. Factions formed around Chirac and Alain Juppé as a mainstream; the 'odd couple' Charles Pasqua and Philippe Séguin, who set up an organization *Demain la France* which campaigned for a 'no' vote in the 1992 Maastricht referendum (this paradoxically broadened the RPR's audience), and issued policy statements independently of the RPR in the 1993 election campaign; Richard Cazenave, who took over a social justice oriented faction called *Vie* when Alain Carignon was suspended in 1990; and Michel Noir and Michele Barzac, who left the party in 1990 and fought by-elections against official candidates. The problem with the RPR in the 1990s is that it has found it difficult to remain faithful to an easily identifiable political project. Indeed, in the 1990s, consensus, particularly within the larger parties in France, is being undermined by new issues such as the future of the EU in the light of the Maastricht Treaty.

The most dramatic manifestation of intra-party conflict in the 1980s and 1990s was in the PCF. In an effort to emerge from the long period of opposition which had begun in 1947 (usually referred to as a 'political ghetto'), the PCF in the 1960s and 1970s adopted a less uncompromising stance and showed signs of ideological flexibility. But the close co-operation with the PS which produced a joint policy programme to be applied once the left came to power was abruptly halted in 1977. This heralded a period of internal dissension hardly muted by the 1981–84 participation in a left-wing government. Factions representing differing strategies later appeared:

1987 *rénovateurs*, at first led by Pierre Juquin, who was soon expelled (he stood as an independent left-wing Presidential candidate in 1988, and in 1991 joined *Les Verts*);

1987 *reconstructeurs*, led by Marcel Rigout, who remained members but were stripped of leadership positions. They formed the *Association de recherche et d'initiatives pour l'autogestion et le socialisme*, later called *Alternative pour la démocratie et le socialisme*;

1989 *refondateurs*, led by the four former PCF ministers of 1981–84, whose strategy was to reform the party from within. In the run-up to the 29th Congress in December 1996, they were described as the *'aile progressiste'* of the party, advocating wide internal consultation in the drawing-up of the policy document to be approved by the Congress.

The natural concomitant of this fission was a further decline in electoral support; the PCF presidential candidate's showing in 1988 was less than 7 per cent, the lowest since 1945; and in 1995 this showing had climbed to only 8.6 per cent.

INTER-PARTY RELATIONS

Relations between parties in France have traditionally been focused on the need in a multi-party system to maximize chances of electoral success, however slim these may be in reality, by co-operation with other parties. The Greens (*Les Verts*) try to apply the maxim *'ni gauche, ni droite'*, but local factors often force them to ally with the left, or with the smaller *Génération écologie*, which claims to be more 'realistic'. Even parties which have been dominant at a given time – the Gaullist party in the 1960s, the PS in the 1980s – cannot ignore the fact that the circumstances which gave them this advantage (usually disarray in the opposing camp) may not endure in the longer term.

The post-war party system in France is best seen as the concretization in party terms of six main 'political families'. This term implies a tradition of shared memories, attitudes and beliefs which may predate the parties themselves: thus there was a body of thought and doctrine appearing at different points in history for each of communism, socialism, radicalism, Christian democracy, liberalism, and (historically more recent of course) Gaullism, before the existence of the respective parties – PCF; SFIO then PS; *Parti radical*; MRP then CDS then *Force démocrate*; CNI/RI then PR then UDF; the successive Gaullist parties (see page 40).

Elections in 1958 to the new Fifth Republic parliament continued the post-war pattern of a National Assembly in which the six political families mentioned above were represented by a party. But whereas this six-party configuration was preserved after the election in November 1962 of a second parliament, a new phenomenon also appeared which has profoundly affected inter-party relations since that date. This was *'le fait majoritaire'*, that is, the existence in the National Assembly of a majority group of *députés* willing to give support to the government's policies – a government party, or closely co-operating group of parties, owing its majority position to the fact that voters were impressed by the past record of the President and the government appointed by him, or on the other hand preferred, as in 1981, 1986 and 1993, opposition policies. This *alternance* (peaceful transfer of power) of the 1980s made parties more 'respectable' in that an election could now mean a change of party or coalition of parties in power and not just a reshuffle of the previous governing coalition; but it took a long time to materialize. The majority in 1962 comprised the UNR plus the RI led by Giscard; the Christian democrat MRP was also very briefly associated, until de Gaulle alienated it by his anti-European utterances. The existence of this right-wing majority obliged the remaining parties to reassess their position. The MRP dissolved itself in 1966 to become the *Centre des démocrates sociaux* (CDS), dropping explicit allegiance to reformist Catholicism, but preserving its pro-European leanings and hoping to keep alive a separate centrist identity at a time of increasing bipolarization of the party system between right and left. It renamed itself *Force démocrate* in November 1995, abandoning its Christian 'reference' and adopting a secular stance, but still insisting that it was centrist.

Bipolarization was fostered, firstly, by the new method, applying from 1965, of direct election of the President by a two-round system where only the two best-placed candidates went through to the second round, and secondly by the requirement from 1966 that a candidate in the first round of National Assembly elections, to be permitted to stand again in the second round, must receive a number of votes equal to 10 per cent of registered voters – raised to 12.5 per cent in 1976. This meant that the *Front national*, as a 'third-force' party, was able to contest the second round of the 1993 National Assembly elections in only 12 constituencies.

It was particularly on the left that adjustment to the new reality of a majority in parliament was necessary if it was itself to constitute a majority of its own, but changes were slow to appear. The PS and PCF found it easy to continue with electoral co-operation, begun tentatively in 1962, whereby the candidate with fewer first-round votes withdrew and urged supporters to back the other party's candidate (*désistement réciproque*). This rational tactic allowed both parties to maximize their parliamentary representation in elections between 1967 and 1981 (and its revival was unsuccessfully mooted in 1991 in anticipation of elections in 1992 and 1993), but co-operation on actual policy was a different matter. The strategy which eventually bore fruit in 1981 was begun in embryonic form by Mitterrand's presidential bid as the candidate of all the left in the 1965 elections. It was Mitterrand who realized that the left must accept that:

- the new Fifth Republic regime was entrenched in public opinion;
- the presidency was the locus of power in this regime;
- a majority in sociological terms could be converted into a parliamentary majority only if the non-communist left first united, and then acted in close political, and not just electoral, conjunction with the PCF.

To try to unite the non-communist left, Mitterrand in 1965 linked the SFIO, his own group of political clubs (CIR) and the *Parti radical*, but this attempt foundered in the aftermath of the Events of May–June 1968. The *Parti radical* then pursued its own course, and split in two in 1972. It was not until after 1971 that the non-communist left was effectively united in the new *Parti socialiste*. Relations between socialists and the PCF, which had been characterized during the 1960s by 'two steps forward, one step back', took a major step forward in 1972 when the Joint Programme for Government was signed by the PS, the PCF and soon afterwards the MRG, and the *Union de la gauche* began actually to mean something. This development, together with the progressive incorporation between 1969 and 1974 of the centre (CDS) and the rump of the *Parti radical* into the governing right-wing majority, gave the party system a distinct bipolar appearance in the mid-1970s.

However, perfect bipolarization was impossible so long as left and right were not solid coalitions. Not only was the Giscardian wing of the right loosely structured and lacking a coherent policy – and the establishment of the UDF in 1978 did nothing to change this – but its relations with the Gaullists have always been far from harmonious. This was especially true after 1976 when Chirac decided he could no longer continue as Prime Minister, and transformed the

Gaullist party into the RPR as a vehicle for his presidential ambitions. Chirac refused to let the RPR be 'giscardized'; and when Paris was finally allowed to have a mayor in 1977 he soundly beat Giscard's candidate in the election for the post, remaining mayor (as well as Prime Minister, 1986–88) until his own successful campaign for the presidency in 1995.

On the left, the *Union de la gauche* suffered a setback in 1977 by its failure to update the 1972 Joint Programme, and the PCF, unwilling to accommodate a shift in the centre of gravity (*rééquilibrage*) within the left, resumed hardline criticism of its socialist partners. When in 1981 the dimension of joint participation in government became available, it should have marked the supreme achievement of the left's objectives, but instead it merely served to underline the divergent perceptions and strategies within the Union. The PCF indulged in *participation sans soutien*, and this only until 1984. In any case the PS parliamentary landslide in June 1981 allowed it to constitute a majority on its own without having to rely on communist votes. The *Union de la gauche* appeared dead and buried by 1986 in national terms though there was some degree of local electoral co-operation in the 1989 and 1995 municipal elections, and talk of it in anticipation of 1998 National Assembly elections. It had, since 1962, taken the form of joint opposition and joint government, but had never been put to the supreme test of joint parliamentary majority, a test which the right passed with difficulty in 1976–81 and 1986–88.

The fact that Jacques Chirac failed to convert his two years as Prime Minister into a successful presidential bid in 1988 was a bitter blow to the parties of the right; moreover, in the 1988–93 parliament they could overturn the left-wing government on a motion of censure only if the communists voted with them. In the late 1980s and into the 1990s, moves to closer co-operation between the RPR and the UDF were always doomed to failure. Disagreement in 1989 over whether the co-ordinating organization should be called an *union* or an *alliance* was symptomatic of constraints on RPR–UDF co-operation. With a history of significantly divergent political cultures and policy stances (particularly on Europe), and with two long-established politicians and several younger aspirants in leadership contention, all that initially united the *Union pour la France* (UPF), set up in June 1990, was a determination not to countenance electoral co-operation with the *Front national*; the small CNI, which favoured co-operation, was therefore excluded from the UPF. Moreover, the UDF brought to the UPF not a dynamic mass organization, strong at grassroots level, but merely a loose amalgam of smaller groups with separate identities. Of these groups, the *Parti républicain* contemplated a separate direct participation in the UPF, rather than through the UDF; and the CDS, in an effort to re-assert centrism as a political force, had formed an autonomous parliamentary group, the *Union démocratique et du centre* (UDC) in the 1988–93 parliament. The RPR–UDF held single-issue conferences (*'états généraux'*) in 1990–91 in parallel with the establishment of the *Union pour la France*, but the latter was seen by opponents as little more than a device for future electoral co-operation in the selection of single first-round right-wing candidates, like the URC in 1988.

The political fortunes of the extreme right in France were at a low ebb after 1945, but decolonization and especially the Algerian war (1954–62) gave a boost to virulent anti-system (which from 1958 meant anti-de Gaulle) nationalism; however, Jean-Marie Le Pen, as the leader of one of the extreme right factions – among which fusion and fission were rife – received only 0.76 per cent of first-round votes in his 1974 presidential bid. In 1981 he was unable to collect the 500 signatures legally required for a presidential candidature (raised from 100 in 1976) and the FN received only 0.18 per cent of the total vote in the National Assembly elections. But by making race and immigration an electoral issue – or as Le Pen would have it, by 'saying out loud what everybody thought in their hearts' – support climbed to 11 per cent in the 1984 European elections, 14.4 per cent for Le Pen's 1988 presidential candidacy, and 15 per cent in 1995.

The mid-1990s party system, therefore, revealed two elements:

- elements of bipolarization, in that an inchoate majority coalition on the right (supporting Chirac as President) faced a party on the left – the PS – which had dominated the 1980s and which by winning the 1998 parliamentary elections could profit from an ensuing period of *cohabitation*, with this time a left government and a right-wing President, and potentially twice as long as 1986–88 and 1993–95;

- elements of a multi-party system with parties still representing the six traditional 'political families', one of which (the PCF) together with the FN was excluded from the major 'poles', thereby reinforcing their anti-system tendencies.

LIMITS TO PARTY INFLUENCE

In fulfilling their traditional function of 'intermediaries' between governors and governed, political parties in France, as elsewhere, aggregate interests, channel demands and draw up policies. Yet much political action takes place either outside political parties or involving them only marginally. Some elements of this exclusion arise from factors specific to France:

- the particular circumstances of the first decades of the Third

Republic, proclaimed in 1870, militated against the formation of a broad party of labour. Political action in defence of the economic interests of labour has been undertaken as much by trade unions as by the parliamentary left;

■ • groups in the French second chamber predated the foundation of political parties, and there are still groups in the Fifth Republic Senate not identifiable with a party;

■ • during the nineteenth century, political clubs kept alive republican humanism associated with the 1789 Revolution. They still undertake political education and, especially in opposition, doctrinal renewal – functions which are not always performed well by the parties themselves;

■ • the phenomenon, not exclusively French, of broad-based nationalist movements has also militated against political parties – Bonapartism, particularly in its plebiscitary phase under the Second Empire, and in more recent times Petainism (1940–44) and pre-1969 Gaullism.

In his bid to re-establish the authority of the state, de Gaulle made a deliberate attempt to reduce the role of political parties in the new Fifth Republic regime: the President of the Republic was to be elected not by the two Chambers of parliament as before, but by a much larger *'collège'* (since 1965, of course, by the whole people); single-member constituencies were intended to reduce the salience of parties and increase the focus on individuals in electoral choice (this stratagem, of course, failed as parties gradually reasserted themselves); the upper Chamber, peopled by largely non-party *notables*, was renamed the Senate and its role increased.

Moreover, political parties which played a crucial role in France, if not in establishing representative democracy, at least in defending it under the Third and Fourth Republics, have not always found it easy to come to terms with participatory democracy in the second half of the twentieth century. The *'participation'* which was a central element of de Gaulle's political thought has always occupied a minor place in the policy programme of the Gaullist party, though it occasionally resurfaces in groups on the Gaullist left.

Advocacy of the self-management (*autogestion*) of units of economic – and by implication political and cultural – activity was half-heartedly undertaken by the left in the 1970s, particularly in the Rocardian faction of the PS; by the early 1990s, however, after the PSU dissolved itself, *autogestion* was reduced to a strand of left-wing Green thinking. Directly elected regional councils and a measure of administrative decentralization had to wait until the 1980s. Parties will be further bypassed if significant use is made of the 1995 constitutional change to Article 11, allowing broad issues of public concern to be the subject of direct consultation of the people by referendum.

A further measure of how political parties are far from all-pervading is that politicians, particularly on the left, are at pains to show awareness of a *'société civile'*, which is best understood as those non-state economic, social and cultural forces which give life to a society through their own initiative, outside spheres where the state has a monopoly of action or maintains a bureaucracy. Commentators have suggested that located within, or arising from, this civil society are countervailing forces (*contre-pouvoirs*), including the expanding phenomenon of 'associations' (not all of which are explicitly political) which serve to limit the power of the state. As they struggle to cope with rising electoral abstentionism, falling membership and the increasing unpopularity of political leaders, political parties in France may find it increasingly difficult to reconcile their desire to foster or exploit or supplant these forces, with their own close involvement in the institutions of the state.

THE ROLE OF PARTIES IN THE SYSTEM

It was this close involvement which, as the Fifth Republic developed, allowed political parties to recover the influence of which the framers of the 1958 Constitution tried to deprive them. It was accepted that parties, as traditional defenders of representative democracy, would dominate the National Assembly – which was why the latter's powers were significantly curtailed in 1958. But parties came into their own again in three ways: firstly, the unforeseen emergence after 1962 of a parliamentary majority, and the coincidence of this with a presidential majority, if necessary by a newly elected President dissolving the National Assembly and provoking new elections as in 1981 (dubbed *la grande alternance*) and 1988; secondly, the growth of bipolarization which made electoral choice between party policy programmes or presidential candidates with party labels the determinant of political decisions; and thirdly, the close relationship between political parties and the presidency.

The original Gaullian concept of a non-party President is tenacious. It was suggested in 1965 that somebody like Albert Schweitzer could take over from de Gaulle, and the equivalent line of thought in the 1980s produced names such as the singer Yves Montand or Bernard Tapie (then a successful businessman), and in the first half of the 1990s Jacques Delors, whose identification with party was not strong. However, the parties have become indissociable from political power by offering what they did before 1958 – a path to the highest political office. Because this office in the Fifth Republic is the directly elected presidency, every party in France has to be in the basic sense a *parti d'électeurs*. The phenomenon can be looked at in two ways.

Firstly, one can speak of the presidentialization of political parties. Public acceptance in the 1962 referendum of a directly elected presidency meant that politicians recognized as serious potential candidates (*'présidentiable'*) gained in stature within their party, and parties began to discard ideological baggage and detach themselves from too-specific class clienteles. The formal structure of parties, or at least the leadership composition and role of grassroots members, tended to be modified (for example the Gaullist party in 1967, and the PS gradually during the 1970s) to give support to its *présidentiable* and, more importantly, to increase his or her general popularity; the obvious reason was that, to win a second-round presidential run-off, candidates need much wider support than the traditional electorate of a single party. Thus Pompidou needed the support of some centrists in 1969, Giscard of some Gaullists led by Chirac (rewarded with the office of Prime Minister) in 1974, Mitterrand of communists in 1981 and centrists in 1988, and Chirac of Giscardians in 1995. A party needs a candidate of stature in the eyes of the electorate, but a serious candidate needs more than a party. Moreover, having more than one *présidentiable* can be a source of weakness for a party. For example the PS had Mitterrand and Rocard in 1981 and 1988, and in 1995 Jospin, Lang and Emmanuelli (plus Delors until he ruled himself out); and Chirac and Balladur came from the same RPR camp in 1995 (for a time there was a strong possibility that they would be rivals in the second-round run-off, and indeed the RPR did not officially support either candidate). The idea of American-style presidential primaries, very popular in the 1990s in the public mind (see *Le Monde*, 2 August 1994), was rejected by all political party leaderships.

The second aspect of the close association of a political party with the presidency is when a presidential strategy is successful and a party's candidate becomes President. Already under the Giscard presidency (1974–81) the decisive role of the parties in both government composition and presidential action was being felt – the President needed the Gaullist party and ministers were in the government as representatives of their party; also, party nepotism and administrative clientelism began to take root. So it might have been thought, when the 1981 and 1988 elections produced a socialist President and a PS majority in the National Assembly (actual in 1981, virtual in 1988), that the PS would be in a position to determine the major orientations of policy. But while it is true that there could be hard bargaining before the party gave its support to the government (for example the 1990 recasting of the social welfare contribution scheme as a *contribution sociale généralisée*), the *Parti socialiste* was never allowed to impose its will on the President or the government. The party leadership was not allowed to assume a mediating function between the 1981–86 and 1988–93 governments and the PS parliamentary group.

Similarly, Balladur as Prime Minister in 1994 wrote to party leaders of the majority coalition in the National Assembly (Chirac for the RPR and Giscard for the UDF) to try to reduce disharmony; when Chirac countered by inviting Balladur to meet the RPR leadership, Nicolas Sarkozy (Balladur's right-hand man in the government) countered that the Fifth Republic regime was not one where *'les chefs de parti font la pluie et le beau temps'*.

In the final analysis, a party in power is subject to the institutional logic of the Fifth Republic. Mitterrand used presidential powers to reduce party influence in Chirac's 1986 government by rejecting party leaders from the majority coalition as Defence and Foreign Affairs Ministers, and imposing non-party ministers. Mitterrand's electoral triumphs in 1981 and 1988, and Chirac's in 1995, were on the basis of a programme worked out by the personal team of each, not by the party leadership, though obviously there was cross-membership. When people spoke of a 'PS state' in 1981–86, as they had of a 'UDR state' in the late 1960s, they were saying no more than that there was a dominant political party which had successfully adjusted to a novel situation. French political parties have

François Mitterrand handed over presidential powers to Jacques Chirac in May 1995. It was only after Mitterrand's death in January 1996 that Chirac, always prone to irrational and hasty action, appeared to assume a more balanced 'vision'

largely recovered from the subordinate position to which the Fifth Republic regime as initially conceived in 1958 had consigned them.

However, increasingly in the 1990s French people speak of a 'crisis in politics', of 'democracy in danger' and the need for a 'renewal of politics'. Political parties are accused of reacting tardily to the everyday concerns of consumers, young people, environmentalists, residents of run-down suburbs, and those in insecure jobs. With their mediating role between individuals and state being increasingly usurped by the media, opinion poll organizations and various forms of direct communication, the role, perceived function and mutual relations of political parties in 1990s France are far from settled.

BIBLIOGRAPHY

General

Chagnollaud, D. (ed.), *La Vie politique en France*. Paris, Seuil, 1993. Especially Part II.

Charlot, J., *La Politique en France*. Paris, Livre de Poche, 1992.

Portelli, H., *La Ve République*. Paris, Grasset, 1994. Provides a historical narrative on Fifth Republic politics from an institutional and analytical perspective.

In English, the following introductory books are suggested:

Charlot, J., *The Political Parties and the Party System in France*. Paris, Ministère des Affaires Etrangères, Direction de la Presse, 1986. A very basic survey, obtainable from 37, Quai d'Orsay, 75007 Paris, or French embassies.

Hall, P. A., Hayward, J. and Machin, H., *Developments in French Politics*. Basingstoke, Macmillan, revised edition, 1994. Chapters 1 and 2.

Morris, P., *French Politics Today*. Manchester, Manchester University Press, 1994. Chapters 7 and 8.

Stevens, A., *The Government and Politics of France*. Basingstoke, Macmillan, 1992.

Wright, V., *The Government and Politics of France*. London, Routledge, 1994.

Books which are relatively easy to read and digest from the point of view of content are:

Addinall, N. A. (ed.), *French Political Parties – A Documentary Guide*. Cardiff, University of Wales Press, 1995.

Bell, D. S., and Criddle, B., *The French Communist Party in the Fifth Republic*. Oxford, Clarendon Press, 1994.

Bennahmias, J.-L., and Roche, A., *Des Verts de toutes les couleurs – histoire et sociologie du mouvement écolo*. Paris, Albin Michel, 1992.

Borella, F., *Les Partis politiques dans la France d'aujourd'hui*. Paris, Seuil, 1990.

Cole, A. (ed.), *French Political Parties in Transition*. Aldershot, Dartmouth Press, 1990.

Knapp, A., *Gaullism since de Gaulle*. Aldershot, Dartmouth Press, 1994.

Marcus, J., *The National Front and French Politics*. Basingstoke, Macmillan, 1995.

Petitfils, J.-C., *La Droite en France de 1789 à nos jours*. Paris, PUF, 1994.

Portelli, H., *Le Parti socialiste*. Paris, Montchrestien, 1992.

Prendiville, B., *Environmental Politics in France*. London, Westview Press, 1994.

Rémond, R., *La Politique n'est plus ce qu'elle était*. Paris, Calmann-Lévy, 1993. Especially Parts I and II.

Vermont, O., *Bienvenue au(x) parti(s)*. Paris, Archipel, 1995.

Ysmal, C., *Les Partis politiques sous la Ve République*. Paris, Monchrestien, 1989.

Books which are useful, but which may be of greater conceptual difficulty are:

Avril, P., *Essais sur les partis politiques*. Paris, Payot, 1991. Not all on France.

Bon, F., and Cheylan, J.-P., *La France qui vote*. Paris, Hachette, 1988. Based on maps showing party electoral support.

Brechon, P., *La France aux urnes – cinquante ans d'histoire électorale*. Paris, La Documentation française, Série Notes et Etudes Documentaires, no. 5008, 1995. The analysis is on a party basis.

Brechon, P., *Le Discours politique en France – évolution des idées partisanes*. Paris, La Documentation française, Série Notes et Etudes Documentaires, no. 4996, 1995.

Camby, J.-P., *Le Financement de la vie politique en France*. Paris, Montchrestien, 1995.

Courtois, S., and Lazar, M., *Histoire du Parti communiste français*. Paris, PUF, 1995.

Daley, A. (ed.), *The Mitterrand Era – Policy Alternatives and Political Mobilization in France*. Basingstoke, Macmillan, 1996. Chapters 10 (PS), 11 (PCF) and 12 (Greens).

Dupin, E., *L'Après-Mitterrand – le Parti socialiste à la dérive*. Paris, Calmann-Lévy, 1991.

Habert, H., et al. (eds), *Le Vote sanction – les élections législatives des 21 et 28 mars 1993*. Paris, Presses de la FNSP, 1993. Has chapters on specific parties.

Mossuz-Lavau, J., *Les Français et la politique*. Paris, Odile Jacob, 1994.

Philippe, A., and Hubscher, D., *Enquête à l'intérieur du Parti socialiste*. Paris, Albin Michel, 1991.

Todd, E., *The Making of Modern France – Ideology, Politics and Culture*. Oxford, Basil Blackwell, 1991. Translation of *La Nouvelle France*. Paris, Seuil, 1987.

Ysmal, C., *Le Comportement électoral des Français*. Paris, La Découverte, 1990.

The reference book *Quid* (Paris, Laffont) appearing annually lists *'Partis, clubs et mouvements actuels'* with addresses of each and histories of the main ones.

The following journals are useful:

Pouvoirs (quarterly), especially 'La Ve République' (no. 49, 1989); 'Le Parlement' (no. 64, 1993); 'Qui gouverne la France?' (no. 68, 1994).

Revue française de science politique (quarterly), especially vol. 40, no. 6 (December 1990) which deals with the classical right, vol. 44, no. 3 (June 1994) which includes 'Le Parti socialiste face à l'écologisme'.

Regards sur l'Actualité (monthly, published by La Documentation française), especially nos 169, 170, 171, 176 (1991); 178, 184 (1992); 190 (1993); 203 (1994); 212, 213 (1995).

L'Etat de l'opinion, published as a yearbook by Le Seuil for the opinion poll organization SOFRES (*Société française d'enquêtes par sondage*), has excellent essays on parties and general politics.

Other media

French-speaking radio stations can usually be received adequately on long wave and are a source of information on the current political scene (all times quoted are French local time).

France-Inter
(1 852m): the early morning weekday news has political analysis at 7.55 a.m.; a guest, though not always a politician, at 8.20 a.m.; and a review of the press at 8.30 a.m.; at 7.20 p.m. on weekdays a phone-in programme on current issues is the long-established pattern.

Europe 1
(1 639m): the early morning weekday political coverage is at 7.20 and 7.45 a.m.; on Sundays at 8.45 a.m.

RTL
(1 271m): 'La Vie politique en France' is at 7.42 a.m. on weekdays; 'Fait politique' at 8.42 on Saturdays; the hour-long 'Grand jury' interview with a politician is at 6.30 p.m. on Sundays.

3

TRADE UNIONS

Richard McAllister

Introduction

The situation of trade unions in France is something of a paradox. It is most obviously described in terms of weakness: France has a smaller proportion of its workforce unionized than any other west European state. Its trade unionists are divided between several rival and usually antagonistic confederations – as indeed are other interest groups. And it appears that trade unions participate less in the processes of economic policy-making than those in most west European states.

Yet in late 1995 and early 1996, trade unions appeared to have made themselves felt. They played a part in the resignation of the Minister of Finance Alain Madelin in the right-of-centre government. They appeared able to create major chaos through a series of strikes centred on the public sector which in turn put pressure on the French franc. And they were being courted by government and employers alike, both because of their important role as partners in administering the country's welfare system, and for their potential usefulness in imposing a degree of order on a volatile workforce.

This chapter aims to describe and explain this curious situation. First, we need to note briefly the context in which trade unions in France have had to operate in the 1980s and 1990s.

Most observers are struck by the basic continuity and similarity of the economic policies pursued by successive French governments, whether notionally of the right or left, in the whole period since about 1982. These policies, including 'rigour' and austerity, have often been defended as a necessary, perhaps an inevitable, result of several developments. These have included: globalization of markets (including financial markets); the whole move towards a single market ('1992') within the EC; the continuous pressure exercised on French manufacturing and traded-goods sectors especially via the country's membership of the Exchange Rate Mechanism (ERM) of the European Monetary System (EMS); and the austerity imposed by the so-called 'convergence criteria' for entry into Economic and Monetary Union (EMU) under the Treaty on European Union ('Maastricht').

Such conditions have not been propitious for French trade unions. A report by the national statistical institute INSEE in late 1991 suggested that the industrial share of total employment in France dropped from about 24 per cent in 1970 to 18 per cent in 1990; that French industry had seen the loss of about 2 million jobs in that period; and that the steel and textiles sectors had lost more than half their workforces in that time. During the 1980s French industrial growth was several percentage points below the EC average.

It is true that many of these conditions applied, *mutatis mutandis*, to trade unions in other west European states. It is also true that unions in other European states as well as France have seen their membership figures slide downwards during this period. But alongside these shared trends and common experiences there are a number of features which are specific to the French situation. Unions in France have suffered from at least five kinds of weakness: numerical weakness; ideological divisions and difficulties in relationships among the various confederations; difficult relationships between leaderships and rank and file; between all confederations and the *patronat*; and with government and the political parties. This chapter will explore each of these. Although there have been some signs of change and some attempts at accommodation in recent years, many of these difficulties are of long standing, their roots going far back into French history.

Yet trade unions continue to be influential: and this was clearly shown, amongst other occasions, in October 1991. Then, certain French trade unions promised a socialist-led government that they would create, in the words of one of their leaders, 'economic death for 24 hours' via a general strike. In the event, the response was poor, and for many people the strike passed almost unnoticed.

This episode illustrated several of the weaknesses just mentioned. Firstly, the position of the unions in general, frail a decade earlier, had weakened considerably further by this time. Secondly, although early in the dispute several union confederations had managed a measure of agreement, there remained important elements of disunity and disagreement. Thirdly, even the Cresson government, weak though it was, was, like its predecessors of a different political hue, adept at exploiting these differences. Fourthly, most of such action as there was centred on the public rather than the private sector, highlighting the long-standing dichotomy of the fortune of French trade unions. Fifthly, though the unions threatened much, their bark was (as often) worse than their bite, even when faced by a government of rare unpopularity.

But if the October 1991 episode illustrates both the long-term and the more recent difficulties of trade unions in France, the events of late 1995 showed that they can sometimes retain a surprising degree of influence. They were partly responsible for the resignation of Alain Madelin as Minister of Finance, replaced by Jean Arthuis. And in October, a 24-hour strike of civil servants and public sector workers in protest at a pay freeze planned for 1996 was widely followed and brought much of the country to a halt: several other strikes followed. This was a show of unity not seen since 1986, when again the unions had managed to agree on united action in the face of a similar pay freeze. In December 1995, the government convened a 'social summit' to try to involve the unions in its proposed reforms and in defusing a tense economic situation.

Cartoon from
Le Monde,
11 October 1995

BACKGROUND

When Giscard was elected President in 1974, one of the first things to be commissioned was a report on reform of enterprises, the Sudreau Report. It traced the origins of the 'crisis of confidence between the social partners' back to the d'Allarde decree and the *Loi le Chapelier* of 1791. The latter, in particular, had prohibited members of any trade or profession from combining on the basis of their 'supposed common interests'. Reform of this situation was a long time coming, grudgingly given and limited: the recognition of unions (significantly, *syndicats*) by the law of 1884 had not given them the freedom to operate within individual plants, and most public services (including the railways) were prohibited initially from unionizing. The right to organize union sections in the workplace did not finally arrive until a law of December 1968, in the wake of 'the Events'.

Divisions were apparent almost immediately after the passing of the 1884 law. Indeed, despite changes of name and on occasion of stance, it is remarkable how closely the original lines of division match those of much later times: revolutionary and reformist; 'confessional' and secular. Right from the start, the divisions between the main strands of socialism in France found their echo in the industrial organizations. The strategy of political action – the need to conquer the machinery of state to better the workers' lot – was represented by the Marxist *Fédération nationale des syndicats*, founded in 1886. A different approach seeking originally to 'domesticate' the labour movement, the 'self-help' and self-improvement strategy, was represented by the *Bourses du travail*, combining employment-exchange with educational and friendly society functions. These formed a national federation in 1892. The *Confédération générale du travail* (CGT), founded in 1895, was to become the most important national organization. It preached industrial action; but, although it commanded the loyalties of the majority of the militant working class in the period up to the First World War, it has never succeeded in uniting all the main unions. Almost as if following the Leninist precept ('split, split and split again!') it has itself split three times – in 1921, 1939 and again in 1948. Yet another contrasting strain was 'social-Catholic' in origin, pre-dating, in the *Cercles ouvriers* of the 1870s, the actual legalization of unions; but given a powerful push by the papal encyclical *Rerum novarum* of 1891. This urged Catholics to become actively involved in the problems of workers.

At various points during the last century, a greater degree of unity in the trade union movement has seemed possible; but at each point it has been overwhelmed by the forces making for disunity. Lack of unity was no surprise in the swirling tides of the generation that followed the Paris Commune. But it seemed that, when the different strands of French socialism came together in 1905 to form the *Section française de l'internationale ouvrière* (SFIO), this might lead in turn to greater unity in the trade union movement. It did not do so because the CGT at that time was dominated by revolutionary syndicalists who believed that a revolutionary general strike was essential and despised those who became embroiled in parliamentary charades. The other principal occasion when unity seemed possible was the electoral victory of the coalition of the left, the Popular Front, in 1936. For three years, indeed, the CGT was reunited: but the 'Muscovite' allegiance of its leading communists was clear (not for the first or last time) in their support of the Nazi–Soviet pact in 1939, and again a split occurred.

The Second World War brought great repression and suffering to all trade unionists, and this, together with the important part played by a number in the Resistance, helped to recreate a sense of solidarity. Once again, it proved short-lived. The Fourth Republic was only a couple of years old when 'cold war' tensions once again caused a split which has so far proved enduring.

The main divisions in the French trade union movement date from this period. Since then, there have been three large confederations, as well as two other important bodies and a host of minor ones. The biggest (though the extent of its dominance has never again reached the same heights as at the time of the Liberation) was, and perhaps still is, the CGT. Its two main rivals were the *Confédération générale du travail – force ouvrière* (CGT–FO) and the *Confédération française des travailleurs chrétiens* (CFTC). The CGT has been, throughout its post-war history, very closely allied indeed to the French Communist Party (PCF). It has always retained token non-communists in certain positions, but the key offices are nowadays virtually monopolized by PCF members: even now when the party is so enfeebled. It was precisely to counter this obedience to the PCF line – and behind it, it was usually thought, the Moscow line – that the CGT–FO was set up in 1948. It was mildly socialist, and reformist in outlook and tactics. The CFTC was much older: its roots were in the social-Catholic tradition of the nineteenth century already mentioned; but it was actually set up in 1919. Although both Catholics and Protestants could be members, it was of course predominantly Catholic. As time went by, it generally became more radical; in doing so, it exchanged the earlier suspicion felt towards it by other unions that it was 'yellow', a creature of the *patronat*, for the suspicion of many Church leaders that it was a tool of communist and socialist revolution – even if an unwitting one. As this strain grew, it gradually lost its Church links, and these ended finally in 1964. It then split; the great majority marking the shift by a change of name to that which it bears today: *Confédération française démocratique du travail* (CFDT). Only about a tenth opted to retain the 'Christian' formula and the old name CFTC, thus creating another, minor, breakaway confederation.

In addition to the 'big three', certain other organizations should be mentioned. Next largest is a trade union federation specific to a particular sector, and thus not affiliated to a confederation: the *Fédération de l'éducation nationale* (FEN), which has grown rapidly in line with the expansion of education since 1945. Next in importance is the *Confédération française de l'encadrement* (CFE–CGC). The original CGC (Confédération générale des cadres) was founded in 1944, representing those *cadres* – managerial, technical and scientific personnel – who disliked the political affiliations of the other confederations and wished to defend their status and income differentials. There are other minor groups as well: the

Confédération des syndicats indépendants; the *Confédération des syndicats autonomes*; the distinctly 'mild' and non-striking *Confédération française du travail* (CFT), and so on.

The fragmentation and division of the French trade union movement is both cause and effect of its ineffectuality – which is examined in greater detail below. Nor is this sort of fragmentation uncommon in western Europe. There are united trade union movements in Britain and Germany for example; but in Belgium, Holland, Italy, Spain and Switzerland, the situation is more like that in France.

In general, such division is but one aspect of deep political cleavages that may be based on social, ideological, or geographical factors or a combination of all three. In such a situation the political left is almost always split too (though this is less true of Holland), and this holds whether or not there are close organizational links between parties and unions. In France, a number of factors in the general environment of the trade unions have tended to heighten or sharpen divisions between them. The most important appear to be: the revolutionary tradition, the religious factor, and the pattern of economic development of the country over the last century and a half.

The tradition of seeking fundamental change through revolution is well known. In both the late eighteenth and the nineteenth centuries, the lessons to be derived from seeking social change by revolutionary means have been much contested in France. This was no less true of the blood-bath of the 1871 Paris Commune than of earlier episodes, and sharpened the divide within the working class between reformists and revolutionaries. Likewise with the religious question: despite the existence of 'progressive' Catholicism, religion was regarded as fundamentally reactionary by much of the left. In France, religious practice has for long been regionally differentiated; and has been strong in, amongst other places, several of the parts of the north and east which have also become main industrial centres. The religious question dominated political debate in the first years of the present century, and since then has helped sustain a major division within the trade union movement.

The pattern of economic development in France has also enhanced division within the trade union movement. Although rapid economic change occurred patchily in most countries, it was particularly patchy in France, and the places most affected by the new developments – including the development of an industrial working class – were often physically far removed from each other. Local conditions, too, were very diverse: again, not conducive to the growth of a unified and powerful mass movement with a sense of common cause underpinned by similarity of experience and relative ease of communication. The main industrial concentrations were around Paris, and in the north and east; there were patches (for example in mining areas) elsewhere. The result was a ghetto mentality: the industrial working class was aware of being in a minority; and in addition, often worked in relatively small plants and factories harder to organize than large units; and local conditions, including wage-rates most notably, differed strikingly until quite recently.

Recent economic changes have been numerous, but their effects somewhat ambiguous. By the mid-1970s, it was clear that twenty five years of rapid economic growth were coming to an end. During that period, France had become a much more industrial country, and in some ways, more of a mass society than ever before. By the late 1970s, however, the talk was of de-industrialization. The high-growth period was itself marked by one major explosion, in the tradition of the *'drame révolutionnaire'* – the events of May–June 1968. This produced quite considerable changes in industrial attitudes – on both sides of industry. The period also saw the growth to a dominant position in the economy of a number of large firms: some already nationalized, such as Renault; some originally not, but nationalized under Mitterrand (such as Rhône-Poulenc); and some remaining in the private sector (Peugeot-Citroën). Questions not merely of ownership, but of how firms should be run, came more to the fore. France from this period had become much more urbanized, and has experienced a very large growth of salaried employees. Despite this, in general the number of trade unionists has declined; French trade unionism remains numerically weak as well as organizationally divided. And despite the many changes under the Fifth Republic, the influence of the more distant past continues to weigh heavily.

THE TRADE UNIONS AND IDEOLOGY

The influences of ideological differences upon the French trade union movement appear to be many and varied, but are in practice hard to evaluate. Two points stand out. The first is that it is not always the *same* beliefs or ideologies which have been prominent. The second is that there has always been an element of ideological competition: a tendency for some groups to indulge in leapfrogging with others in the escalation of demands (a phenomenon not limited to the unions), and for other groups to distance themselves deliberately from this process. An interesting question, but a hard one to answer, is whether ideology has had any 'independent' effect on members or non-members of trade unions in France, whether it can be said to have attracted or repelled them, or to have shaped their perceptions of the world and how they relate to it.

The ideologies that have had prominence have changed; or a particular trade union grouping has sometimes changed its ideological attachment. Revolutionary syndicalism, the belief in a great general strike to bring about massive societal change, though it remains present, is now the belief of rather few (though often influential) people. It was the original credo of the CGT at the end of the nineteenth century; and it was especially influential around 1900–10. It was not a single, self-consistent doctrine but rather a reflection of an attitude and a mood. Thus its most famous expression, the Charter of Amiens adopted by the CGT Congress of 1906, talked about improving the workers' lot in essentially reformist ways, but added that complete emancipation required the expropriation of the capitalist class; this would be brought about by a general strike which would establish the *syndicats* no longer as mere 'resisters' but as the basis of the new social order. Revolutionary utopianism was therefore very much part of the credo too.

These years were perhaps the high watermark of revolutionary syndicalism. But in 1908 a sharp increase in unemployment was followed by severe repression by the authorities of the syndicalist movement. In the very next year, 1909, the CGT leadership was taken over by one of the hardiest perennials ever of the French trade union movement, Léon Jouhaux. He remained its General Secretary from 1909 to 1947, when, logically for one of his views, he transferred his allegiance to the CGT–FO. It was he who converted the CGT to a much more reformist approach.

This approach, however, had been directly challenged by the Russian Revolution of 1917 and events immediately following it. A growing body of opinion looked to the Soviet model of a successful revolution: others favoured continuing along a parliamentary road to socialism. This divide showed itself first in the political parties, leading to the setting up of the PCF at the Tours conference in 1920. But its effects did not stop there, for the Leninists of the PCF believed that the trade unions required the lead of a revolutionary political party with a high degree of class consciousness. They also maintained that the unions should be subordinate to the party which should infiltrate and control them, since, left to their own devices, they would concentrate only on the narrow sectional interests of their members and could achieve little. This view was totally opposed to that of the social democrats and reformists: the conflict came to a head in the violent 1921 Lille conference which culminated in the expulsion of the communists. At this point the communists were in the minority, and set up their own organization, the CGTU (*Confédération générale du travail unitaire*).

This episode left a deep legacy of hatred between communists and non-communists, within both parties and the unions. Only on certain occasions since were the PCF and CGTU willing or able to associate closely with non-communists on the left, notably during the 1930s when the Soviet Union, alarmed at the rise of fascism and national socialism, was prepared to back the Popular Front. But the events, first of the 1930s – deep economic depression, and the fight against fascism – and then of the Second World War, served to increase the appeal of the communists. Their excellent organization helped them in the Resistance: in turn, their excellent Resistance record gave them a dominant position in the immediately post-war trade union movement. At the CGT 1946 Conference, the communists could count on about 80 per cent of the vote.

For a short while all seemed workable: Jean Monnet's proposals for planning looked to trade union involvement; even de Gaulle's Bayeux speech had looked to increased functional representation. It did not last long. The tensions of the cold war period reached very directly into French politics: after the expulsion of the communist members of government in 1947, the CGT called a wave of strikes which were widely described as 'insurrectionary' and certainly seemed aimed at bringing government and the economy to its knees. Non-communists within the CGT became more and more alarmed; an unease increased by the Prague coup of February 1948 which confirmed the worst fears of many about Moscow-inspired methods. Once again there was a split; but this time, with the communists firmly in the majority, it was most of the non-communists who left the CGT to set up the CGT–FO in 1948. The bitterness of this period marked relations between the two groupings for a long time thereafter. The new union, CGT–FO, sought to distinguish itself from the CGT by concentrating directly on issues of 'relevance' to its membership, rather than honing them for the wider political struggle, or, indeed, as the CGT did, taking up cudgels on behalf of the non-unionized in an effort to widen its constituency. In its turn, the CGT–FO was also very much a child of the cold war: it was widely reported to have not only the (domestic) support of the SFIO, but that of unions in the United States and the CIA as well.

The third main confederation had, as we have seen, a very curious history. The CFTC drew much of its membership from the lower-middle classes and from women; it was rather despised by the other confederations, yet its membership was greater than that of the CGT–FO for much of the time. Post-war, its original ideological position may be described as 'liberal-Catholic'. As with other French trade unions, however, it claimed for itself independence of all political parties, and, with the shift to the right of the Christian democratic MRP and of economic policy, the CFTC took its distance. The final victory of its reconstruction group led to the split and formation of the CFDT in 1964. From that point on, as we shall see, events (and the Events) took over: the CFDT went through an 'ultra-radical' phase, before swinging rather more recently to trying to find a middle way between social democracy and Marxism. Its successes during the 1970s and 1980s owe not a little to the influential General Secretary of the period, Edmond Maire, to whom we shall return.

The fact that a number of different ideologies and perspectives are catered for in the unions might be thought conducive to overall numerical strength. The opposite is the case. France is virtually at the bottom of the European league in the proportion of the workforce unionized. In Switzerland, that proportion is about 90 per cent; the EU average is some 40 per cent, with West Germany, Italy and the UK all near the 40 per cent level. In France, the figure has been falling steadily: equally significant, there are serious disagreements about just what the membership figures actually are, both overall and for individual confederations. It is certain that the overall figure is far below 15 per cent; several estimates put it around 10 per cent and one as low as 9 per cent. Thus, despite the range of ideology, there is a real problem about the 'representativeness' of trade unions in France which when added to the hostile instincts of the *patronat*, especially at plant level, has made for prickly and difficult relations between the two sides.

ORGANIZATION AND RECORD

The picture that emerges then, is one of under-development and weakness. French trade unions have had an uphill struggle to be taken seriously by the *patronat*, by government, and by the mass of workers. There have been surges in their numerical strength – after the First World War, after the Popular Front victory of 1936; following the Second World War, and following the Events of 1968 – but there have also been relapses.

The unions have usually been regarded by employers as unreliable partners: as unable to make a settlement stick with the shopfloor and even as unable to control strike action. The Sudreau Report commented on the tendency of the grassroots to 'spontaneous' action. The trade unions as such have generally been seen as being only one of a number of channels for contact, negotiation and management of industrial relations and, depending upon the situation in the particular factory or plant, by no means always the preferred one. There are also the *délégués du personnel*, finally confirmed in law in 1936. In addition, there are the *comités d'entreprise* (or works councils) set up after the Second World War in all undertakings with a staff of 50 or more. The *délégués* have generally been the more effective 'grievance' channel. The *comités* (chosen by the staff from among candidates usually nominated by the unions), which deal with welfare and social activities, and are supposed also to act as a channel for information and advice between management and workers, have usually been less effective. Unions have also had to vie with each other to obtain the status of 'most representative' union. This status confers important rights (of negotiation and representation), is bestowed by the state, and may be – and has been – challenged in the administrative courts.

The organization of trade union activity in France is both territorial and functional. Most main bodies are confederations, with a decentralized and usually rather weak structure. The CGT, for example, has both a geographical structure (*unions locales*, *unions départementales*) and a professional (or occupational) structure (*sections syndicales d'entreprise*, *syndicats*, *fédérations nationales*) together making up the *confédération*. The total membership of French trade unions is small, almost certainly below 3 million. All confederations have habitually claimed more adherents than their paid-up membership. The CGT probably has less than 700,000 paid-up members and the numbers have fallen in most of the last eighteen years, mainly in response to the perceived 'wrecking tactics' of the communists over the 'united-left' negotiations and the 1978 legislative elections. A 1984 estimate put the CFDT's membership at between 800,000 and 900,000; a more recent estimate has been somewhat under 600,000. It had grown substantially following its radical stance in the Events of 1968. The membership of the CGT–FO is also disputed: the lowest recent estimate is 400,000; it is unlikely to be above 650,000. It also grew for a while, partly as its 'moderate' stance of co-operation with management found some echoes among the more reformist and innovative sections of the *patronat* during the 1970s. The FEN probably had about 500,000 members in 1984 and this number may have fallen to little more than 300,000 by the mid-1990s; and the CGC has between 300,000 and 500,000. It is striking, firstly, that the estimates vary so widely; secondly, that everyone agrees that numbers have fallen steadily, and that the traditional union weaknesses in the private sector have now spread to the public sector also.

All the organizations suffer from limited financial resources and consequently limited numbers of paid headquarters staff. At 'confederal' level, the CGT and CFDT each have headquarters staffs of between one and two hundred only: the FO has well below a hundred. Constituent organizations, with small budgets of their own, also support very small staffs. There is heavy reliance upon unpaid 'militants' at local level, which in turn decreases the control between the various levels. Nor do the confederations have substantial strike funds to support a prolonged strike, and one result is a marked preference for token one-day stoppages, work-to-rule, go-slow and rotating lightning-strikes, affecting one plant after another unpredictably. Action at the plant level is very often unsuccessful, even if spectacular (for example occupations of sites, locking-in of management and so on). Negotiations frequently have to be referred to a much higher, and usually national, level if they are to succeed.

Such has been the tradition. There is also evidence of change; but the changes have not been in a constant direction. Certain changes of a 'modernizing' kind seemed to be set in train by the Events of 1968: others, including the steady haemorrhaging of membership, have rather been the result of the changed conditions of the 1980s and into the 1990s.

THE EVENTS OF 1968 AND THEIR AFTERMATH

It is generally agreed that the Events took most people, and certainly much of the union leadership, by surprise. The CGT was especially alarmed at the outbreak of 'spontaneity' (demands for a transformation of work-relations and so on) and sought to alter and limit demands and to channel them into the traditional mould – rates of pay and hours, benefits and so on. Although they succeeded in doing this to some extent, in other ways the Events did signal a long period of reflection and reconsideration, on all sides, of the role of trade unions and their relationships both with employers and with the activities of the state.

From the point of view of the union leaderships, the grievances that had appeared at the time of the Events were not novel. They felt left out in the cold by government economic policy; victims of a 'reform' of the social security system in 1967 in which they had not been involved and which appeared to combine higher contributions with unchanged or diminished benefits. Unemployment was rising, and real wages were held down in the name of 'competitiveness' and the wider 'financial rigour' by which France in the late 1960s sought to build a substantial balance of payments surplus which could be turned – literally – into gold; transported to the vaults of the Bank of France, hence forcing the 'Anglo-Saxon profligates' – the United States and Britain – to mend their ways. The protests began at the grassroots; they were not directed by union leaderships. They were directed, most of all, at antiquated social relationships, rigid and outdated attitudes especially of management. Much of what happened, too, was in imitation of the students – the occupation of factories in particular – even though no united front between students and workers was established.

At the time, it was claimed that the general strike peaked with some 9 million involved. Though this was almost certainly an exaggeration, the government was badly shaken and at one time looked as if it might fall. But the longer chaos continued, the stronger the reaction to it became, as the massive Gaullist victory in the election a month later proved.

The main forces involved differed sharply in their reactions at the time, and in their attitudes afterwards. The CGT, along with the PCF, declared that a revolutionary situation 'did not exist'. Regardless of the ability of the government to 'defend the Republic' by military means (de Gaulle was absent, endeavouring to reassure himself on this point, at the height of the crisis) it was fairly clear that there could be no 'revolutionary situation' if the CGT and PCF declared that there was none. The CGT settled for accommodation in the Grenelle agreements – mainly involving an across-the-board 10 per cent pay increase and a one-third rise in the minimum wage (then known as SMIG, later rechristened SMIC – *Salaire minimum interprofessionel de croissance*), which also served to reduce differentials. They had no intention of seeking 'transformations' of work-relationships which might take the edge off class antagonism and alienation. Yet Georges Séguy, then General Secretary of the CGT, was heckled and booed for his acceptance of the Grenelle agreements; militant workers, many of them not unionized, were seeking – realistically or not – much wider changes of outlook and regarded Grenelle as a betrayal.

This was truest in the CFDT, which was quite deeply affected by the Events, confirmed in the more radical course announced by the 1964 split. At its 1970 Congress, it linked the call for collectivization of the means of production and exchange to more novel demands which distinguished the CFDT from the other confederations. These were calls for democratic (as opposed to merely 'technocratic') planning and *autogestion* (workers' self-management). It was in the years immediately following the Events that the CFDT seemed most hostile to the existing order. Under Edmond Maire, its General Secretary from 1971, it generally returned to the pursuit of immediate benefits, but without dropping calls for long-term and radical change.

The response of the FO was distinctly confused, but in general it emerged even more 'moderate', anti-communist and anti-gauchiste than before. Despite its animosity to the CGT and PCF, the FO, under its General Secretary André Bergeron, was a crucial backer of the Grenelle agreements, thus helping to ensure that 'reform', mild at that, would be the outcome.

Promises and sounds of sweeping change were fairly rapidly diminished. The 'wilder' schemes of René Capitant (briefly Couve de Murville's Minister of Justice, charged with preparing a new labour code) expired, stifled by the combined hostility of the CGT and *patronat*. Although participation was severely limited, a number of changes were made. Profit sharing, introduced in very modest degree in 1967 and opposed by the unions, was given some boost; and the role of the *comités d'entreprises* was modestly strengthened. Most significant was the recognition, at long last, of union rights to organize and operate within the plant. There were more diffuse and less concrete changes of attitude and mood. For a period (1969–72) the government (under Chaban-Delmas) talked of *politique contractuelle*, the involvement of representatives of labour in a fuller and more organized way at national level in economic decisions – a process of tripartite consultations which, if it fell far short of corporatism, yet seemed to move in that direction. Union membership rose, modestly; the number of *sections d'entreprises* grew much more rapidly, on the back of the 1968 law. There began a process which, with varying success, continued through the 1970s and early 1980s, one of more active involvement of workers in the organization of work-patterns and practices, and active consultation of them, much favoured by the FO. The glacial attitude of the *patronat*, too, showed signs of change, especially when François Ceyrac became its President in 1973. Between them, Ceyrac and Edmond Maire may be taken as talismen of the new mood.

UNION RELATIONSHIPS

Relations with each other

Enough has been said to show that the main confederations differ amongst themselves not merely over economic strategy and issues, but also over political issues, and over the relationships between the political struggle and pursuit of economic aims. The FO takes a basically non-political approach, in the sense of distancing itself from all the parties, and stressing the independence and separation of political action from the 'rightful' aims of trade unions. The CGT believes both in the political role of trade unions (or at any rate of itself as the largest, generally in support of the PCF though it occasionally takes a tactical and tactful distance) and in the 'statist' tradition, placing main emphasis upon the role of the state in intervening, and of state ownership along traditional lines. The CFDT, although generally sympathetic to the PS, is by no means so close to it organizationally as the CGT to the communists, and tends to favour economic changes which rely far less exclusively upon the state. It is hardly surprising, therefore, that even in terms of general policy and orientation, relationships between them are strained.

But there are at least three other sources of difficulty. The first concerns personalities and styles. The second is that, broadly, the three have rather different characteristic 'constituencies', with different areas of strength and weakness in terms of both economic sectors and regions. Third, and notwithstanding this second factor, the three are ultimately in competition, not just to poach members from each other (which happens on a small scale) but rather to obtain the allegiance of some substantial part of the great majority of French workers – who are non-unionized. To do this, they believe they need to maintain a degree of 'product-differentiation', to appear distinctive and different from the others.

Georges Séguy was for a long time General Secretary of the CGT, until succeeded, in turn, by Henri Krasucki and by Louis Viannet. Séguy was very much a tough, if on occasion genial, worker who saw the CGT through a number of important shifts of policy in the 1970s. In the days of the common programme of the left after 1972, the CGT generally showed its 'liberal' face: later, it obediently followed the PCF in making a united left victory in 1978 virtually impossible. There were those who, after that, hoped the CGT could be opened up, and its tight control by PCF activists and its role as recruiting sergeant for the party loosened. In the event exactly the opposite happened. Henri Krasucki was regarded by most as very much a Stalinist amongst the party faithful. By contrast, Edmond Maire, CFDT General Secretary from 1971 until replaced by Jean Kaspar in the late 1980s, proved an influential and reflective individual, his manner quiet and rather shy, combining realism about what was immediately achievable with longer-range idealism, or in some eyes utopianism. Though himself a PS member, he also proved one of the most influential critics of the 1981–86 governments, asserting that it was a duty of trade unionists to speak truths which the parties did not dare, concerning the government's policies and the country's economic options. The CFDT had also proved ready to enter a 'real dialogue' earlier, with the Giscard-Barre government from about 1978 to 1981, and positioned itself to retain the ear of the Chirac government of 1986–88.

The CGT's great strength lies in heavy industry, in public sector industrial activities, and in such areas as the automotive sector. That of the FO has been in the lower and middle echelons of the public service (including white-collar) and also frequently in establishments where the *patronat* made clear its disapproval of the other confederations. The CFDT's following is spread more evenly throughout activities and industries, but without a heartland of support of the kind that both the CGT and FO have. It has attempted to attack CGT strongholds, especially where the CGT's attitudes have alienated immigrant workers.

Competition for the allegiance of the non-unionized seems to fly in the face of what evidence there is about the preferences of most workers themselves. Surveys suggest that a majority believe the existence of several confederations damages workers' interests and weakens the movement. In general, relations between the main confederations have grown worse since the late 1970s, and few formal arrangements for co-operation bind them together. For example, when in October 1991 the FO called for a general strike, and met with the CFDT, this was described as an 'historic encounter', the first official meeting of its kind for twenty years: but since then co-operation has been only sporadic. Until 1970, the FO and CFDT had enjoyed official relations: these were broken off in 1972 when the chemical branch of the FO rejoined the CFDT; subsequently, at least twice – in 1979 and 1980 – the FO refused to meet the CFDT.

Relations with the political parties

The trade union confederations are almost always at pains to assert their independence from all political parties. They are just as regularly accused by the bulk of French workers of having too close affiliations with one or other party. The CGT–FO goes farthest in avoiding partisan party allegiance, not surprisingly since a significant minority of its members are supporters of parties of the right and centre.

At the other end of the scale comes the CGT, practising the Leninist principle of overlapping membership, with party membership as the determinant of suitability for a union job. Almost all secretaries of CGT *unions départementales* are said to be PCF members, as well as about 90 per cent of heads of the CGT's industrial federations. The CFDT rides a little uneasily between these two situations, and has felt it of great importance not to be seen to be the spokesman of the PS.

The closeness of the CGT–PCF link was apparent throughout the period of left governments from 1981–86. The level and nature of its criticisms followed those of the party throughout: muted at first; more strident once the 'U-turn' in economic policy became apparent in 1982–83 and until the PCF ministerial participation came to an end in 1984; moving to the 'day of action' in October 1985 in protest at the government's policies. The general verdict on this 'great day', as the CGT leadership called it, was that it had been a flop. *Le Monde* opined that most wage-earners had been 'spectators'; that even the heartland of the public sector had been far from fully supportive. It was a good bench-mark of 'united action' and 'fraternal solidarity': André Bergeron spoke of the 'predictable failure' which had 'tarnished the image of the union movement': Louis Viannet of the CGT accused the FO, CFDT and CGC of being 'passive' and only acting 'against' the CGT's initiative.

As the 1986 legislative elections approached, it was commented that seldom had the CGT been more tightly bound to the party; and that, given the declining popular appeal of each, this was a risky strategy. To date, so it has proved for both. Nevertheless, those elections produced a notable 'first' in French political life: none of the main trade union confederations gave explicit instructions to its members on how to vote.

Nor did the CFDT find itself in a much easier position. Maire persuaded his colleagues in the leadership not to advocate officially support for the left; but several grassroots revolts occurred. Having established his credentials for constructive dialogue, Maire warned Chirac that if the government could not control its more extreme elements, then it was putting at risk the development of orderly and structured relations with the unions. He criticized in particular the government's proposals to make redundancies easier, which were enacted in June 1986.

At the FO, Bergeron was able to follow the 'traditional' line of 'no instructions' on voting; but knew that he could not let himself be outflanked by the CFDT and CGT, or accused of inaction. His known excellent personal relationship with Chirac was in this respect something of a two-edged weapon, and it was clear that he would have to be careful not to be seen as the government's 'poodle'.

The return of a PS-led government without an overall majority in 1988 did not appear to herald major change. For one thing, this time there was no governmental talk of 'break with capitalism'; rather, only very mild changes of emphasis or policy, as over the wealth tax or (presentationally but not actually) over privatization. For another, unemployment remained stubbornly high. Large demonstrations against government policy in both 1988 and 1989 led neither to a general surge in union popularity nor to the fall of the government, which, under Rocard at least, could claim some success for its economic policy. The decline of union membership in the 1980s and 1990s in France occurred without the kind of trade union legislation that took place in the UK. It seems rather to have reflected the unions' outdated organizational structure; their lack of adaptation to changed circumstances, new technologies and work patterns; the legacy of the unpopular strategies they had pursued in the 1970s; and the shrinking numbers from whom they could hope to recruit, as many industries continued to contract and unemployment stayed high.

What of the link between union membership and political allegiance or preference for the ordinary rank-and-file union member? The trends which appear are hardly startling, and the direction of causation difficult to identify, but we may note two in particular. First is family background: it appears that workers from left-voting backgrounds are considerably more likely to join the CGT than are others. Second, the question of level of political commitment: whilst fairly apathetic right- or centre-leaning workers may be prepared to join the CGT, those more politically interested are much less likely to do so; also political interest among left-wing workers seems still to incline people strongly to joining the CGT.

Relations with government

From the trade unions' point of view, relations with government have not depended merely upon what particular governments were trying to do, important though this has been. A good deal has depended on how they have felt themselves to be received and regarded by the various organs of the state and the administration. Traditionally, they have not been held in high esteem most of the time. Initial attempts to involve them in the planning process were at best only a slight success. The CFDT showed itself the most willing to be involved for the longest time, but finally it too felt it should indicate displeasure at not being able to influence inputs and priorities in time to have much impact. The importance attributed to 'planning' has in any case been highly variable: the left made somewhat hesitant attempts to restore it between 1981 and 1986; the apparent commitment of much of the right post-1986 to economic 'liberalism' and deregulation appeared to leave little room for it; yet it survives with very modest ambitions into the 1990s.

In general, the unions are aware that the administration, in framing legislation or in seeking advice or sounding out opinion, distinguishes rather sharply between what it sees as professional associations, who are carefully cultivated and listened to, and mere lobbies or interest groups, who are usually not thought able to contribute much (apart from requests or demands) to the process of policy formulation or implementation. For most of the Fifth Republic, trade unions have been uncomfortably aware of being labelled as the latter. They have, indeed, an even longer history of regarding the doings of government with suspicion, and the tradition remains hard to overcome.

There is evidence that they enjoyed a brief increase in participation in 1974, followed by a decline, then a sharp but short-lived increase again in 1981–82. Under the left governments from 1981, the unions saw several of their leading figures co-opted into governmental positions: for instance, André Henri of the FEN was made Minister for Leisure; Michel Roland of the CFDT was put in charge of the Energy Control Agency. Yet most trade unionists (especially the rank and file) remained suspicious of the 'intellectuals and technocrats' of the government. This was seen, for example, at the time of the 1982 wage-and-price freeze, whose introduction coincided with the CGT Congress at Lille. Whilst union leaders gave a mixed response to the economic policy of a government containing PCF members, the grassroots response was distinctly chilly.

If such was the pattern under the left, there seemed little reason to expect greater 'incorporation' or co-optation under the right after the 1986 legislative elections. To be sure, such appointments as those of Edouard Balladur as Minister of Economy, Finance and Privatization, and of Pierre Séguin at Social Affairs, were widely interpreted as signalling Chirac's concern to avoid provoking labour unrest. Yet the Chirac government was speedily warned not to pursue policies 'without wage-earners, let alone against them'.

This raises a very central issue for government–trade union relations in any country: namely, how far do the unions wish, and does the government encourage them, to be 'incorporated' into the structures of decision-making? In the French case, the answer from most quarters most of the time has been – not very much. In the early 1980s, communist ministers in the Mauroy government made plain that they felt trade unionists retained a right and freedom to attack policy which they themselves did not have. Yet non-communists fretted that the PCF, in conjunction with the CGT, would operate through the nationalization programme and the Auroux reforms to establish a much wider bridgehead of 'workers' power', as they claimed had happened back in the cold war days of 1947–48.

But perhaps one of the most telling episodes regarding the ability of unions to 'dictate' policy, even to a left government, occurred over the Savary education Bill. The 1981–86 period was, after all, dubbed *'la République des professeurs'*; the teaching professions were extraordinarily heavily represented amongst deputies and ministers. Yet it proved to be the case that the wide control enjoyed by unions over 'personnel' and 'internal' professional matters did not extend to an ability to dictate terms over national education policy at the level of 'high politics', the shaping of the system, even under the 'ideal' conditions of 1981–86.

More recently, however, governments of the right have felt the need to maintain some dialogue with and to involve the trade unions. The reasons are interesting. The unions have had an important role as partners in administering the welfare system, which has been under great strain in the 1990s. Although France's high unemployment is partly blamed on the way the welfare state is funded (high welfare charges on company payrolls have meant that companies are unwilling to take on unskilled labour), the unions remain in favour of the present welfare system because they have had a large hand in running it. Tens of thousands of trade unionists, particularly from the FO, have been involved, along with employers' representatives, in running these major functions. The FO was very wary of reform proposals in 1995 to shift the funding of these from employer/employee contributions to general taxation and the budget.

For once, the unions' wishes to be involved coincide to a degree with the preferences of government and employers. The latter are clear that, in regard to the crisis in the unemployment insurance scheme in 1993 for example, the unions were better able to impose higher contributions and reduced payments than could the state itself. In September 1995, Prime Minister Alain Juppé, having the previous month lost his Minister of Finance after the latter had proposed cutting public service numbers and perks, paid the unions the compliment of a full day of discussions on public sector pay and the future funding of the welfare system.

There are other, related, reasons. The French government in the mid-1990s has been under heavy pressure from the EU Commission to liberalize or deregulate, if not to privatize, the great public utilities: gas, electricity, post and telecommunications. These are exactly the areas of the economy where the unions retain their greatest influence, and it is clear that the government will initiate change only slowly and cautiously.

The government's other central commitment has been to try to fulfil the so-called 'convergence criteria' for membership of European Economic and Monetary Union (EMU) at an early date. The policies required to try to do this have been extremely painful, in terms of unemployment, public services and welfare budgets. The Prime Minister is well aware of the nervousness of the foreign exchange markets to any suggestion that the economy, which has many structural weaknesses compared to its German neighbour, is headed for further chaos. As these constraints tighten, so does the need to try to keep the trade unions on the government's side. In this, he has been supported by the head of the *patronat*, Jean Gandois, who has an interventionist approach. It is clear that many among the *patronat* believe that they have much to lose if the unions become yet weaker. Hence the curious paradox of *patronat* and a right-of-centre Prime Minister throwing the unions a lifeline.

Relations of union leaderships with the rank and file

It is well known that French workers express greater resentment and a greater general sense of grievance and social injustice than, for example, similarly placed British workers. Why this is so is a more difficult issue. It is sometimes suggested that the unions themselves are the most important agents shaping the attitudes of the working class. But in France, where union membership is so low, it appears that the direct effect of the unions may be limited. It seems, rather, that the unions have played a major part in reinforcing a climate of antagonism and division inside French factories; but that this may be as much the result of their sense of weakness and inability to influence decisions as it is the result of conscious policy on their part. The resentment about their position, and about social inequality in general, seems much more the result of the actual climate of French industrial relations in most factories (at least until very recently) combined with the acknowledged high degree of inequality of income and wealth in France – higher than in almost all other west European countries.

Further, it appears that there is not any very strong correlation between the opinions of leaders of any particular union organization, and the opinions of that organization's rank and file. For example, on *autogestion*, a main hallmark of the CFDT leadership for many years, the rank and file were less in favour of it than rank-and-file FO or CGT members. Further, it has not seemed to matter a great deal whether individuals were unionized or not: all French workers, unionized or not, appeared to have a greater sense of resentment and grievance than comparable groups in several other countries.

The legitimacy accorded to the union organizations by most workers appears low. A SOFRES (*Société française d'enquêtes par sondage*) survey in October 1979 indicated that whilst in general terms it was thought to be useful to be a union member, there was much more scepticism about unions' efficiency in defending their members' interests. Low membership figures are only one indicator of low legitimacy.

Relations with management

French management, traditionally, has been characterized as 'at best paternalistic and at worst thoroughly autocratic'. This situation has been to a large degree sustained by both union and management attitudes and by circumstances. Many major milestones of union rights and recognition have either been very late in being reached, or have yet to be reached. Yet in certain respects the opposite has been true: labour practice is quite evolved, and legislation was strong on the protection of workers – over dismissal and compensation, retraining, maternity and other leave. Alongside this, however, has been a situation where, in many plants, the idea of regular bargaining and consultation is a real novelty. The unions have often found that they were only consulted in times of crisis – be it the 'global' one of the Events of 1968, or an acute sectoral crisis such as that in steel from 1979.

A main purpose of the proposals which Jean Auroux, as Minister of Labour, introduced in 1982, was to achieve a major update of the labour code by revising about a third of it. The proposals showed that much that was already supposed to be in operation – notably in the field of *délégués du personnel* and *comités d'entreprise* – had simply not up to that time been applied. For the large employers of the *Confédération nationale du patronat français* (CNPF), Yvon Gattaz appeared ready to enter into a dialogue with the government. In many respects, however, it was in smaller firms that basic workers' rights seemed farthest from realization; and here it was not the writ of CNPF which ran, but that of the increasingly militant SNPMI (*Syndicat national de la petite et moyenne industrie*), whose 'neo-Poujadist' guerrilla warfare, under its leader Georges Deuil, seemed in the 1980s intended to sabotage the Auroux reforms. Nor was the SNPMI any longer a tiny and insignificant minority. From the unions' point of view, the future direction of management attitudes still appears highly uncertain: there is a considerable tension within the *patronat* between those of the Gandois persuasion, and others who would much prefer to break off dialogue with the unions, regarding them as now representing only a cushioned and wasteful public sector.

CONCLUSION: THE PRESENT POSITION AND PROSPECTS

In 1986, both the political context and the economic context appeared very unfavourable from the point of view of trade unions in France. Government and the parliamentary majority appeared more wedded to 'liberal' economic policies, including privatization and the reduction of the role of the state, than any French government for a long time. The speed with which this programme was carried out, and its extent, were clearly influenced by electoral considerations and the demands of *cohabitation*, but also by the stock market crash of 1987.

The response of the unions, after a period of *morosité*, was to promise a hot autumn of strikes and disruption. Whilst the policies of the Chirac government might seem to give their militancy some edge, they continued to promise 'hot autumns' to socialist-led governments in 1988, 1989 and 1991, without conspicuous success. Their numerical strength and morale have been sapped considerably in recent years and seem unlikely to recover swiftly.

Any estimation of the position has to take account of the relations between the leading confederations. Whilst in several respects relations between the CFDT and CGT have improved over the last twenty or so years, ambiguities remain. The CGT still appears to be hitching itself firmly to a star which has been falling rather than rising: that of the PCF. The CGT and CFDT still represent almost what have been described as two 'separate sub-cultures' within French working-class life.

In the autumn of 1991 four groupings – CFDT, CFTC, FEN and CGC – managed to join together in a single delegation to talk to the government about its economic policy and about selective budgetary stimulus to the economy in particular. They had a cool reception: for the government, Bérégovoy spoke rather of 'competitive dis-inflation': not the language they wished to hear. We have already noted the disarray that attended their other attempts at 'unity of action' at this time.

For the unions in general, the picture appears to be of considerable continuity with their past attitudes and traditions. They have become numerically very weak, and the likely economic evolution of France does not encourage belief that this trend is about to be rapidly reversed. 'United action' appears with rare exceptions as elusive as ever. They were not sucked very far into a 'corporatist' dialogue with the left governments of 1981–86; nor have they been since, under governments of any colour.

At the time of the 1986 elections, there was a good deal of slightly airy talk about an 'emerging consensus' in French political life. Events since then have given only limited support to such views. Indeed, in one very central area of concern for France, that of policy toward the European Community/Union, controversy and division have seemed to be increasing. The referendum on the Maastricht European Union Treaty was not only a knife-edge affair: it revealed a major split between a rich, urban France voting 'yes', and a working-class and rural France voting 'no'. Increasingly in the late 1980s and into the 1990s, trade unions in France have felt that prospects for them, for their members, and for the swelling numbers of unemployed have deteriorated. They tend to regard Brussels as one of the villains of the peace, along with the liberalizing pressures of the 'Anglo-Saxons' and the globalizing pressures from the GATT Uruguay Round. It is still unclear how far they will try to resist such pressures; whether, if they try, they will be able to make common cause with other nationalist, interventionist or protectionist forces within France; and whether, even if they did, this would have any great effect. In the autumn of 1995, French trade unions made their point in local terms. But, if the question, 'Can unions survive?' is being widely canvassed, there are particularly compelling reasons to pose it in the case of France.

BIBLIOGRAPHY

Adam, G., *Le Pouvoir syndical*. Paris, Dunod, 1983.

Adam, P., Bon, F., Capdevielle, J., and Mouriaux, R., *L'Ouvrier français en 1970*. Paris, Colin, 1970. An opinion and attitude survey of over a thousand workers.

Andrieux, A., and Lignon, J., *Le Militant syndicalist d'aujourd'hui*. Paris, Denoel, 1973. A survey of the motivations and attitudes of trade union activists.

Ardagh, J., *France Today*. London, Penguin, 1987. See in particular Part 2 'The economy, modernised but menaced'.

Compston, H., 'Union participation in economic policy making in France, Italy, Germany and Britain, 1970–1993'. *West European Politics*, vol. 18, no. 2, April 1995.

Johnson, R. W., *The Long March of the French Left*. London, Macmillan, 1981.

Labbé, D., 'Trade unionism in France since the Second World War'. *West European Politics*, vol. 17, no. 1, January 1994.

Labbé, D., and Croisat, M., *La Fin des syndicats*. Paris, L'Harmattan, 1992.

Lefranc, G., *Le Mouvement syndical de la libération aux événements de mai–juin 1968*. Paris, Payot, 1969. An excellent history of the trade union movement in this period.

Noblecourt, M., *Les Syndicats en question*. Paris, Les éditions ouvrières, 1990.

Nugent, N., and Lowe, D., *The Left in France*. London, Macmillan, 1982.

Reynaud, J. D., *Les Syndicats en France*. Paris, Colin, 2nd edition, 1975. Two volumes. A comprehensive introduction with document and bibliography.

Rosanvallon, P., *La Question syndicale*. Paris, Calmann-Lévy, 1988.

Ross, G., *Workers and Communists in France*. University of California Press, 1982.

Sudreau Report. *Rapport du comité d'étude pour la réforme de l'entreprise* (Presidé par Pierre Sudreau). Paris, La Documentation française, 1975.

Touraine, A., *Le Mouvement ouvrier*. Paris, Fayard, 1986.

West European Politics, vol. 3, no. 1, January 1980. A special issue on trade unions and politics in western Europe, edited by J. Hayward. See in particular the section on France by D. Gallie.

4

FOREIGN POLICY

Alan Clark

The Gaullist heritage (1958–69)

The essential principles of de Gaulle's foreign policy in the 1960s were few and uncomplicated. Their vital initial postulate was the paramount importance of national independence, the reassertion of which would enable France to regain its traditional position of international eminence. In independence, it was argued, France would be free to enter into multiform co-operation with other nations and thus to fulfil its historical 'vocation' of promoting peace and certain civilized values. Without independence, valid international co-operation would not be possible since it would inevitably involve the subordination of one of the co-operating partners. National indignity apart, such co-operation/in-subordination would, in practice, be bound to fail: pragmatism and idealism taught the same lesson.

From 1958 French foreign policy quickly became *le domaine réservé* of the President of the Republic who accorded it prime importance, determining its major orientations and deciding particular, often crucial, issues. De Gaulle conducted a personal policy in an individual fashion. For some observers it was a policy characterized more by its diplomatic style – its gesture and its rhetoric – than by the solidity of its achievements. Yet, substantial or stylistic, important changes in French foreign policy did take place under de Gaulle. Following the rapid and broadly effective decolonization of France's African possessions, and the settlement of the Algerian war by 1962, de Gaulle had worked to establish national independence on the only basis that, in his mind, was valid: French control of an effective national security system. This led him in 1966 to withdraw France from the integrated military command of a NATO dominated by the USA, and to develop a French nuclear strategy and strike capacity. As the converse of this disengagement from the American orbit, a policy of co-operation and *détente* with the USSR and the 'satellite' countries of eastern Europe was pursued with enthusiasm.

In European affairs, French intransigence concerning the implementation in the EC of a common agricultural policy (CAP), effective though it proved to be, took second place in de Gaulle's estimation behind his political ambition to establish a confederal association of west European states, a 'Europe of nations' in which France would play a leading political role. Between, and distinct from, the superpowers of East and West, de Gaulle's western Europe was to have become indispensable to world stability. In practice, his political Europeanism was eventually reduced to an unshakeable opposition to any proposals which might lead to the emergence of a supranationalist Europe, more or less aligned with the USA.

The Gaullist gospel of the independence of nation states was appreciatively received in many parts of the Third World. France's international standing was enhanced by the vigorous co-operation and aid policies it pursued, particularly in the newly independent African francophone states. Nevertheless, the function of arbiter in international conflicts which de Gaulle had on occasion loudly assigned to a 'neutral' France lost credibility at least with Israel as, in the Middle East, French sympathies came increasingly to lie with the Arab oil-producing states.

For Couve de Murville (Minister of Foreign Affairs, 1958–68) de Gaulle was beyond doubt *un homme d'une passion intransigeante et sa passion était la France'*; his foreign policy pursued *'l'intérêt national au sens le plus élevé du terme'*. Couve de Murville's assessment should not be accepted uncritically. Critics within and outside France have accused de Gaulle's foreign policy of being anachronistic, unrealistic and therefore dangerous, merely negative, or – most damning – of being the product of an old man's idiosyncrasies. But, in principle, the pursuit of national independence by de Gaulle was never a matter of ignoring harsh world realities; rather, he constantly affirmed the priority of the national reality as the unavoidable precondition of international dealings. His basic position was not inevitably nationalist in the pejorative sense of the word, to the extent that France's 'nationalness' sought peaceful rather than conflictual relations with other nations. Until recent years, de Gaulle's ideas and priorities have exercised easily the single most powerful influence on the foreign policy of succeeding Presidents of the Republic – *'le dogme le plus envahissant de la Ve République'*, Alain Duhamel called them in 1991. More than thirty years later, in the massively different international context of the 1990s, President Mitterrand's foreign policy was far from having achieved complete emancipation from its Gaullist heritage.

FOREIGN POLICY UNDER POMPIDOU (1969–74)

At de Gaulle's resignation (April 1969) French national prestige stood higher than at any time since 1940 and, arguably, since before the First World War. During the 1960s France had exerted a determining influence on the economic and political evolution of Europe and of a large portion of Africa. The voice of France had been heard – if not always listened to – in far wider fields, from Washington to Moscow and in many capitals of the Third World. Foreign reaction to the renewed French standing in the world was doubtless an unstable amalgam of resentment and respect, of envy and affection. Complaints at the cost of Gaullist co-operation and nuclear policies apart, domestic French feelings remained on balance appreciative of the needed restoration of national dignity.

In defence policy, Pompidou was faithful to his predecessor's approach: in contrast to the rigidity of France's 1966 position, he adopted the more moderate line perceptible from 1968 without, however, committing himself to any positive developments of that line. Criticism of the tiny size and doubtful efficacy of *la force de frappe* grew. The cost of the nuclear effort weighed more heavily both financially and, as the left increased its electoral following, politically.

France had not signed the 1963 and 1968 international treaties on nuclear disarmament and arms control, and the agreement on the prevention of nuclear war signed between the USA and the USSR in June 1973 justified, in Pompidou's eyes, the earlier intransigence of de Gaulle. For France, the 1973 treaty was tantamount to the self-promotion of the two superpowers to the shared office of nuclear policeman for the rest of the world. According to Pompidou's Foreign Minister Jobert, it was a condominium which was not to be confused with genuine progress towards international *détente*. The final twelve months of Pompidou's presidency amply underlined basic Gaullist principles and attitudes relating to national security. At the Helsinki conference on European security and defence (July 1973), and elsewhere, France emphasized the need for each nation, and for a united Europe, to exercise their defensive responsibilities: subjugation to the superpowers of East or West in so vital an area as defence was unacceptable.

Pompidou's relations with the superpowers were not always as difficult as they became in 1973 and were at no stage sharply marked by the temperamental anti-Americanism to which de Gaulle on occasion succumbed. However, relations deteriorated considerably in 1973 when, as well as the USA–USSR treaty on the prevention of nuclear war, further discord emerged. In an effort to ensure agreement with a Europe working more or less slowly towards economic and political union, the USA proposed (June 1973) a 'new Atlantic charter' designed to promote an Atlanticist orientation of Europe. For the USA and for France's European partners the project had its merits: quite apart from its substantial economic interests in western Europe, the USA provided the lion's share of a NATO defensive system which sooner or later would be affected by the decisions of any politically united Europe of the future. For France, the move constituted yet another attempt at domination by the Americans; this time not only the sovereignty of France but also the autonomy of a possible union of Europe were threatened. By the end of Pompidou's presidency (he died in office, April 1974), France appeared again in the familiar Gaullist stance of isolated opposition to American intentions in several fields.

Pompidou continued to develop political links with the USSR in the context of Gaullist 'balanced' relations with the superpowers. Until 1973, exchanges remained cordial and limited progress was made in Franco-Soviet commercial and technical exchanges. But the treaty of June 1973 demonstrated that in matters of importance the USSR preferred to leave France out of account and deal directly with its American rival/partner. On his visit to Peking (September 1973), Pompidou found himself talking the same diplomatic language as the Chinese leaders: both disapproved of the 'collusion' between the USA and the USSR. For Pompidou, their joint 'imperialism' was no less potentially dangerous than had been the conflict between the two blocs in the 1950s and 1960s.

From 1971, the bulk of Pompidou's activity was given to the promotion of greater European union, especially in the monetary and political spheres. Pompidou's desire to set Europe in motion again was evident at the European summit held at The Hague (December 1969) which agreed to open negotiations with candidate countries, notably Britain. Following a meeting in Paris between Pompidou and the British Prime Minister Heath (May 1971), it was decided that Britain (and Ireland and Denmark) should enter the EC on 1 January 1973. Called at the French President's suggestion, the Paris meeting of the Nine (October 1972) went further and drew up a calendar for a political union that was to be achieved by 1980. Pompidou did not depart from de Gaulle's insistence on a confederal union of states, although he was more sensitive to the isolation of France that was liable to result if that policy was promoted in too unbending a fashion. His temperamental preference was for progressive, concrete realizations. Only ineffectual goodwill was plentiful however, and 1973 ended with Europe struggling in the aftermath of a global oil crisis, still unable to agree on common monetary, energy and raw materials policies.

Pompidou remained firm in the pro-Arab stance adopted by de

Gaulle in 1967, conducting his Middle East policy with a sure sense of national economic interests. The diplomatic position remained much as before (namely, guarantees for both Israel and the Palestinian people and a negotiated settlement based on mutual concessions), but French energy supplies were also involved and had to be protected. Pompidou's pragmatism became apparent when, while maintaining the embargo on selling arms to Israel, he agreed that France should supply Libya with 100 Mirages (January 1970). Gaullist claims to impartiality fell to pieces: Pompidou's France was no longer a peacemaker but was concerned rather to exert influence and cultivate interests. French diplomats covered the Middle Eastern states thoroughly in the context of a long-term policy intended to develop French industrial, commercial and cultural interests in the region.

Pompidou's action in the Middle East should be seen within his wider policy context of expanding France's role in the Mediterranean region. By emphasizing southern interests Pompidou thought France could re-balance the northern predominance that would result from the Europe of Nine, and regain some of its eroded importance by occupying a leading position in the 'new' Mediterranean that might emerge. Efforts made from 1969 met with moderate success. Contacts with Morocco, Spain and Portugal improved. Relations with Algeria were often difficult: the loss of French oil concessions in the Algerian nationalizations of 1971 was a heavy blow, the proportion of French aid going to Algeria declined steadily and, following racial tension in Marseille in 1973, Algeria suspended the heavy emigration of its workers to France. Pompidou nevertheless persisted in his efforts to cultivate good relations, looking to France's longer-term economic and strategic interests. His concept of an Arab-Latin Mediterranean was far-sighted and perhaps feasible, although it was not without its opportunism. It was a policy defensible as prudent manoeuvring, but one which also contained the implicit admission that France's role, after being played on the world stage, might in future be limited effectively to western Europe and the Mediterranean. And to a presence in Africa.

While President, Pompidou visited, at least once, most of the former French territories in black Africa; after 1958 de Gaulle had not ventured further south than the countries of the Maghreb. The contrast illustrates Pompidou's greater concern for a co-operation policy that was less paternalistic, more open to the evolving circumstances of the Third World. Wherever possible, the privileged relations between France and its former colonies were maintained. While it increased in volume, the proportion of the French budget given to co-operation declined in the period to 1974; aid from the private sector (banks, industry) became almost as important as public aid – and less disinterested. Further, the French co-operation programme began to spread its funds and expertise beyond its traditional African spheres of influence: in 1970, 40 per cent of aid from Paris went to developing countries outside the French franc zone.

As the oil crisis deepened, Pompidou saw the problems of the Third World (the stability of prices received for raw materials, trade relations with the developed world) in global, long-term perspectives and, by 1974, the familiar Gaullist thesis of an international mediatory role for France had cropped up again. France's refusal to follow the American 'common front' strategy on oil prices (October 1973), and its stress on the need for developing countries to be fully involved in discussions related to international trade, were welcomed by the many countries of the Third World dependent on prices received for their exports to the West.

FOREIGN POLICY UNDER GISCARD D'ESTAING (1974–81)

A number of features of Giscard's reputation in the field of foreign policy were widely acknowledged at the start of his term of office. He was first and foremost a convinced European who looked to a politically united Europe having its own defence, currency and foreign policy. Although he always denied it, critics (many Gaullists, most Socialists and all the Communists) accused him of Atlanticist leanings, of working for greater French and European association with the USA, particularly with regard to economic and defence structures. By his own admission Giscard was more deliberately internationalist in his approach to foreign policy: problems now posed themselves on a world scale, state-to-state relations *à la* de Gaulle were no longer sufficient in many cases; what he termed *'une politique mondiale'* was vital, although national sovereignty was to be firmly preserved. Such a global perspective necessitated what Giscard regularly referred to as a policy of *'concertation'*, that is of dialogue and harmonious co-ordination rather than of intimidation and conflict. To what extent an implied criticism of de Gaulle's resolute defence of (his version of) French national interests was to be detected in these Giscardian emphases was a matter of political opinion.

Change was undeniable too in Giscard's own political position. As leader of the *Républicains indépendants* (RI), a minority party of the centre-right, he was the first non-Gaullist President of the Fifth Republic. It was clear from the start that the Gaullists in parliament would see that departures, real or imagined, from their founder's principles (in particular with regard to defence and national independence within Europe) did not pass uncriticized. The narrowness of his electoral victory (fewer than 2 per cent more votes than

Mitterrand, the candidate of the combined left in the 1974 presidential election) might have been expected to restrict Giscard's freedom to conduct his own foreign policy. In fact Giscard's political base expanded significantly later in his term: gains were made by the Giscardian UDF both in the 1978 legislative elections and in the European Assembly elections of the following year. Presidential foreign policy in the three years to May 1981 often appeared in consequence innovative and dynamic, particularly when that policy concerned disarmament, Africa and Europe.

Giscard came to power at a time of serious and persistent international difficulties. The world oil crisis from late 1973 promised to involve other raw materials and threatened shaky international financial systems. Europe was in conflict, stagnant if not actually regressive. The USA was in the final throes of the Watergate scandal. The new French President's wide financial experience (Giscard had been a liberal Minister of Finance under both de Gaulle, 1962–66, and Pompidou, 1969–74) was expected to produce in the conduct of foreign policy an intensification of Pompidou-style sensitivity to French economic interests. Complex and rapid change on all sides also encouraged Giscard to develop his predecessor's pragmatism: in a world characterized more by chaos than by order, *'le pilotage à vue'* and *'la gestion de l'imprévisible'* (the phrases are Giscard's) became the only effective attitudes to adopt. Critics nostalgic for de Gaulle's heavily affirmed fundamental principles and long-term strategies were reluctant to admit Giscard's constant emphasis on change and on what he called *'le grand réaménagement des relations internationales'* in the late 1970s. The same critics could have been more sensitive to the sombre conflict that underlay Giscardian foreign policy: on the one hand, the advocacy of a humanitarian *mondialisme*, biased towards the indispensable implementation of greater international economic justice and the needs of the developing world; on the other, the no less necessary defence of national strategic and economic interests.

Even had he wanted to do otherwise, Giscard would have been under pressure, for reasons at once political and technological, to adopt a defence policy acceptable to the Gaullists. Before his election he promised to maintain and develop French nuclear weapons and guaranteed the absence of France from disarmament and non-proliferation talks which sought only to maintain the blocs of the superpowers. Between 1974 and 1977, however, perceived deviations from established defence policy occurred with disconcerting frequency. Nuclear tests at Mururoa were confined underground and their frequency reduced. Presidential declarations in 1976 implied a geographical extension of the hitherto strictly national dissuasion policy and an increased degree of French involvement in NATO's military structures. Giscard's insistence on the need to modernize France's conventional forces, and in particular to develop mobile, multi-purpose interventionist units, was also seen to be symptomatic of a relative departure from de Gaulle's priorities.

Deviation in defence policy was in fact more apparent than real. Following the relative pause of 1976–78, nuclear dissuasion policy was redefined along identifiably Gaullist lines. Commissioned in 1979, France's sixth strategic nuclear submarine, *L'Inflexible*, was programmed to enter service in 1985 armed with the M-4, a new generation of longer-range, multi-headed missiles. Existing FOST (*Force océanique stratégique*) submarines were to be renovated and similarly equipped from the later 1980s. As a result, the megaton capacity of France's strategic forces was projected to quadruple in the seven years to 1985. More specifically Giscardian emphases on flexibility and innovation were discernible in longer-term programmes announced in mid-1980: mobile, land-based strategic missiles for the 1990s, the technological development of enhanced radiation weapons. Consequences of Giscard's energetic reaffirmation of defence policy were soon evident. Underground nuclear testing in the Pacific expanded again. French defence costs rose significantly: by 30 per cent in real terms between 1977 and 1981, a rate of expenditure not achieved by most European NATO countries.

International interest was stimulated by Giscard's presentation to the UN (May 1978) of a number of disarmament proposals. His address, which marked France's return to the world disarmament scene after some twenty years' absence, was characterized by a typically subtle combination of Gaullist orthodoxy and Eurocentric innovation. His efforts to regionalize, and in particular to Europeanize, progress towards international disarmament were as idealistic as they were necessary. Not only French but west European disquiet intensified as, in a context marked by increased Soviet military power in eastern Europe, the signing of SALT 2 (June 1979) brought into question the long-term reliability of American nuclear commitment to European security. Subsequent deterioration of strategic tensions in Europe served to intensify fears in French political circles, from the Gaullist RPR to the PCF, that the superpowers of East and West were effectively disposing between themselves of European security. It did not diminish the potential value of Giscard's Europeanist approach to security problems which in fact, in 1981, continued to underlie much of the work of the Madrid conference on disarmament in Europe.

Giscard's predicted determination to effect a *rapprochement* with the USA became evident during the months following his election. In the aftermath of President Carter's visit to France (January 1978) relations between the two nations were, Giscard claimed, *'cordiaux, ouverts et respectueux des droits de l'autre'* – that is, to a degree never previously equalled, the USA recognized France's right to pursue autonomous national policies. However, such formal assertions of the excellence of Franco-American relations became increasingly difficult to reconcile with multiplying points of conflict of a commercial or industrial nature; differences of position over energy and security matters also emerged. By 1979 France had become prominent (for example, at the Tokyo summit of industrialized nations, June 1979) in voicing EC resentment at the absence of a concerted American policy on oil imports.

As with the USA, France's relations with the USSR from 1974 were characterized by an evolution towards uncertainty and, especially after 1977, prolonged ambivalence. At first, France stressed its determination to develop further the policy of *détente* and co-operation which, initiated by de Gaulle, had become established by the mid-1970s as a central feature of its foreign policy. Indeed, the triple formula of *détente, entente et coopération* was still employed by France, at the end of the decade, to convey the essence of its formal relations with the USSR. Nor was this a mere diplomatic slogan, for Franco-Soviet co-operation had, by the later 1970s, become varied, substantial and, ultimately, expansive. By the end of 1974, major energy and industrial agreements had been concluded, together with a general accord on economic co-operation intended to triple bilateral trade to 1980. By mid-1979 extensive co-operation agreements to 1990 were in place. All seemed set fair for the next decade.

Subsequent diplomatic relations proved to be decidedly less smooth. Following almost three years of Soviet disquiet both at the uncertain evolution of French defence policy and at Giscard's more conciliatory attitude towards the USA, the period 1977–78 was marked by a deterioration in relations so serious as to temporarily hamper commercial exchanges. Secondary areas of dispute were not lacking: Soviet rejection of the French disarmament proposals of May 1978, the Middle East, human rights, China. However, central to Franco-Soviet dissension were Moscow's virulent attacks on Giscard's African policy, and in particular its criticism of French 'imperialist' intervention against 'progressivist' forces in Zaire and Chad (see page 96). Then of some fourteen years' standing, the Franco-Soviet *détente* may, as Giscard claimed, have made a significant contribution to peace and stability in Europe: but just as clearly, no French impingement on the USSR's African strategies would be tolerated. So vulnerable a dichotomy between *entente* and *coopération*, between diplomacy and trade, constituted at best an unpredictable basis on which to build future Franco-Soviet relations.

The numerous uncertainties of relations with both the USA and

the USSR reflected the recent shift in France's foreign policy perspectives away from the bipolar world of the superpowers towards
an international scene conceived, where possible, in multipolar,
regionalist terms. Complex and subject to constant redefinition, it
was a movement compatible both with de Gaulle's criticism in the
1960s of the superpowers' hegemony and with his largely symbolic
recognition of the importance of Third World nations. Pompidou's
initiatives in Africa, the Mediterranean and the Arab world had maintained the movement. In his turn, Giscard attempted to co-ordinate
French foreign policy more tightly than ever around the triple
regional 'poles' of Europe, the Arab states and the Third World, especially Africa.

As Pompidou had done in 1969, Giscard set out with an ambition to relaunch Europe. Even more than his predecessor, Giscard
was obliged from the mid-1970s to pit his ideals against a Europe
that was retrogressive and disunited. In particular, common monetary and energy policies were still lacking at a time when member
countries were experiencing more or less acute economic difficulties. Pessimistic analyses of the impotent condition of the Nine
flourished, and late in 1976 French observers even speculated
sceptically on the future survival of the EC's fundamental customs
union.

Particularly from 1977, however, Franco-German relations mate-
rially underpinned European integration, providing much needed
stability and stimulus. It was, for example, a text jointly presented by
Giscard and West German Chancellor Schmidt to the European
Council (July 1978) that supplied the basis for the European Monetary System (EMS) which came into operation in March 1979. After a
difficult birth, the EMS's early functioning was sound. A substantial
advance in monetary co-operation had been achieved.

Persistent French efforts were made from 1974 to promote
political union in Europe. Giscard's early tactics in this area owed
much to de Gaulle's European 'union of states': the new President
suggested that the nine heads of government should meet regularly
but informally to discuss current or longer-term matters of European
concern. His objective in initiating this European Council was to
progressively accustom the Nine to top-level political discussion
from which co-ordination and perhaps, by accretion as it were,
greater unity might emerge. This process was to be supplemented
by formal institutional change, in particular by a European Assembly
elected by universal suffrage. After initial moves in 1975–76, regular
progress towards realizing this major Giscardian ambition was made,
culminating in the inauguration, in mid-1979, of the first democrati-
cally based European Parliament.

In the 1979 Euro-elections almost 40 per cent of the French electorate abstained from voting. With economic interests more pressingly at stake, the next stage in the construction of Europe – the expansion of the EC to twelve members by the inclusion of Greece (from January 1981), Spain and Portugal – did not benefit from such broadly sympathetic public disinterest. Giscard's unequivocal, if not unconditional, support for the Europe of Twelve was exceptional in the France of 1978–79: to the PCF, parts of the PS, the RPR, to farmers' groups and some industrialists in the Midi, the entry of Spain in particular threatened French social and economic interests. If to such hostility were added both left-wing and Gaullist charges that Giscard intended to establish an 'Atlanticized', supranationalist Europe, and the need for sweeping institutional reform of an enlarged EC, it seemed probable that the qualified success achieved by Giscardian European policy to 1981 would be difficult to equal, or even to maintain.

For both economic and strategic reasons, Giscard developed relations with the Arab world to a point far beyond that reached by Pompidou. The French diplomatic position with regard to Israel shifted in emphasis if not in fundamentals when, by late 1974, Giscard had already stressed the vital importance of arriving at a durable settlement of the Palestinian problem, one which included establishing sure and recognized frontiers for all concerned, and in particular for Israel and the Palestinian people. By 1977, France maintained that Israel should withdraw to its territorial limits of 1967, while the Palestinians should have access to a homeland. The need for a global settlement in the Middle East caused France to share the majority of the Arab world's anxiety and reserve about the Camp David agreements (between Israel and Egypt, March 1979), seeing in them – a further point of Franco-American dissension – a fragmentary and potentially divisive response to what in reality was a much wider issue.

If relations with Israel were eventually normalized (in 1977) after France's effective recognition (UN debate, October 1974) of the Palestine Liberation Organization (PLO), French identification and involvement with the Arab world expanded enormously throughout the 1970s. Such association ranged in later years from mercenary pro-Arab reactions to the promotion of dialogue between the EC and the OPEC states. Above all, however, Franco-Arab relations were governed by economic constraint. Obliged since 1973 to pay escalating prices for its oil imports, France, like other industrialized countries, strove as never before to increase its industrial and technological sales to the Arab states. The inevitable identification of French policy towards the Arab world with the promotion of commercial and strategic interests was firmly underscored by Prime Minister Barre's productive visit to Iraq (July 1979). Iraq undertook to guarantee up to one-third of France's annual oil imports, thereby more than doubling its rate of supply. In return France was to sell to Iraq a range of arms and military equipment, and a civil nuclear research centre. If in the wake of the Iranian revolution and the Gulf War between Iran and Iraq France redefined some of its strategic relations in the Arab region, the perilous and fragile formula of 'oil for arms' had not outlived its usefulness, or its necessity.

France's relations with the Third World in the 1970s were characterized by an unstable combination, not unknown in de Gaulle's day, of generous intentions and imperfect realizations of those intentions. Giscard consistently presented himself as a renovator of French co-operation policy. Long-established links with north and black African countries were to be retained, but also revised. More importantly, the taint of imperialism was to be removed from French co-operation in all its forms – technical, cultural or merely linguistic: 'l'Afrique aux Africains' was the slogan Giscard brandished in talks with African leaders from 1975. In consequence, the numbers of French medical, teaching and administrative personnel based in Africa diminished gradually as greater emphasis was placed on co-operation through investment and the establishment of self-sufficient structures within the developing countries: formation rather than assistance.

This revamped policy did not hinder the expansion and revival of French bilateral relations in Africa and elsewhere. Complementing significant *rapprochement* with previously critical 'progressivist' states such as Angola, Ethiopia and Madagascar, Giscard's historic visit to Guinea (December 1978) at once restored relations between Paris and Conakry (relations which had been ruptured in 1958 in the early days of de Gaulle's presidency), symbolized the more dynamic, outgoing character of Giscardian co-operation – and promised to be profitable. Unprecedented French initiatives were subsequently undertaken in former British and Portuguese territories with a view to expanding and co-ordinating French co-operation on a broader regionalist basis throughout West Africa. Of potentially equal importance was the long overdue revival of French diplomatic, industrial and economic interest in South and Central America.

More controversial was Giscard's policy of military intervention in Africa. In Western Sahara, Chad, and the Shaba province of Zaire in particular, French military personnel and equipment were repeatedly engaged in stabilizing chaotic internal situations. But at what point did stabilizing assistance end and 'neo-colonialist' interference begin? Reactions were divided and often extremist. The USSR and 'progressivist' African states (for example Tanzania and Madagascar) were unreservedly hostile. Among Arab nations, Libya denounced French policy in Chad as archaic colonialism, while Franco-Algerian diplomatic and economic relations went into serious decline from mid-1977 in the face of French assistance to Morocco and Mauritania, and after the Algeria-backed Polisario Front held several French civilians hostage. On the other hand, numerous black African states, not invariably francophone, expressed varying degrees of relieved approval of France's supportive actions. More discreetly, the EC, the USA and even sections of the Organization of African Unity associated themselves sympathetically with Giscard's initiatives.

By 1978, the risks inherent in such interventionism were felt, not least by the ascendant French left led by Mitterrand, to be acute: the prolongation and escalation of military involvement (in Chad), the detrimental identification of France with repressive regimes (Mobutu's Zaire, Bokassa's Central African Empire) and unenlightened policies (continued French intervention in the Comores, and ambivalent commercial relations with South Africa). If by 1979–81 French interventionism in Africa appeared less militarily activist, diplomatically more balanced and reserved, the longer-term coherence of what Giscard termed *'la fidélité africaine de la France'* was still not evident. Many in France feared that the need to protect French economic and western strategic interests, as well as African security, could give rise to further piecemeal responses.

More durably innovatory was the importance Giscard repeatedly attached to the need to adopt international regionalist perspectives when responding to the Third World. While France still had a useful role to play in Africa and elsewhere, often limitedly national, bilateral action was now insufficient: economic, political and strategic problems posed themselves on so complex and extensive a scale that only multilateral approaches, involving effective negotiations between industrialized and developing nations, were appropriate. Unfortunately Giscard's various proposals in this vein too often remained at the level of prestigious diplomatic initiatives, with little or no practical application. The North–South conference on international economic co-operation was launched in 1974 at the joint suggestion of France and Saudi Arabia. It ended (in June 1977) with the participating Third World countries disillusioned by the industrialized world's reluctance to agree to large-scale structural reform of international financial and trade systems. Fundamental problems – energy supplies, commodity prices, Third World indebtedness – remained virtually unchanged. Two years later, Giscardian assertions of *'concertation'* and *'interdépendance'* as the keys to a more just and workable international economic order were still more numerous than effective. The Lomé Convention (between the EC and African, Caribbean and Pacific countries) was renewed only with difficulty and in confusion (June 1979).

FOREIGN POLICY UNDER MITTERRAND (1981–95)

The election in May 1981 of a Socialist President of the Republic roused more extreme hopes, and fears, for French foreign policy than had the arrival of Giscard d'Estaing, his liberal conservative predecessor, seven years earlier. Within France rather than abroad, on the left rather than on the right, the hopes sprang from Mitterrand's long-recognized concern for European and international disarmament, for the economic and humanitarian development of the Third World and, more diffusely, for an approach to international relations that would be more firmly principled than that which, it was claimed, either Pompidou or Giscard had exhibited.

The early fears concerning Mitterrand's foreign policy were at once more numerous, more acute since more closely defined, and more widespread, being evident both abroad (in Washington and Moscow, from Bonn to numerous Arab and francophone African capitals) and at home (among all centre-right opinion, but also in the PCF). After all, until the second half of the 1970s both the PS and PCF had still favoured dismantling the national nuclear strike capacity: what would happen to defence strategy under Mitterrand? The consequences for NATO and European security at a time of increasing continental tensions were potentially critical. Surely French relations with the major powers of West and East would suffer disruption, especially following the introduction of four PCF ministers into Prime Minister Mauroy's cabinet (June 1981)? Ideological common ground between the new US President Reagan (who took office in January 1981) and Mitterrand appeared minimal. Prospects for improving co-operation in a deeply recessive EC were not enhanced by the Mauroy government's anomalous reflationary economic policies (1981–82). Previous French policies towards Africa and the Arab world had been variously criticized among the French left as mercenary, opportunist and ineffective: what upheavals might be in store in those areas? And so on.

By the 1990s most of such speculations had long proved to be groundless. Certainly the more extreme fears – but also the more lofty hopes – had not been realized.

> *La politique extérieure de la France s'ordonne autour de quelques idées simples: l'indépendance nationale, l'équilibre des blocs militaires dans le monde, la construction de l'Europe, le droit des peuples à disposer d'eux-mêmes, le développement des pays pauvres, [... et] l'ouverture de notre pays vers la Méditerranée et l'Afrique.*

These words might have been written by de Gaulle in 1960. They were in fact composed a quarter of a century later, in 1986, by

Mitterrand (in his introductory essay to *Réflexions sur la politique extérieure de la France*). The thrust towards continuity in the fundamentals of French foreign policy remains a powerful one. Even the two-year period (1986–88) of executive *'cohabitation'* between Mitterrand and RPR Prime Minister Jacques Chirac that was produced by the legislative elections of 1986 did not substantially deflect that thrust. Albeit often more rhetorical than real, policy differences did exist between Mitterrand and the Chirac government in 1986–88: the level of defence spending, the objectives and pace of the European integration process, French involvement in Central America, Third World indebtedness, co-operation policy in general. Nevertheless, conflict over policy content proved less significant than the struggle for political control over that policy. And the outcome of that struggle was settled, in May 1988, by Mitterrand's decisive presidential re-election, at Chirac's expense, for a second seven-year term (1988–95).

From 1981 French commitment in security matters was notably firm and clear. Having reaffirmed his government's adherence to the Gaullist line of autonomous national membership of the Atlantic Alliance, Mitterrand went further than Giscard had ever done by supporting (July 1981) the USA's insistence on the need to respond to the build-up of Soviet military power by installing NATO Pershing missiles in western Europe (January 1983 speech to the Bundestag). His invariable argument in later years was to say that worthwhile disarmament negotiations could proceed only once a position of equilibrium had in this way been re-established. *'Je crois, de toute ma conviction, que la paix tient à l'équilibre des forces dans le monde, à l'équilibre des forces en Europe'*, Mitterrand wrote in 1986.

This apparently paradoxical *rapprochement* between French and Atlantic perspectives produced little effect on the more specifically national dimensions of Mitterrand's defence policy. In the face of widespread opposition in the South Pacific, underground nuclear testing programmes continued at Mururoa until 1991. In the course of Mitterrand's fourteen years in power the nuclear dissuasive arsenal was extended and modernized in ways that attempted to combine Gaullist orthodoxy with the more pliable, Europeanist concerns of Giscard. Among numerous programmes, a seventh strategic nuclear missile-firing submarine was constructed, and by the end of the 1980s a re-equipment programme had increased six-fold the M-4 missile warheads carried by the strategic submarine fleet, while by 1986 Franco-German talks were grappling with the possible deployment of both French forces and pre-strategic arms on West German territory.

The unprecedented shifts in the European geo-strategic situation that have been under way since the late 1980s (German reunification, the collapse of the Soviet Union and of the communist bloc in eastern Europe, the Gulf War against Iraq, persistent difficulties over European integration . . .) exerted continuous, intensifying pressure for change in most sectors of French defence policy, as indeed in foreign policy more widely conceived. The policy responses of the Mitterrand administration in matters of external security since 1989 on occasion appeared to critics to be hesitant, unimaginative or even incoherent, and above all of limited effectiveness. Given the rapidity and bewildering scope of the shifts involved, such criticisms were doubtless unavoidable. Nevertheless, major defence reforms were undertaken.

Since 1990, French positions towards the Atlantic Alliance have often been contentious. Critical of American efforts to expand the political and territorial roles of NATO following the dissolution of the Warsaw Pact (July 1991), Mitterrand persisted in stressing the importance of developing a specifically European security dimension, *'une défense réellement plus européenne dans l'Alliance Atlantique'* as he termed it. Organized within the Western European Union (WEU), the EU's military capacity should in the future operate within the Alliance on a basis of partnership with, rather than subordinated to, the USA. Mitterrand's positions were certainly far-sighted, looking to a time when American defence forces had been withdrawn from Europe. Moreover, erecting a European 'defence pillar' would be an important stage in building a politically united Europe. French progress in this matter was, however, slight and diplomatic rather than substantive. In mid-1991 the Copenhagen NATO Council meeting did formally acknowledge 'the emergence and development of a European security identity and the role of Europe in defence matters'; complementarity between the Alliance and the WEU was also recognized. At the same time France refused to participate both in the rapid reaction multinational units of NATO's new military organization (decided in May 1991), and in the Co-operation Council established by NATO (in November 1991) as a forum for security debate with the countries of eastern Europe and the CIS (Commonwealth of Independent States). Traditional concerns for specifically national defence interests combined with futuristic aspirations towards a politically united Europe to increase the risk of French isolation in a pan-European security context in rapid evolution.

Both defence policy imperatives – the national and the European – were subject to persistent reform in the first half of the 1990s; durable policy coherence between them remains to be achieved. French participation in the Gulf War (1990–91) demonstrated paradoxically both the fragility and the indispensability of French military autonomy and strategic independence. His country's continued diplomatic eminence (for example, as a permanent member of the UN Security Council) was repeatedly associated by Mitterrand with France's capacity for autonomous participation in the allied operations against Iraq. This Gaullist concern for their wider diplomatic significance did not, however, prevent France's strategic nuclear forces from undergoing modification and re-evaluation. De Gaulle's original nuclear triad was effectively abandoned when it was decided, in July 1991, not to replace the land-based S-3D missiles on the Plateau d'Albion with the S-45 strategic missile. In the same year, in response to the vastly changed circumstances of the European security theatre, the short-range Hadès missile programme was withdrawn before entering operational service, while the French army lost half of its Pluton nuclear missiles. A new generation of four *Triomphant*-class submarines was scheduled to enter service from 1995. To be armed in turn with M-45 and M-5 missiles, this renewed FOST was intended to function as the vital core of a more compact, high-quality French strategic capacity well beyond 2000.

Reductions in conventional forces had been programmed since the *'Armées 2000'* plan was adopted in 1989. For reasons both budgetary and military, the French army was by 1997 to shed more than a fifth of its manpower, with the loss of some 35 regiments. Military service was reduced from a year to ten months in late 1991. The 1993–97 defence spending programme contained a reduction in overall defence expenditure – the first time that this had occurred in post-war France.

In June 1981 Minister of External Relations Claude Cheysson far-sightedly suggested that the USA would find in his country *'un solide partenaire, sinon facile'*. Broadly common Franco-American international responses (from the Euromissiles question in the early 1980s to the Gulf War, and since) subsequently demonstrated their durability. Only a year later, however, Cheysson referred openly to *'le divorce progressif'* which was dividing Washington not only from Paris, but from western Europe in general. Sharply divergent approaches to monetary and commercial policies, and the impact of these on East–West relations, underlay this erosion of Atlantic solidarity. Washington's calls for increased NATO defence spending caused resentment among European states which from 1980 had seen their recessions worsen as a consequence of persistently high American interest rates. Reagan's advocacy of unrestricted international trade did not extend to EC steel exports to the USA, while active American opposition (1981–82) to the construction of a natural gas pipeline from Siberia to western Europe appeared to European eyes to be both incompatible with American cereal sales to the USSR and an infringement of European economic sovereignty. Subsequent Franco-American relations continued to be mixed.

Mitterrand's overriding commitment to Atlantic solidarity did not alter his disagreement with American views of and responses to revolution in Central America, although effective French involvement in that region diminished greatly after 1982. Unlike West Germany and Britain, France declined (May 1985) to participate at the national level in the Strategic Defense Initiative (SDI) proposed by Reagan: Mitterrand saw in it a menace to the hard-won strategic balance in Europe by increasing the likelihood of a security 'decoupling' of the USA from Europe.

Supported on occasion by other EC nations such as Germany and Britain, Mitterrand regularly – and conveniently – distinguished in the 1980s between political and commercial relations with the USSR. While the former could not be regularized until, for example, Soviet troops withdrew from Afghanistan, the latter should continue (for example a massive contract for the supply of Soviet natural gas to France was signed (January 1982) just one month after martial law was imposed in Poland). De Gaulle, and Giscard, had proceeded along similar lines. From July 1984 the French cabinet no longer contained any communist ministers. Released from this residual political constraint, and with irreproachable Atlantic and defence policy records already behind him, Mitterrand moved to restore full diplomatic dialogue. The results were more symbolic than substantial. Soon after Gorbachev's official visit to France (October 1985), Mitterrand's controversial decision to receive the Polish leader General Jaruzelski at the Elysée Palace (December 1985) underscored his firm resumption of traditional Gaullist dialogue with the eastern bloc states.

'Commençons par rendre son âme à l'Europe', Mitterrand urged from the outset (June 1981), while at the same time exhorting the European Council to develop the EC's social legislation, what he called 'l'espace social européen'. Even by 1995 his essential positions on Europe had not varied. In an EC suffering high unemployment, Mitterrand's early euro-socialist idealism was lyrical, entirely appropriate – but unlikely to be realized; indeed, until the middle of the 1980s, it went largely neglected. What co-ordinated action was accomplished by the EC remained, perhaps inevitably, partial, defensive or circumstantial: common mobilization against Japanese exports, for example, or against monetary policies and against 'le véritable protectionnisme déguisé' (the phrase is Mitterrand's) deployed by the USA, or, in 1986, the adoption of concerted measures to combat international terrorism. On the positive side, the EMS functioned with increasing effectiveness and the EC expanded to admit Spain and Portugal (January 1986). Otherwise European affairs until the mid-1980s too often remained dogged, as they had during the later years of Giscard's presidency, by politically linked disputes focusing on the size of, and (until 1984) British contributions to, the EC's budget, on reform of the CAP, and on the persistent problem of agricultural surpluses and international trade policy disputes with the USA.

As for European political relations, Mitterrand extended to the (West) Germany of Chancellor Helmut Kohl the high level of co-operation that had been maintained by Giscard and Schmidt, and complemented this by cultivating more diversified bilateral links, with Britain (Channel Tunnel agreement, January 1986; nuclear arms co-operation from 1991), and with Italy and Spain in particular. As Giscard had before him, Mitterrand remained convinced that political union (involving a recasting of the original Treaty of Rome) was indispensable to the viability of an expanded Europe. While working towards this longer-term institutional objective, Mitterrand strove to extend European technological co-ordination by expanding French involvement in and promotion of extensive European technological research and development programmes (JET, CERN, ESPRIT, RACE), as well as major European industrial ventures such as Airbus and Ariane. His Eureka initiative (April 1985) offered a flexible range of market-oriented extensions of these ideas: at the end of the first year, some forty international high-technology projects had been proposed by the eighteen western European countries involved. *'J'estime complémentaires l'indépendance de la France et la construction de l'Europe'*, Mitterrand wrote early in 1986. In particular, the technological and political advance of Europe were interdependent. Their joint success would determine France's national future.

The collapse of the Soviet Union, the disintegration of its east European bloc and the process of German reunification gave rise from 1989 to major economic, security and institutional consequences for the future evolution of Europe. Such a radically redefined pan-European context would have posed problems of adjustment to any existing pattern of French foreign policy; by no means all of those problems had been resolved by 1995. Although early French policy responses to the tumultuous gestation of the new Europe were criticized as hesitant and incoherent, it is hard to see that significant long-term damage resulted. Indeed, Mitterrand's record over the longer period 1988–93 suggests rather the steady, lucid management of a complex, shifting context. Faced with the rapid transformation of Germany and eastern Europe, Mitterrand sought to balance national interests with the double need to underpin the European integration dynamic while maintaining pan-European security. Kohl shared Mitterrand's central concern to integrate a single, expanded Germany within a more deeply united Europe. Prompted by a Franco-German joint initiative, the Dublin European summit (June 1990) agreed to work towards both economic and monetary union (EMU) and political union. The Maastricht Treaty on European Union (December 1991) that was the outcome of this summit established the EU's policy agenda and institutional timetable for the rest of the decade, culminating in the projected establishment of a single European currency from 1999. Recession in Europe, repeated monetary crises, public discontent with the PS and Europe (the Maastricht Treaty was only narrowly ratified in France, in September 1992), stresses associated with expanding the EU eastwards . . . all failed to disrupt the underlying dynamic. It is, however, true that two years of governmental cohabitation (1993–95) dulled France's foreign policy vitality as presidential authority was largely transferred to the Balladur government following the massive defeat of the PS in the 1993 legislative elections. Not that Mitterrand's own European conviction was shaken: *'Pour construire l'Europe, il faut le souffle long, c'est une course de fond, pas un sprint. [. . .] C'est maintenant qu'on va savoir si notre ambition de Maastricht se réalise. [. . .] l'idée d'Europe sera l'idée-force des temps à venir ou bien elle se perdra. J'ai fait mon choix,'* he declared in mid-1994.

In the Middle East the pursuit of diplomatic equilibrium was unremitting, frustrating and, in multiple ways, costly. Recognized at the outset as a long-standing friend of Israel, Mitterrand initially worked for what he considered to be a more even-handed approach to the Palestinian conflict: guaranteed recognition of all sides, including a Palestinian state and a negotiated settlement within the Camp David framework. The effort gave rise to considerable Arab apprehension as, for the first time since 1967, France voiced active concern for the interests of Israel. Humanitarian, non-partisan diplomacy was courageous but perceived to be provocative as, from 1982, inter-Arab, anti-French and anti-Zionist terrorism flared spasmodically in Paris. Arab criticism reached heights unknown throughout the 1970s when, in spite of Israel's annexation of the Golan Heights (December 1981), Mitterrand paid an unprecedented presidential visit to Jerusalem (March 1982). From the middle of that year, however, Franco-Israeli relations deteriorated in their turn following French condemnation of the Israeli invasion of Lebanon (June 1982). In consultation with the USA and in concert with Egypt, Paris's diplomatic involvement persisted at a high pitch, culminating in the repeated participation of French troops in UN multinational peace-keeping forces in Beirut. Arab, especially PLO, appreciation of French positions was progressively restored following Cheysson's meeting with Yasser Arafat in October 1982. Yet, in the context of war between Iran and Iraq, continued French arms and civil nuclear sales to the Arab world (to Saudi Arabia and Iraq, in particular) provoked Iranian hostility towards France. The old contradiction in

French Middle Eastern policy between an interventionist role and a (commercially and therefore politically) partisan position exacted a high price in terms of soldiers' lives and (from March 1985) of French civilian hostages held by Islamic extremists in Lebanon.

The gap between intention and performance was, not surprisingly, widest in policies concerning the Third World. The Socialist government multiplied assertions of the pressing need for what Mitterrand referred to variously as *'un co-développement généralisé'* or *'une restructuration d'ensemble'* of economic relations between developed and developing worlds. North–South relations had to be co-ordinated globally, enveloping monetary, energy, industrial and commercial strategies with more orthodox development aid. Not that this last was to be neglected: in 1981 Mitterrand undertook to double French public aid to the Third World – to the UN target figure of 0.7 per cent of GDP – during his first term of office. Although even by 1995 this target had not been reached, French spending on public aid was the highest among the G7 countries (see graph).

Spending on non-military foreign aid, 1993
Source: *Agency for International Development/OECD data*

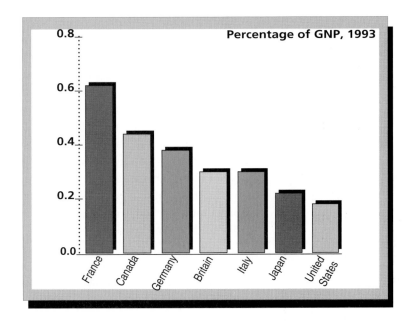

France's solidarity with the Third World was repeatedly affirmed: in its early stages it was to be structured on the triple basis of exemplary relations with Algeria, Mexico and India. A substantial contract for the supply to France of natural gas on commercial terms generous to Algeria (February 1982) was presented by Paris as an example for other industrialized nations to follow. But was it a legitimate example? Or was it, as conservative critics alarmed at France's record trade deficit in late 1982 alleged, simply bad business? And what of the fact, disturbing to some PS parliamentarians, that

Mitterrand's redefinition of Third World policies did not impede substantial sales, *à la* Giscard, of Mirage 2000s to India, or of (defensive) arms to Nicaragua? Or that socialist trade embargoes imposed on pre-democracy South Africa excluded strategically important exports to France of uranium?

Global reorganization was not in any case to be pursued to the exclusion of France's established bilateral ties with many African, especially francophone, states. Existing treaty obligations with such countries were respected and in some cases (for example, Zaire) French financial commitment was increased. In the light of Giscard's experiences in Western Sahara and Central Africa, interventionism was, however, minimized, *'la non-ingérence'* observed and *'le développement autocentré'* promoted. Nevertheless, French military and logistical forces continued to support the established Habré government in Chad against the rebel incursions backed by Libya, although they did so in a more coherently organized, restrained and (to mid-1986) effective fashion than had been the case in the late 1970s.

Annual Franco-African summits suggested that under Mitterrand relations with African states were restored to high levels of mutual understanding for most of the 1980s. On the whole they remained there in spite of both deepening Third World indebtedness and a struggling metropolitan economy. At the La Baule summit in 1990 however, Mitterrand introduced a new, more controversial note when he overtly linked the future availability of French co-operation aid to African states with their progress towards multi-partism and other democratic modes of organization. Not all the African states involved either appreciated – or adopted – the La Baule recommendations, preferring to see in them yet a further example of neo-colonial interference. Fewer still approved when, in January 1994, France and the International Monetary Fund devalued the CFA franc by 50 per cent in an overdue attempt to inject more liberal orthodoxy into their financial relations with francophone Africa. Indeed, questions concerning French development assistance to Africa became ever more controversial as Mitterrand's second term drew to a close. Inter-ethnic genocide in Rwanda (April–August 1994) exposed Paris's ambivalent support for the government in Kigali at a time when France had become the largest supplier of arms to the developing world. And yet, early in 1995, France found itself virtually isolated in its willingness to increase EU development assistance to the African, Caribbean and Pacific Ocean member states of the Lomé Convention. Incoherent and counter-effective as aspects of its African policy were, only France defended aid levels for Africa against the competing needs of eastern European states.

If his policy record on European integration came closest to realizing the hopes raised back in 1981, it was in reforming France's relations with the developing world that on balance Mitterrand's performance had, by 1995, most disappointed expectations.

FOREIGN POLICY UNDER CHIRAC (1995–   )

According to Jacques Attali, his long-time special advisor in the Elysée, Mitterrand in 1988 had considered his presidential successor to be incorrigibly unpredictable, irresponsibly capable of saying and doing anything. Were he to be elected President of the Republic, Chirac would, according to Mitterrand, quickly become the laughing-stock of the world. Severe as it was, Mitterrand's judgment did reflect something of Chirac's established reputation in the area of foreign policy prior to his election in May 1995. From as far back as the mid-1970s his positions on European integration in particular had been hesitant, inconsistent, even at times contradictory. In more recent years, Chirac had been only minimally supportive of France's ratification of the Maastricht Treaty (September 1992); at one point in his 1995 presidential election campaign he had even appeared to call for Maastricht to be renegotiated. The modest levels of electoral popularity that he commanded (less than 21 per cent of the vote in the first round of the 1995 presidential election, a modest margin of victory over the less experienced PS candidate Lionel Jospin in the second round) combined with unreliable party support (both the principal party formations of his parliamentary majority, the RPR and the UDF, were internally divided between supporters of European integration and Euro-sceptics) to generate a dimension of uncertainty concerning prospects for foreign policy under Chirac. Against such factors, however, had to be weighed Chirac's impressive political experience: thirty years in national-level politics as founding leader of the RPR, France's largest party, including spells as Prime Minister under both of his presidential predecessors, Giscard d'Estaing (1974–76) and Mitterrand (1986–88). Alain Juppé had been an effective Foreign Minister in the Balladur government (1993–95): his appointment as Chirac's Prime Minister bolstered further the foreign policy qualifications of the new administration.

Chirac's decision to complete the nuclear test programme at Mururoa and Fangataufa was announced (June 1995) less than a month after he took office. The move brought to an end the testing moratorium that Mitterrand had declared in April 1992. In a post-cold war context of diminished strategic risk (the global Non-Proliferation Treaty had been extended indefinitely in May 1995), hostile international reaction was predictable. Protests quickly expanded beyond Australasia and the South Pacific to spread worldwide, although they were made more frequently – not to say noisily

– at the informal level of mediatized public opinion than through more formal diplomatic or governmental channels. Where Japan was critical, the USA and Britain were restrained if not actually sympathetic in their responses. In the EU, the European Parliament passed a motion condemning the resumption of testing while the International Court of Justice and the EU Commission declined to criticize France's action. In France itself opinion was divided and arguably incoherent, with 59 per cent of people opposed to the resumption of French testing while 58 per cent approved in principle of retaining a national nuclear dissuasive capacity (SOFRES poll, August 1995).

Chirac's decision, in mid-1995, to authorize a final series of six nuclear tests attracted more widespread criticism than his presidential predecessors, de Gaulle and Mitterrand, had had to bear (cartoon from Le Monde, *2 August 1995)*

30 TIRS

86 TIRS

TIRS EN TOUS GENRES

Ironically, over the decade 1981–91 Mitterrand had authorized 86 nuclear tests without being subject to the widespread criticism suffered by Chirac over his modest programme of six tests between September 1995 and January 1996. In other areas of defence policy, moreover, Chirac subsequently provided ample evidence that, far from being an anachronistic nuclear warrior, he was committed to scaling down and radically revising the Gaullist nuclear policy heritage. After Juppé's mini-budget (June 1995) had continued the trend begun under Mitterrand towards reduced military spending, Chirac committed France to end all levels of nuclear testing (in a Comprehensive Test Ban Treaty scheduled to be signed by late 1996). He ratified in company with the USA and Britain (March 1996) the protocoles of the Treaty of Raratonga establishing a nuclear-free zone in the South Pacific, programmed the closure of testing facilities in French Polynesia, scrapped both the strategic missiles housed in silos on the Plateau d'Albion in southern France and the Hadès tactical missiles, and postponed until 2001 the construction of a fourth strategic nuclear submarine of the new generation *Triomphant* class.

Early initiatives to enhance long-term nuclear security co-operation with Germany and especially with Britain (August and October 1995) were but the prelude to a flood of reforms. From the end of 1995 Chirac announced his intentions to: professionalize France's armed forces, reducing their numbers by 150,000 and ending obligatory national service from 1997; cut defence spending by more than 100 billion francs over five years; and restructure national defence industries. Most tellingly, France would be substantially re-integrated into NATO – albeit into an adapted and reformed NATO more sensitive to long-standing French and German concerns to develop what (at the Berlin NATO Council meeting in June 1996) Foreign Minister Hervé de Charette called *l'identité européenne de défense*. The draft military programme law 1997–2002, which incorporated many of these changes, was adopted by the Chirac–Juppé cabinet in May

Chirac: 'Stop crying! You'll still be able to intervene in Africa!' Major cuts in the French armed forces and defence budgets were announced from late 1995 (cartoon from Le Monde Sélection, *23-29 May 1996)*

1996; the programme of reforms may not be fully implemented before 2015. These historic moves served to underline Chirac's distinctly un-Gaullist recognition of the need to continue efforts – initiated by Giscard and Mitterrand – to rationalize and progressively to tailor national security policies to fit both the transformed strategic environment and a future integrated Europe. Chirac's energetic promotion (July 1995) of a more active military involvement by western forces to relieve the Serbian siege of Sarajevo had offered a promising example of this last priority.

During his first months of office Chirac regularly re-asserted France's determination to qualify as a founder member of EMU in conformity with the Maastricht Treaty. A single European currency from 1999 remained his objective. As it had been since the 1950s, Franco-German co-operation would remain at the heart of the EU in the future. Chirac's commitment to this direct prolongation and development of Mitterrand's European policy was made plain throughout his first year as President, from the Cannes EU summit (June 1995) through to the launch in Turin (March 1996) of the inter-governmental conference of the EU, in his state visit to Britain (May 1996) as at the Dijon Franco-German summit with Kohl (June 1996). That he will continue to enjoy, domestically and abroad, the political and economic autonomy necessary to realize these objectives seems, however, less certain. Reducing France's budget and welfare deficits (in order to conform to the Maastricht Treaty's convergence criteria for the establishment of a single European currency) could prove unacceptably painful to a French electorate ravaged by persistent high unemployment (11.9 per cent in April 1996) and holding sceptical views on the EU and EMU.

In spite of their having ratified the Maastricht Treaty, the fifteen members of the EU continued in 1995–96 to display their differences and reservations concerning the terms and timetable for EMU. The substance and relative priorities to be accorded over the next few years to the integration and expansion of the EU remained to be determined. In the second and third quarters of 1995, Chirac's overt policy positions still reflected on occasion the confusion of this advance towards an integrated Europe. Yet in a major television interview (26 October 1995) he re-asserted that his first priority for the foreseeable future would be to ensure that the Juppé government reduced its budget deficit so that France would be able to participate in EMU from 1999. When, a few days later, a Franco-British summit (29–30 October 1995) made notable progress towards developing bilateral nuclear defence co-operation, a shift in French European policy emphasis appeared to some observers to be under way, one that was moving from the Mitterrand–Kohl federalist idealism of the 1980s and early 1990s, back towards the more pragmatic nation-state Europeanism of . . . de Gaulle. In March 1996 a prospective analysis published in *Le Monde* suggested that *'Le président Chirac pourrait se révéler, à côté des Monnet, Adenauer, Schuman et autres Kohl, comme l'un des fondateurs de l'Europe, le père en fait d'une nouvelle Europe faite de multiples souverainetés partagées'*. Time will tell. In mid-1996 Chirac's definitive policy line on Europe had still to establish itself fully. The direction of that line might well determine the future of the EU.

Not that recent French foreign policy has restricted itself to the confines of Europe. In contrast to the somewhat narrow concentration on European integration that had characterized Mitterrand's final few years, it was on the contrary the expansiveness and global projection of Chirac's policy enterprises that attracted attention. Tensions relating to trade issues and the Middle East notwithstanding, relations with the USA have been re-invigorated, in large part due to the improved security co-operation within the Atlantic Alliance engendered by France's new enthusiasm to work within NATO. The initial Euro-Asia summit, held in Bangkok (March 1996), allowed Chirac to reaffirm that, in company with its EU partners, Paris was – belatedly – determined to accord far higher priority to diplomatic and economic relations with the Asian region. Recalling a much earlier policy priority of Pompidou, Paris restated at the Euro-Mediterranean Forum in Barcelona (November 1995) its long-term commitment to fostering trade, development and security links with the countries of the Mediterranean rim as a whole – *'un véritable partenariat euro-méditerranéen'*, was Chirac's sonorous formula. Perhaps most striking were French efforts to re-launch relations with the Arab world. Speaking in Cairo at the end of an extended visit to Lebanon and Egypt (April 1996), Chirac first asserted his Gaullist credentials (*'La politique arabe de la France doit être une dimension essentielle de sa politique étrangère. Je souhaite lui donner un élan nouveau.'*), before going further and calling on the EU to assume a more prominent political role as a co-partner in the Middle East peace process. Backing up his President's words with action, and in response to Israeli air attacks against Hizbullah guerrillas in southern Lebanon, de Charette mounted – in the face of Israeli indifference and American resentment at such French 'interference' – a persistent and eventually effective diplomatic offensive on behalf of Lebanese territorial sovereignty (April 1996). Elsewhere in the Middle East particular emphasis was placed by Paris on the delicate development of relations with Iraq and Iran.

By mid-1996, as the second year of the new presidential term began, it had become clear that distinctive new foreign policy patterns were emerging: 'Jacques was back'. Even *The Economist* conceded that 'Not since de Gaulle himself, perhaps, has France been so conspicuous around the world'. Yet problems of substance remained unresolved, some effectively inherited from the earliest days of de Gaulle. It was for example difficult to reconcile Chirac's unilateral, *national* initiatives – the resumption of nuclear testing, his delay in implementing the Schengen agreement on dismantling EU internal borders, or French diplomatic initiatives regarding Lebanon – with his no less firmly declared commitment to developing *common* foreign and security policies with the EU. Equilibrium also remained to be established between support for democracy and human rights and pursuit of national commercial interests: a controversial state visit by China's Prime Minister Li Peng (April 1996) produced human rights protests in Paris – and the anticipated 11 billion francs of industrial contracts for Airbus, Citroën, Sofregaz, Saint-Gobain and others. King Hassan II of Morocco was received with pomp in the National Assembly (May 1996) – but also with parliamentary criticism from the PCF and members of Jospin's PS. Yet Chirac's assertion on this last occasion that Morocco was a force for democracy in North Africa that deserved French economic support was lent relative strength by the collapse in relations with an Algeria torn by civil war: following the kidnapping and murder of seven French monks by Algerian Islamist terrorists, the Juppé government called (May 1996) for all remaining French expatriates to leave the country. Elsewhere in Africa, military involvement in France's former colonies resurfaced as it had under Giscard and Mitterrand: French troops twice (April and May 1996) intervened in Bangui to maintain order – and the régime of President Patassé – in the face of mutiny by part of the Central African Republic's army. Some things had not changed, although this was foreign policy continuity of a more ambivalent nature.

An IFOP poll conducted within days of his predecessor's death, in January 1996, suggested that 84 per cent of French public opinion thought that France had made progress in European integration under Mitterrand's presidency, while 68 per cent considered that, since 1981, France's place in the world had been enhanced. These seem difficult targets to equal, let alone surpass. Chirac lacks neither energy nor determination nor, on the evidence of his assertive, high-profile first year in office, scope of ideas. Most of his foreign policy's outcomes have of course yet to be achieved.

BIBLIOGRAPHY

Aldrich, R., and Connell, J., *France in World Politics*. London, Routledge, 1989. Nine chapters on various aspects of France's international relations – defence issues, European unity, Africa and the Third World, the DOM-TOM, Francophonie, among others. An invaluable introduction.

Chafer, T., and Jenkins, B. (eds), *France. From the Cold War to the new world order*. London, Macmillan, 1996. Essays on various aspects of French foreign policy: Franco-German relations, France and European security, defence policy, French aid to Africa, relations with Algeria.

Clark, A., 'François Mitterrand and the idea of Europe'. In Nelson, B., (ed.), *The Idea of Europe: Problems of National and Transnational Identity*. New York, Berg, 1992.

Frears, J. R., *France in the Giscard Presidency*. London, George Allen & Unwin, 1981. Chapters 5 and 6 on foreign policy and defence under Giscard.

Godt, P. (ed.), *Policy-Making in France. From de Gaulle to Mitterrand*. London, Pinter, 1989. Section V contains chapters on France's relations (1958–88) with the USSR, Europe and the Third World.

Howorth, J., 'Foreign and defence policy: from independence to interdependence'. In Hall, P. A., Hayward, J., and Machin, H. (eds), *Developments in French Politics*. London, Macmillan, revised edition, 1994.

Kramer, S. P., *Does France still count? The French Role in the New Europe*. Westport (Connecticut), Praeger, 1994. A recent American perspective on France's security and integration policies in Europe since 1991. Chapter 5 examines Franco-American relations.

McCarthy, P. (ed.), *France-Germany 1983-1993. The Struggle to cooperate*. New York, St Martin's Press, 1993. A collection of essays examining aspects of Franco-German relations during the Mitterrand years.

Mitterrand, F., *Ici et maintenant*. Paris, Livre de Poche, 1981. Chapters VI and VII: a lively *tour d'horizon* of major international questions, conducted a few months before Mitterrand was first elected President.

Mitterrand, F., *Réflexions sur la politique extérieure de la France*. Paris, Fayard, 1986. The introduction (pp. 7-135) contains an extended account of French defence, European and Third World policies.

Mitterrand, F., 'The Future of Europe'. In *The World Today*, vol. 43, no. 3, March 1987. A speech made in London in January 1987 which contains much of Mitterrand's policy views and vision of Europe.

Mitterrand, F., *De l'Allemagne, de la France*. Paris, Editions Odile Jacob, 1996. Mitterrand's final views, written in the last weeks of his life, on European integration, Franco-German relations, German reunification.

Pickles, D., *The Government and Politics of France*, vol. 2: 'Politics'. London, Methuen, 1973. Although now dated, Part II offers a full account of foreign policy under de Gaulle and Pompidou.

Ross, G., Hoffmann, S., and Malzacher, S., *The Mitterrand Experiment. Continuity and Change in Modern France*. Cambridge, Polity Press, 1987.

Section V: 'France and the world under Mitterrand', contains essays on Mitterrand's foreign and defence policies, and on France's relations with the Third World.

Tiersky, R., *France in the New Europe. Changing yet Steadfast*. Belmont (California), Wadsworth, 1994. An elegant recent study. See the chapter entitled 'Geopolitics and foreign policy'.

Tiersky, R., 'Mitterrand's legacies'. In *Foreign Affairs*, vol. 74, no. 1, January–February 1995. A brief appraisal of Mitterrand's foreign policy achievements.

Invaluable official statements, updated daily, from the Quai d'Orsay relating to the main elements of France's foreign policies (defence and disarmament; development aid; European Union, Francophonie; cultural, scientific and technical co-operation; bilateral relations, etc.) are located on the Internet at:

http://www.france.diplomatie.fr/actual/index.html

5

IMMIGRANTS

Brian Fitzpatrick

Introduction: numbers and definitions

According to the most recent national census taken in 1990, there were 3,597,000 foreigners in France out of a total population of 56.7 million. This official figure reflects a decline of 117,000 on the 1982 figure. Moreover, figures released in December 1995 by the *Direction de la Population et des Migrations* suggest that the number of foreigners entering France has declined significantly in recent years: while 116,000 new immigrants were admitted in 1993, that number fell to 83,000 in the following year. The official figures do not tell the whole story, however. Unlike most European states, France does not have a complete register of aliens residing on her territory. While the census distinguishes between French citizens and foreign residents, the distinction is based on a voluntary declaration made by individuals and households. The *Institut national de la Statistique et des Etudes économiques* (INSEE), which carries out the national census, admits that '*il faut tenir compte des erreurs de déclaration de nationalité*'. The errors are said to relate to declarations made by or on behalf of people born in France and who assume, therefore, that they are French citizens. According to INSEE, taking account of births, deaths and inaccurate census returns, the number of people who are technically foreigners has in fact increased and should be reckoned at about 4.2 million.

Even this figure requires qualification. The census figures depend, we have seen, on returns made freely by residents who are not afraid to make their presence known to the authorities, even if they give inaccurate information. But France has long experienced illegal immigration, and illegal immigrants do not figure in the official census. Thus, an independent commentator, Jean Mottin (see bibliography), a former *Conseiller d'Etat*, using a variety of sources, including the *Ministère de l'Intérieur*, the *Secrétariat d'Etat à l'Immigration* and the *Ministère des Affaires sociales*, argues that INSEE's census figures underestimated the foreign population by as much as 14 per cent in 1982 and 31 per cent in 1990. This analysis implies that there may be as many as 5.5 million foreigners living in France at present.

Immigrants and their children may eventually apply for French citizenship. Thus, not all immigrants are 'foreigners' in legal terms. Many have sought and acquired French citizenship since settling in the country, and increasingly their children claim it. As restrictions on immigrants increase, more and more foreigners are seeking citizenship to avoid the loss of privileges and the possibility of expulsion: in 1994, 126,000 foreign residents sought and obtained French nationality, an increase of 32 per cent on 1993. In the case of young people born in France of immigrant parents, the acquisition of French citizenship is no longer automatic at the age of eighteen. Since the introduction of the Pasqua/Méhaignerie laws in 1993, children born in France to two foreign parents must formally apply for it between the ages of sixteen and twenty-one by a procedure known as *la manifestation de volonté*. Until then, they are deemed to be foreigners and can be deported along with their parents if these are considered to be a threat to public order or if they are illegal immigrants. (The one exception to this involves children born in France to Algerians themselves born before Algerian independence, that is when Algeria was an integral part of France. Such children are considered to be French unless they choose Algerian citizenship.) Since 1993 some 33,000 young residents have obtained French citizenship by applying for it. In terms of the census, these are French people, yet in many respects – family culture, qualifications, income, attitudes – such people may remain much more representative of the 'immigrant' than of the *Français par acquisition* they have become. Thus, many of the social problems associated with young *Beurs* (from *verlan*, slang for *arabe*) involve people who are legally French, but who cannot identify with typical French culture, and who are frequently rejected out of hand by the French because they have not been able to exchange their North African or African physical features for European features on acquiring French nationality.

Well over 3 million of France's declared foreign residents remain nationals of their country of birth and are governed by residence and work permits which determine how long the holder can remain in the country and in what circumstances.

Significant distinctions can be made between immigrants from countries now in the European Union (EU) and those from other parts of the globe. On the whole, EU members have considerable rights in France – notably in terms of health care, social security and

Mass demonstrations against the Front national's *attitude to immigrants, March 1997*

participation in local politics – which are reciprocated to French nationals living in other EU countries. At present, about 36.5 per cent of France's foreign population comes from EU member states. The enlargement of the European Community, now the European Union, has led to a reclassification of many of France's foreign residents and to a consolidation of their position. Probably the Portuguese are the greatest beneficiaries of this enlargement. When Portugal joined the then EC in 1986, more than 750,000 of her citizens were living and working in France and they made up about one fifth of the overall foreign population. While they were culturally better integrated than the growing numbers of immigrants from beyond Europe's confines, the Portuguese were still subject to strict residence and work regulations. European Union membership has certainly helped to enhance their security and status in France, and

Portuguese nationals remain by far the largest immigrant group in France.

Other European citizens have taken advantage of the rights conferred by EU membership. While the English presence in France was for long a wealthy minority confined to parts of Paris and the Côte d'Azur, the UK's entry into the EC in 1973 led to an extensive colonization of selected regions in the 1980s – Normandy and the Dordogne, notably.

Foreigners make up at least 6.3 per cent of the population of France, more probably 7 or 8 per cent. In comparison, in 1990, officially registered foreigners made up the following percentages of: Austria 5.3 per cent; Belgium 9.1 per cent; Denmark 3.1 per cent; Finland 0.5 per cent; Germany (West) 8.2 per cent; Italy 1.4 per cent; Netherlands 4.6 per cent; Sweden 5.6 per cent; Switzerland 16.3 per cent; UK 3.3 per cent.

A more detailed inspection of the foreigners in France reveals that almost 41 per cent are Europeans. Eighteen per cent are Portuguese; 7 per cent are Italians; 6 per cent are Spaniards. The proportion of Europeans has been decreasing steadily since the 1920s, when Europeans made up 94 per cent of France's foreign population. Within that decline, particular nationalities have been eclipsed. Italians have fallen from 30 per cent, Spaniards from almost 17 per cent and Belgians from 23 per cent to 1.5 per cent. Conversely, the Portuguese made up less than 1 per cent of the foreigners in France in 1921.

Hard on the heels of the Europeans come the North Africans (*Maghrébins*) whose numbers in France have increased dramatically from 2.4 per cent of foreigners in 1921 to almost 39 per cent in 1991. Algerians remain the largest national group at just over 17 per cent, followed by Moroccans (16 per cent) and Tunisians (6 per cent).

The third largest group is made up of Asians (almost 12 per cent), of whom Turks constitute almost 6 per cent.

Black Africans account for about 5 per cent of the foreigners in France. Again, it is important to note that these figures are based on INSEE census returns, and they can almost certainly underestimate the size of the North African, Asian and Black African populations in France.

FRANCE AND IMMIGRATION – A BRIEF HISTORY

Like most countries, France has always housed expatriate communities – merchants, traders, students, artists and others whose exile has been largely voluntary and, on the whole, comfortable. With other European liberal democracies, France has a tradition of sheltering political refugees and stateless persons. This tradition goes back to

Table 5.1: *The principal immigrant communities in France*

Nationality	Size*
Portuguese	645,578
Algerian	619,923
Moroccan	584,708
Italian	253,679
Spanish	216,015
Tunisian	207,496
Turkish	201,480
Yugoslav	51,697
Polish	46,283
Senegalese	45,260
Cambodian	44,029
Malian	34,937
Laotian	31,643
Vietnamese	31,171
Camerounais	19,145
Ivoirien (Ivory Coast)	16,987
Source: INSEE census, 1990	
* Subject to the limitations discussed above.	

the Bourbon monarchy which made welcome Irish and Scottish Jacobites in the seventeenth century. It was reinforced by the French Revolution, and since then many refugees have found a home in *France, terre d'asile*. In the twentieth century, Armenians, Poles, White Russians, Spaniards, Yugoslavs, Chileans and Argentines have figured prominently among the exiled communities.

The spread of small, local wars in many parts of the world, often fuelled by ethnic rivalries, has led to increasing pressure on countries like France to offer asylum to victims of persecution. In 1992, 10,300 applications for asylum were made, and in 1994 nearly 26,000. Requests from Romanians increased by 48 per cent, from Chinese 218 per cent. However, only 24 per cent of these requests were successful (*Le Monde*, 22–23 April 1995). At present there are more than 70,000 officially recognized refugees and stateless persons among the foreign population, many of whom are refugees from Turkey and the Near East (Kurds, notably), Asia and Asia Minor, North and sub-Saharan Africa. With the spread of Moslem fanaticism in some of France's former colonies, the 1990s have seen a growing trickle of liberals from North Africa seeking to escape the fury of groups like the *Front islamique du Salut* (FIS). In 1994, 2,385 Algerians who felt themselves threatened by 'Islamic salvation' requested asylum. It is ironic that the Ayatollah Khomeini enjoyed asylum in France before returning to Iran in 1979 to establish one of the most intolerant regimes of the century.

The racial composition of France's foreign population largely reflects the country's colonial past. Having lost many of her overseas possessions (North America and parts of India, notably) in the second half of the eighteenth century, from about 1830 France began to rebuild an empire. By 1914, France governed most of Africa northwest of the equator, Madagascar and Indo-China (Cambodia and Vietnam). After the Second World War, the empire was unable to withstand demands for independence. France was forced out of Indo-China in 1954 after a bloody conflict; Morocco and Tunisia became independent in 1956; and Algeria, which was constitutionally as much a part of France as Corsica, secured independence in 1962 after six years of savage and deeply divisive armed conflict with France. During the early years of the Fifth Republic, France's sub-Saharan territories also achieved independence: Guinea in 1958; Mauretania, Mali, Niger, Haute Volta (now Burkina Faso), Chad, Cameroon, Central African Republic, Gabon, Ivory Coast and Senegal in 1960. All of them, except Guinea, kept close cultural and economic ties with France which became a natural focus for emigration. The partition of Indo-China in 1954, with a communist government in power in the North, then the collapse of South Vietnam in 1975, ensured two waves of migrants and refugees towards France.

French economic expansion in the 1960s was responsible for the influx of Turks, of whom there are more than 200,000, and Yugoslavs (almost 52,000).

Immigration is historically linked very closely to France's demographic and economic evolution. Population growth in France was slight between the Revolution and the end of the Second World War, and during the period 1935 to 1946 there were more deaths than live births each year. Many reasons are given for this, notably a conscious effort among a largely rural population to limit the number of claimants on land that may have been obtained painstakingly and at great cost, and, of course, the effects of the two world wars. One million, four hundred thousand deaths resulted from the First World War, that is to say one French citizen in twenty-five died. As far as male deaths were concerned, one in five of the country's young men died prematurely. Apart from the immediate losses, one has to take account of the effects on the next generation. There were fewer men and women of a reproductive age available to renew the population. The conflict between 1940 and 1945 resulted in the loss of a further 900,000 French men and women. Again, a large number of these died prematurely.

The size and age structure of the population affected economic development. Industrial expansion relied from the outset on immigration labour – Belgians and Poles worked in the coalfields and iron foundries of the north east, for example. Labour intensive forms of agriculture, like the grape harvest in the Midi, relied on seasonal workers from Spain and Italy. Reconstruction after the First World War led to a significant influx of foreign workers so that foreigners made up 6.6 per cent of the total population (and 7.4 per cent of the workforce) by 1931.

At the end of the Second World War, French economic reconstruction was planned centrally by the *Commissariat au Plan*, and it became clear that growth could only be achieved with the aid of a sizeable, imported workforce. An *Office national de l'Immigration* was established to oversee large-scale immigration. Moreover, entire families were encouraged to settle in France to help boost consumption as well as production.

The period from 1946 to the early 1980s was marked by extensive modernization and careful planning which transformed France into a major industrial power and Europe's second most powerful economy. Immigrant labour played a significant part in this economic development as employers demanded ever greater numbers of workers. Thus Mottin calculated that more than 11 million foreigners migrated to France between 1948 and 1990, more than 8 million of them after 1962. By the mid-1970s, legal immigrants made up slightly more than 7 per cent of the workforce.

Since the mid-1970s, when boom began to turn to slump with a consequent rise in unemployment, immigration from outside the EU has slowed to the point where only the spouse and children under eighteen years of settled workers are permitted to enter the country in accordance with a policy known as *le regroupement familial*. Since the Pasqua/Méhaignerie laws were enacted, the number of foreigners admitted in the context of *le regroupement familial* has decreased. Fewer than 21,000 spouses and children entered France in 1994 compared to an average of 35,000 a year in the late 1980s and early 1990s. Equally, mayors now have the right to refuse to marry French citizens to foreigners if they suspect that the ceremony is a ploy to enable the foreign party to acquire French citizenship.

THE ECONOMIC IMPACT OF IMMIGRANTS

We have seen that foreigners were sought after 1945 to boost France's inadequate population and to make economic reconstruction and expansion possible. In fact, immigrants have contributed about 20 per cent of the net population increase in France since 1945 by immigration, *regroupement familial*, marriage to French citizens and by a consistently higher birth rate than that of the French. While 9.9 per cent of legitimate babies born in 1977 had two foreign parents, that figure had risen to 11.1 per cent in 1991. In the same year 4.7 per cent were born into families in which one parent was foreign against 2.7 per cent in 1977. Nevertheless, the immigrant birth rate is falling, and is now generally lower than its equivalent in the immigrant's country of origin (see Table 5.2).

Table 5.2: *Fertility*

Nationality	Children per woman 1981	Children per woman 1990
French	1.8	1.7
Portuguese	2.2	1.9
Spanish	1.7	1.5
Italian	1.7	1.4
Algerian	4.3	3.2
Moroccan	5.2	3.5
Tunisian	5.3	3.9
Turkish	5.2	3.7
Black African	5.1	4.8

Fertility in countries of origin in 1991 was: Tunisia 4.9; Turkey 5.1; Algeria 5.4; Morocco 5.9; Black Africa 6.4; Portugal 1.5; Spain and Italy 1.3.

Source: INSEE statistics, taken from Champsaur, *Les Etrangers en France* (1994), p. 41

The immigrants' contribution to the growth of the French economy since the Second World War is less easy to quantify. Certainly, the Fifth Plan (1966–70) acknowledged that 70 per cent of the larger workforce that France required would have to be imported. That meant an annual immigration of 130,000 workers during the period of the plan. The Sixth Plan (1971–75) envisaged an annual recruitment of 75,000 foreign workers.

Employers were acutely aware of the economic advantages involved in hiring immigrant labour. In the early 1970s, when 40 per cent of the labour employed in the building trade was immigrant, one builder, who wished to remain anonymous, spoke for many French employers when he said: *'Si j'avais des Français à la place des étrangers, je devrais verser des salaires supérieurs de 20 pour cent'*. Some large firms undertook their own recruitment campaigns in Turkey, Yugoslavia and a number of African states, so anxious were they to obtain manpower at low cost. In 1974, shortly after the oil-producing countries demonstrated their ability to cause havoc in the industrial world by withholding supplies and increasing prices dramatically, French employers feared that labour-exporting countries might do the same thing: *'Nous serions bien embêtés si l'Algérie rapatriait du jour au lendemain ses 1,200 ressortissants qui travaillent chez nous'* commented the managing director of Berliet trucks on one occasion.

Immigrants were prepared to do many jobs that Frenchmen turned down as dirty, demeaning or ill-paid. Most immigrants are employed in unskilled or low-skilled jobs. Fifteen per cent of French males are in managerial/executive positions, but only 3.4 per cent of foreigners. At the other end of the scale, 15 per cent of French males are unskilled workers while 32 per cent of immigrants are. This is particularly true of immigrants from countries outside the EU, although the Portuguese have traditionally figured prominently among building workers. The least qualified immigrants are North and Black Africans. The individual immigrant's average wage is, on the whole, 20 per cent lower than the average French income. When we consider household incomes (*revenus des ménages*), households with two French spouses enjoy an income which is 36 per cent higher than that of households with two immigrant spouses – largely because more French households have two wage-earners, each of whom is generally better paid than immigrant wage-earners.

As far as women are concerned, while 25 per cent of French women have no qualifications, 60 per cent of immigrant women have none. While 30 per cent of French wage-earners are women, only 14 per cent of immigrant women earn a wage. That, too, is 18–20 per cent less than the average wage earned by French women.

Since the 1980s, industrial transformation has forced many workers into the service sector and into unemployment. These changes have been particularly significant in the immigrant community.

Unemployment has affected the immigrant community much more severely than the French population. In 1992, 9.5 per cent of the working population was unemployed. Unemployment was higher (13.8 per cent) among *Français par acquisition* - immigrants who have successfully sought French citizenship - than it was among *Français de naissance* (9.4 per cent), but 18.6 per cent of the foreign workers were unemployed. Among the immigrants, certain national groups suffered more than others. Unemployment was around 30 per cent for North and Black Africans, while Portuguese unemployment was below the national average (8.7 per cent). Young immigrants or the children of immigrants fared particularly badly. Unemployment among young French citizens (15 to 24 years) reached 20.3 per cent, again with a distinction between *Français d'acquisition* (31.3 per cent), and *Français de naissance* (20.1 per cent). At the same time, 29.8 per cent of young foreigners were unemployed, with levels reaching 53 per cent of young North and Black Africans. Once again, the Portuguese community proved the exception with an unemployment level of 15.4 per cent in that age group, substantially below the national average for France.

Table 5.3: *Percentage of immigrant workers in main sectors of employment*

Nationality	Agriculture	Industry	Construction	Services
Spanish	6.1	24.4	19.5	50.1
Italian	2.2	28.4	27.1	42.3
Portuguese	2.6	24.1	29.9	43.5
Algerian	0.6	26.9	21.9	50.6
Moroccan	10.6	29.6	18.9	40.9
Tunisian	3.3	21.8	24.6	50.3
Black African	0.3	23.6	6.9	69.2
Turkish	4.3	43.7	28.5	23.5
Asian	1.1	42.7	3.5	52.8

Source: INSEE national census, 1990

THE IMMIGRANT COMMUNITY IN FRANCE – A PROFILE

From the information already provided, it is clear that immigrants have a distinctive profile. One can elaborate by noting that they are on the whole less qualified than the French, are paid less, and are usually found in the more menial occupations. Other general statements can be made about them, but there are also profound differences between the ethnic and national groups which make up the immigrant population. These differences are increasingly significant in determining the attitude of the population at large towards immigrants and in determining the immigrants' capacity to integrate into French society.

Table 5.4: *Percentage shifts in immigrant employment 1982–90*

Occupation	Shift among French	Shift among immigrants
Agriculture, sylviculture, pêche	−28.0	−25.3
Industries agricoles et alimentaires	+1.5	−11.9
Production et distribution d'énergie	−9.9	−55.3
Industries des biens intermédiaires	−8.5	−25.9
Industries des biens d'équipement	−8.4	−30.4
Industries des biens de consommation	−9.9	−15.3
Commerce	+4.7	+10.7
Transports & télécommunications	+5.6	+8.0
Services marchands	+28.2	+38.4
Location et crédit-bail immobiliers	+13.6	+4.8
Assurances	+10.2	+17.7
Organismes financiers	+8.5	+28.8
Services non marchands	+13.1	+13.0

Source: INSEE national censuses, 1982 and 1990

Age and sex

The immigrant population is younger than the French population. Twenty-one per cent of foreigners are under fifteen years of age against 19 per cent of the French. Almost 49 per cent of foreigners are aged between 25 and 54 against 40 per cent of the French. Fewer foreigners (7.8 per cent) than French (15.2 per cent) are to be found in the retired population aged 65 and over. The immigrant community has a higher proportion of males than its French counterpart – 55 per cent against 48.2 per cent. However, the imbalance between males and females in the immigrant community has been decreasing since the 1970s. For many years, immigrants tended to be single males seeking work. Certainly, many were married with families in their country of origin, but the male breadwinner had gone to France alone. The prohibition on immigration for work purposes but not on *le regroupement familial* has increased the female immigrant population. Thus, in 1968, 61 per cent of immigrants were male, in 1975, 60 per cent were and in 1982, 57 per cent.

Housing

Most post-1945 immigrants came to France to work in the industrial sector. Consequently, France's immigrant population is overwhelmingly urban: 38 per cent of them live in the Paris region (Ile-de-France), where they make up 13 per cent of the region's population; 12 per cent live in the Rhône-Alpes region (Lyonnais, Grenoble) and make up 8 per cent of the total population of the region; 12 per cent live along the Mediterranean coast and make up 13.4 per cent of the population; 7.9 per cent live in Alsace-Lorraine, forming 14.6 per cent of the region's population. At the other end of the spectrum, only around 1.0 per cent live in agricultural Brittany, Lower Normandy, Poitou and the Loire valley.

Table 5.5: *Population distribution according to town size (percentage)*

Size of commune	French nationals	Foreigners
Rural	27.3	8.1
Urban, smaller than 20,000 inhabitants	16.7	12.0
20,000–100,000	13.2	13.8
100,000–200,000	27.7	30.5
Paris region	15.1	35.6
Source: INSEE national census, 1990		

On the whole, immigrants are less well housed than the native French. Certainly matters have improved since the 1960s when immigrant workers were frequently found in sprawling *ad hoc* shanty towns (*bidonvilles*) on the outskirts of major French industrial cities. But, while 56 per cent of native French families are home owners, only 26 per cent of foreigners are. Twenty-eight per cent of immigrant households rent HLM (*Habitations à loyer modéré*) apartments, and they make up 11.5 per cent of HLM *locataires* even though they make up only 6 per cent of French households. Among foreigners, certain national groups figure more prominently than others: 74.3 per cent of Algerians, 80 per cent of Moroccans, 80 per cent of Tunisians and 87 per cent of Turks rent HLM apartments against 61 per cent of Portuguese and 52 per cent of Spaniards.

In some respects, the unprepossessing tower blocks that make up many HLM estates are luxurious in comparison with the shabby alternatives that so many immigrants, particularly the *clandestins*, endure. Foreigners figure prominently in the run-down *quartiers prioritaires* which exist in most French cities. The national average shows that 18 per cent of the inhabitants of these urban and suburban zones is made up of foreigners, but the percentage rises to 25 per cent in the Paris region, 26 per cent in Burgundy, 33 per cent in Franche-Comté. Closer inspection shows that non-EU immigrants make up 81 per cent of those lodged in such zones.

Many immigrants who came to France as single men or who left their family in the country of their origin live in cheap hotel rooms or, if they are legal immigrant workers, in hostels (*foyers*). Eighty-five per cent of hostel residents are North or Black Africans, 72 per cent of whom are married men whose family is still in the country of origin.

An INSEE investigation carried out in 1988 showed that 17 per cent of North Africans had no hot water in their accommodation; 20 per cent had to share a lavatory with others; 20 per cent lived in accommodation which had no shower or bathroom; 34 per cent had no central heating; and 56 per cent lived in overcrowded accommodation. Yet the redevelopment of these run-down areas brings its own problems. The *clandestins* and poorly paid workers find it impossible to pay the higher rents that improved accommodation entails.

Education

Immigrants are less qualified than the French. The 1990 census indicated that 60 per cent of the immigrants who replied had no qualifications. Only 27 per cent of the native French are in the same category. *Français par acquisition*, immigrants or their children who have taken out French citizenship, are in an intermediary position: 40 per cent of them have no qualifications. Closer inspection reveals the North African and Turkish communities having the highest proportion of unqualified immigrants: Algerians 70.8 per cent; Moroccans 71 per cent; Tunisians 63.9 per cent; Turks 72.2 per cent. However, the Italians and Portuguese are not far behind: 66.2 per cent of Italians have no qualifications, and 62.2 per cent of Portuguese have none.

Those immigrants who possess qualifications tend to have elementary, vocational or trade qualifications rather than academic or professional qualifications (see Table 5.6).

Table 5.6: *Over 15s and qualifications in percentages*

Nationality	Cert. d'études primaires	CAP	BEP	Bac. or Brevet professionnel	Diplôme supérieur
Français de naissance	19.2	14.3	5.7	11.6	5.3
Français par acquisition	18.4	11.8	4.1	9.0	5.6
Portuguese	18.4	9.1	2.6	2.1	0.3
Algerian	7.2	8.8	2.7	3.1	2.1
Moroccan	6.9	5.4	2.1	4.0	3.5
Tunisian	11.0	7.5	2.4	4.7	3.3
Turkish	13.6	4.1	1.3	2.0	0.9
Black African	6.3	3.4	2.4	9.9	12.0

Source: INSEE national census, 1990

The qualifications gap between immigrants and native French is expected to close somewhat as more foreigners pass through the education system from the very beginning – 80 per cent of immigrants' children under the age of ten are now born in France. In 1992, foreigners made up 9.4 per cent of the total school population of France as opposed to 7.7 per cent in 1975. Of these, 11.5 per cent were Portuguese nationals, and 56 per cent North Africans. For those whose grasp of French is weak, special *classes d'initiation* and *classes d'adaptation* are provided in areas with high immigrant populations. The *classes d'initiation* concentrate on language skills while the *classes d'adaptation* are relatively small in size and are intended to let teachers work more closely with individual pupils.

However, efforts made in the schools may not be completely effective in eradicating the handicaps that immigrants and their children experience. Much hinges on the social and physical environment in which the children live and grow up. Many immigrant families live in ghettos where the *lingua franca* is Arabic, Turkish or Vietnamese. Immigrant parents often find it impossible to promote their children's education because they are poorly educated themselves, and have little grasp of French culture and the education system.

THE SOCIAL AND POLITICAL DIMENSION OF IMMIGRATION

For twenty years, *'le problème des immigrés'* has figured prominently in French politics. During the same period, xenophobia and racial attacks have increased dramatically – so, too, has anti-

*Young immigrant
girls learn about Islam
at a mosque school
(photo: Steve
Mccurry/National
Geographic Society)*

semitism. In the 1995 presidential election, Jean-Marie Le Pen's
Front national achieved its best ever score in a national election –
15.27 per cent of the vote in metropolitan France with well over 18
per cent in the *départements* of the Mediterranean coast, the industrial Rhône-Alpes, the north-east and the working-class suburbs to
the north-east of Paris. These are precisely the regions in which
there are large concentrations of North African, Black African and
Turkish immigrants. As usual, Le Pen's campaign was fought on the
immigrant question, which the other candidates and most political
commentators believed to be irrelevant until the results of the first
round became available – *l'immigration n'est plus au centre du
débat présidentiel'* proclaimed *Le Monde* on 19 April 1995, four
days before the first round. Since the election of a centre-right
government with the former mayor of Paris, Jacques Chirac, as President, the *Front national* has continued to make electoral gains in
towns with a large immigrant population. In municipal elections in
the summer of 1995, the *Front national*'s representation increased
significantly and the party attracted more than 25 per cent of the
votes in twenty towns with more than 30,000 inhabitants, winning
outright control of Marignane, Orange and Toulon. In a spectacular
volte face, Vitrolles (Bouches du Rhône) voted massively against its
socialist mayor in favour of Bruno Mégret, Le Pen's lieutenant, who

was very nearly elected mayor. In a jubilant mood, Mégret told the party's 1995 youth summer school that its successes in the municipal elections had demonstrated that the *Front national* had become *'le premier parti ouvrier de France'* and had *'[fait] sauter le clivage traditionnel entre la gauche et la droite'*. The *Mairie* of Vitrolles finally fell to the *Front national* in February 1997.

The current wave of xenophobia is certainly related to high levels of unemployment, between 10 and 12 per cent in the period 1995–97. Fifteen years ago, it would have been extraordinary to see Frenchmen sweeping the streets. Now it is not at all unusual. Moreover, it is chiefly French people who, in growing numbers, try to sell publications for the homeless and unemployed like *La Rue*, *Macadam* and *La Lanterne* on the streets of France's towns. In times of hardship many are tempted to accept the crude solution proposed by Le Pen since the 1980s that unemployment could be eliminated if immigrants were repatriated. Now that immigrants experience a higher level of unemployment than the French, they are seen as a drain on society. It is a view that reflects pre-war immigration policy when foreigners had few rights if they came to France to seek work and one that refuses to reward immigrants for the part they have played in France's economic growth since the Second World War.

Hostility is directed mainly at the non-Europeans and their children who are perceived by a growing number of Frenchmen and women as a threat to the French way of life. Increasingly frustrated French people point to the rising percentage of foreigners in the country's prison population – it rose from 14.4 per cent in 1971 to 31.2 per cent in 1993 – and their sizeable share in drug peddling (9.2 per cent of convictions in 1991) and theft and robbery (38.2 per cent of convictions). Thus, in relation to their overall numbers, there are five times more foreigners than French people in prison. These figures, and the perception that non-Europeans are parasites incapable of assimilating, have given rise to angry confrontations in areas where there are concentrations of immigrants, confrontations between French nationals and immigrants, between the police and immigrants. The *Front national* is never far from such confrontations. Early in 1995, its members in Marseille attacked and killed a young man from the Comores who was bill-posting for a civil rights organization; in the early hours of the morning following Jean-Marie Le Pen's last presidential rally, staged in the Bois de Boulogne on 21 April 1995, three of his supporters seriously wounded a pregnant Algerian woman at Courbevoie; and at the *Fête Jeanne d'Arc* ceremonies orchestrated in Paris by right-wing groups on 1 May to counter the left's Labour Day, *Front national* supporters flung a North African into the Seine. In certain respects, the *Front national* is articulating anxiety, but it is also encouraging people to see immigrants as a major cause of a widespread malaise, referred to as *l'insécurité*. In short, racism is now overt. An opinion poll taken in 1992 for inclusion in an annual report by the *Commission consultative des Droits de l'Homme* revealed that 40 per cent of the sample admitted to being racist and 25 per cent said they were a bit racist. A poll taken by *Le Monde* in April 1996 indicated that one-third of the French agreed with Jean-Marie Le Pen's uncompromising hostility to the presence of immigrants in France.

There can be little doubt that the rising crime rate among immigrants is related to their marginalization and relative deprivation. We have seen that they are worse paid, worse housed and more prone to unemployment than the French. Moreover, the immigrant population continues to contain a high proportion of young males, precisely the category most likely to become involved in crime.

Often isolated in tower block housing estates like those of La Courneuve or Stains to the north of Paris, many young immigrants and the children of immigrants are cut off from French society by their lack of qualifications and social skills. They are also prime targets for France's many police forces. In almost all airports, major railway stations and métro stations in Paris, squads of CRS (*Compagnies républicaines de Sécurité* – France's riot police) carry out spot checks on identity papers. Invariably, the squads single out individuals whose physiognomy is not obviously European. The checks have the dual function of picking up *les sans papiers*, the illegal immigrants, and reassuring the French that the authorities are taking steps to maintain public order. In recent years, public employees have been instructed to inform on immigrants whose papers are not in order – for instance, a post-office worker is on record for informing the local *Commissariat de Police* that an African's residence permit had expired, while a clinic notified the police that a North African woman who had just given birth was a *sans papiers*, and employees of *préfectures* have summoned the police to offices where officials were dealing with immigrants whose work and residence permits had expired.

It would be wrong to imply that the response of governments to the immigrant presence in recent years has been wholly negative. While considerable energy has been devoted to limiting the number of illegal immigrants whose living and working conditions are necessarily precarious, numerous policies have sought to ameliorate the conditions and security of legally settled immigrants and their families.

The construction of *foyers* for single male immigrants (SONACOTRA), and the establishment of the *Fonds d'Action sociale* (FAS) have helped a significant number of legal immigrants to establish social clubs and to find acceptable standards of accommodation – even though hostel residents have frequently had to protest about costs, conditions and poor service in a number of hostels. The *Aides au logement*, housing benefits aimed at ensuring that people on low incomes can enjoy decent housing, cover more than half of the rent paid by immigrants in public housing as opposed to a quarter of the rent paid by French residents in similar housing. In education, the identification of *Zones d'Education prioritaires* (ZEP), the provision of *classes d'initiation* and *classes d'adaptation* have sought to provide the children of immigrants with the basic requirements to function in France. Efforts have been made to ensure that *Halal* meat is available in school canteens and in barracks where Moslems are doing National Service. A greater sense of security was provided in 1983, when the panoply or residence and work permits was reduced to a single permit entitling the holder to ten years' residence – unless he or she committed a crime which incurred the penalty of expulsion.

Immigrants now have a number of pressure groups which act on their behalf: *SOS Racisme*, the *Mouvement contre le Racisme, l'Antisémitisme et pour la Paix* (MRAP) and the *Groupe d'Information et de Soutien des Travailleurs immigrés* (GISTI) are the best known. Governments have, since the mid-1970s, set up ministerial and quasi-governmental bodies to report on the conditions of immigrants. In the 1970s, a *Secrétariat d'Etat chargé des Travailleurs immigrés* was established; in 1984, a *Conseil national des Populations immigrées*; and in 1990 a *Haut Conseil à l'Intégration*; and the Chirac administration elected in May 1995 has created a *Ministère de l'Intégration et de la Lutte contre l'Exclusion*. Needless to say, almost all the government-inspired bodies have come in for criticism from the right, which regards them as pandering to unjustifiable minority demands, and from groups on the left, which see them as mere cosmetic exercises.

The audiovisual media in France have also begun to reflect the diverse ethnic groups present in the country. Television, traditionally a state monopoly, has responded feebly to pluralism since the privatizations of the 1980s. As in many other countries, more attention has been paid to the number of viewers a station can attract, and so dubbed American serials, cartoons and films fill viewing hours along with live coverage of sport. VHF radio provides minority groups with more entertainment and information. There are stations such as *Radio Beur* (aimed at the first generation born in France), *Radio Communauté Juive* and stations for Portuguese, Spanish, North African and Armenian listeners in most cities with substantial ethnic minorities.

The French parliament has passed a number of laws intended to combat racism. In 1972 incitement to racially or religiously inspired hatred was outlawed, and organizations founded to combat racism were enabled to instigate legal proceedings and to present themselves as the *partie civile* (injured party) in the courts. A law passed in 1985 extended the scope of the 1972 law to include discrimination in job appointments and the sale or rental of living accommodation on the basis of sex, race, religion, health, infirmity or opinions. Most recently, the *loi Gayssot* (1990), named after the communist deputy who sponsored the bill, stiffened the penalties which can be imposed for racist activities or propaganda to include loss of civic rights for five years, the publication in the press of penalties inflicted by the courts and the statutory right of reply for injured parties. The most controversial aspect of the *loi Gayssot* has been its condemnation of historical revisionism with regard to crimes against humanity. By insisting that legal action could be taken against revisionist historians who sought to play down the mass murder undertaken by the Third Reich, the law compelled the courts to become involved in making historical judgments.

On the whole, the anti-racist laws have been most successfully exploited by traditionally well-organized groups like the Jewish community who can articulate their concerns and criticisms through organizations such as the *Ligue internationale contre le Racisme et l'Antisémitisme* (LICRA) and the *Ligue des Droits de l'Homme* which was founded during the Dreyfus affair at the end of the last century. A recent legal action undertaken by the LICRA resulted in the censoring of a new edition of the Bible on the grounds that certain passages in the commentary could be held to encourage anti-semitism by appearing to denigrate Jewish ritual (*Le Monde*, 13–20 April 1995).

In recent years, a debate has arisen in France over the rights of minorities to preserve and promote their particular cultures. Historically, the establishment of republican France has required citizens to give their allegiance as individuals to a unitary, secular regime, with such things as religious belief and practice remaining personal and private matters. It has never been part of the republican tradition to accommodate groups and communities. For years, the major source of conflict between the state and a part of the citizenry was the question of subsidies for Catholic schools. Die-hard republicans rejected the demand that Catholic schools should be subsidized. Catholics, who formed a large part of the nation, argued that they were being taxed twice over by paying state taxes while having to fund their own schools. The matter was resolved in 1959 when recognized private schools, mainly Catholic, were permitted to enter into a contractual relationship with the Ministry of Education and derive a significant part of their funding from the state. In the early

1980s, under the socialist government formed by François Mitterrand, an unsuccessful effort was made to modify the 1959 agreement.

In recent years, the antagonism between Catholicism and the Republic has been eclipsed by the rise of other interests which have begun to make their own demands and to challenge traditional republican values more profoundly than French Catholics have done in this century.

With an estimated 4 million adherents, Islam is the second largest religious denomination in France. In many respects, Islam represents what many French people fear in the immigrant population. Its practitioners are mainly the North Africans and Turks who move to France in search of work, so it is a foreign import, closely identified with the least popular immigrant communities. It came as something of a shock to many French people in the early 1980s to see television pictures of production lines stopping in car factories while the workers knelt on mats facing Mecca for ritual prayer, or entire streets in cities like Marseille blocked by Moslems at prayer, or Moslems slaughtering sheep in tenement courtyards for festivals.

By its distinctive laws, customs and practices, and its links with countries like Iran and Saudi Arabia, Islam seems to many to proclaim the inability or the refusal of its adherents to embrace French norms but rather to give their allegiance to foreign powers. This is an important point because traditionally immigrants have been expected to conform to French values and customs, and to demonstrate their assimilation into French society if applying for citizenship and civic rights.

The issue has become all the more serious because of the rise of an illiberal, uncompromising, fundamentalist and exclusive brand of Islam since the 1970s. There are few facilities in France for training Islamic religious leaders, and these are usually trained in North African and Middle Eastern countries – precisely those areas exposed to the influence of fanatical groups like the *Front islamique du Salut* whose adepts have bombed French cities and assassinated at least one liberal *imam*. Some people are tempted to believe that a number of the religious teachers in France's Moslem communities are preaching subversion on behalf of foreign interests. The large Paris mosque, while subsidized from Algeria, appears not to have been influenced by the fundamentalists who are currently terrorizing that country, and there have been no demands for any separatist institutions like the Moslem parliament that some immigrants to Britain demanded. The French government has been careful to foster good relations with the Paris Moslem authorities: the walls of the Mosque display a number of letters signed by François Mitterrand offering his good wishes to the Moslem community for their major festivals.

Yet the Moslem community is not a monolith. A poll carried out in 1989 by the *Institut français d'Opinion public* (IFOP) suggested that only 37 per cent of Moslems practice their religion, while 38 per cent described themselves as believers. A large number of Moslems have long practised their religion discreetly and inoffensively. Moreover, 40 per cent of the IFOP sample described themselves as having no religious conviction.

Recently, the writer spoke to a Paris-based Algerian journalist in a café in Belleville, a *quartier* of Paris with old, settled, North African Moslem and Jewish communities. On one of the café's walls, a sticker proclaimed *I laïc Algeria*. In discussing relations between Jews and Arabs in general and in Belleville in particular, the journalist observed that the Moslems of Paris had more to fear from their *'frères intégristes'* than from Ultra-Zionist militias like *Betar* and *Tagar* which have begun to flourish because of the upsurge of anti-Semitism fomented by the same elements of the extreme right that attack and vilify North Africans. However much Moslem community leaders try to distance themselves from the violence of the extremists, the murder of Europeans in Algeria and the planting of bombs in public places in France is making life more uncomfortable for all of France's North African population and is undermining efforts to accommodate Moslems.

In the 1980s, socialist governments attempted to modify France's traditional assimilationist approach in favour of *l'insertion*, an approach intended to accept immigrants with their ethnic and religious identities. One of the common expressions of the early 1980s was *'le droit à la différence'*, implying that France could and should become a multi-cultural society which would formally recognize the distinctiveness of immigrant communities. The policy backfired badly, however, as the French right quickly attacked the proposals. The refusal to conform to French norms, it was argued, negated the possibility of offering ethnic minorities French citizenship and rights and could lead to a form of apartheid, with French citizens demanding priority of treatment over foreign minorities.

By the end of the 1980s, *l'insertion* had become *l'intégration*, an approach intended to reach a compromise. In exchange for the right to maintain their own customs as far as is feasible in a western, industrial society, immigrants would have to acknowledge the primacy of French norms and values and not seek exemptions or privileges that could offend the majority population or disrupt French institutions.

School has long been considered by the French as a fundamental instrument in the process of assimilating foreigners. The state system in particular has been the vehicle of the republican values of *égalité* and *laïcité*. The overwhelming majority of non-European immigrants send their children to state schools – 96 per cent of Turks, 97 per cent of Moroccans and Tunisians, 98 per cent of Algerians. It is the cheapest, most obvious form of schooling. Since the late 1980s, there have been clashes in state schools between republican secular values and Moslem values. The authorities are feeling their way towards a compromise, but with difficulty. The first such clash to become a *cause célèbre* occurred in November 1989, when three Moslem girls were suspended from a school in the Paris suburbs because they insisted on wearing the head-covering required of devout Moslem women. This was deemed by the principal of the college to be an ostentatious and provocative assertion of a religious belief in a place subject to the secular principles of the Republic. At the time, the *Conseil d'Etat* ruled that the wearing of veils and head-scarves was not in itself a provocative act – many pupils wear a cross or a *Magen David* around their necks.

Five years later, the opinion of the *Conseil d'Etat* was reiterated by a *tribunal administratif* after 26 Moslem girls were suspended from a school in the Lille area in the autumn of 1994. This time, how-ever, 23 suspensions were upheld on the grounds that the students involved had intended to upset the normal functioning of the school and to provoke the authorities and their non-Moslem classmates.

Such decisions are sensitive and controversial. Many immigrants have embraced intransigent forms of Islam as an alternative to the secular French society that has failed to meet their expectations. They are only too willing to seek out weaknesses in a system they feel has excluded them. On the other hand, right-wing opinion is always ready to castigate every attempt made by governments to accommodate immigrants.

It is worth noting that traditional republican secular values in schools have come under fire from part of the Jewish community, too. In the school year 1994–95, orthodox Jews sought exemption from attendance at classes on Saturday mornings. The *Conseil d'Etat* ruled in April 1995 that each case should be judged on its merits. Thus, Jewish pupils in the *classes préparatoires* for admission to the *Grandes Ecoles* could not be given a exemption as progress tests are normally scheduled for Saturday mornings. Pupils in other classes may be excused attendance on Saturdays if the work missed can be made up effectively and their absence does not disrupt the normal functioning of school life.

It is clear that in the case of Moslem headscarves and the obser-vance of the Jewish sabbath, the state is increasingly willing to toler-ate the particular demands of minorities, provided there is no disruption or flouting of the norms established for the majority. The decisions of the *Conseil d'Etat* therefore reflect a move away from the traditional republican requirement for assimilation.

One way in which the socialists hoped to integrate immigrants more directly was by giving them the right to vote in local elections. It was argued that the right to vote and to stand in municipal elections would recognize taxes paid and work done on behalf of France. It was also seen as a means of gauging immigrant opinion. The point was made that some European countries – Sweden, Denmark, Norway and Holland – allowed settled foreigners some role in the electoral process. But the government gave way to criticisms that the proposal would lead to the establishment of ethnic lobbies and to a second-class citizenship in conflict with the ideals of the Republic which has traditionally linked civic rights with citizenship. A small number of left-wing municipalities co-opted representatives of the local immigrant community as advisers, but these had no legal status.

IMMIGRATION AS A EUROPEAN PROBLEM

The immigrant question is now assuming European proportions. According to the EU, 3.3 per cent of the 369 million people living in the EU by 1993 were foreigners. Turks were most numerous (14.7 per cent of the total), followed by ex-Yugoslavs (7.4 per cent) and Moroccans (6.2 per cent). During the past decade, the EC, then the EU, has sought to rationalize national immigration policies and to establish effective frontier controls. In 1985, France, Germany, Belgium, Holland and Luxembourg met at Schengen and agreed to implement a policy of free movement within the territory covered by their jurisdictions. It was to be an experiment in freedom of movement within part of the EC. In the years which followed, the collapse of socialism in eastern Europe, indeed the collapse of states like the Soviet Union, East Germany and Yugoslavia, gave a new dimension to the Schengen proposals. It appeared increasingly important to protect the territory of the EC against the risk of an invasion of migrants from the east and the south. An agreement to extend the Schengen proposals gradually to Italy, Spain, Portugal and Greece was signed in June 1990. Denmark, Ireland and the UK refused to sign the agreement. From the point of view of immigration, the practical effect is that a person admitted to the territory of a state which is a party to the Schengen agreement has the right to move unhindered to other states which have signed the agreement. However, because the agreement was intended to facilitate the movement of EC citizens, the signatories have not harmonized their policies regarding immigrants and refugees.

The collapse of Soviet-dominated eastern Europe and the civil war in the Balkans have produced a tidal wave of refugees, asylum seekers and migrants who want to move to western Europe. While

Germany is in the front line, with nearly 500,000 formal applications from Easterners for residence permits in 1992, France is concerned that Italy and Spain are becoming recognized routes for migrants seeking to settle clandestinely in western Europe because these countries do not deploy the resources needed to check clandestine immigration and, in any case, they know that they are merely conduits and will not have to cope with a growing immigrant population. In one week in April 1995, over 500 illegal immigrants were arrested by the French frontier police on France's border with Italy. They were mainly Kurds, Turks, Yugoslavs and Albanians whom the Italian authorities had little interest in detaining on their side of the frontier.

The emergence of a free-market economy in former socialist states has led to a lucrative trade in smuggling people seeking to reach rich countries like France and Germany. According to the couriers, it costs 400 US dollars to obtain a place in one of the many boats which sail from the Albanian ports of Dürres and Vlorë and land their human cargoes on beaches between Bari and Lecce. For an extra 200 US dollars, a guide will take his customers to the station and provide them with tickets to one of the cities in the north or to Ventimiglia, Italy's frontier town with France. Besides Albanians, Turks and Yugoslavs, the principal customers appear to be Romanian gypsies, Bulgarians, Kurds from Iraq and Turkey, Pakistanis and Chinese. For 1,000 US dollars, most European passports and visas can be bought easily in the market on Skanderberg Square, Tirana.

Jacques Expert was *Radio France*'s chief reporter in eastern Europe in the late 1980s and the early 1990s. In an account of the transformations he witnessed, published as *Gens de l'Est*, Expert describes similar smuggling networks based in Romania and Bulgaria. Indians, Pakistanis, Bangladeshis, Sri Lankans, Nigerians, Ghanaians, Vietnamese and Chinese have paid up to 1,200 US dollars to couriers to get them from Black Sea ports or Bucharest and Sofia across Hungary and into Austria. The Hungarian route is one of the best established – in May 1988, Hungary dismantled her border controls with Austria – but it is now one of the most heavily policed on the Austrian side. Austria, which has 1,300 km of frontier with Hungary, Slovenia, Slovakia and the Czech Republic, signed the Schengen agreement in late April 1995.

The south-eastern routes to western Europe's industrial heart have been heavily used by would-be illegal immigrants from Africa and the Far East because it was relatively easy to obtain visas to work and study in the former People's Democracies. Hungary, Romania and the former Czechoslovakia had hundreds of African and Vietnamese workers and students, while citizens of the People's Republic of China had no difficulty in obtaining visas to visit Albania. Many workers and students were effectively trapped in the host countries when socialism collapsed, and they chose to take their chance and move westwards. It continues to be easy to travel from Africa and the Far East to Bulgaria, Albania and Romania, which remain popular, if unreliable, starting points for illegal entry into the EU.

North African and some sub-Saharan illegals still take the Spanish route. A passage in a fishing boat or an outboard motor between the beaches around Tangiers to the Spanish coast around Algeciras, barely 20 km away, costs between 500 and 600 pounds sterling. In 1992, at the height of illegal immigration into the EU by this route, the Spanish police were arresting 1,000 illegals a month, and it is reckoned that 400 immigrants lost their lives at sea trying to make the crossing. The Spanish authorities have become doubly vigilant as the stretch of water is also a route favoured by drug smugglers.

The accounts of smuggling routes given above indicates that the EU is facing the prospect of hundreds of thousands of potential immigrants from those parts of the world which are impoverished and politically unstable. In 1993, Tahar Ben Jalloun, himself an immigrant in France, wrote in an introduction to a book on the televisual representation of foreigners (Vargaftig; see bibliography):

L'Europe des douze compte un état de plus. Comme le chiffre treize n'est pas sympathique, on n'en parle pas. Cet état n'est pas un pays. Ou plutôt ce serait un pays imaginaire. Quant à sa population, elle est bien vivante, diverse et semblable. L'état des immigrés est dans l'esprit des gens. Ils savent qu'il existe, mais n'arrivent pas à le situer. C'est peut-être un état de trop pour des hommes en trop, d'après l'expression de Jean Daniel.

La fin de ce siècle sera marquée par un phénomène de déplacement. Des hommes et des femmes vont être obligés de quitter leur terre sèche, leur pays n'arrivant plus à les retenir. L'exemple albanais est dans les mémoires. Mais que dire des Africains qui traversent des milliers de kilomètres pour arriver jusqu'au détroit de Gibraltar en vue d'entrer en Europe?

As in the Americas, the wealthiest regions are attracting the poor outside the gates. The EU's approach to the inevitable demands for admission is to guard the gates with the Schengen agreements and their extension. All signatories will be expected to apply identical conditions for the issues of visas and grants of political asylum. They will have to accept an agreed list of countries whose nationals will or will not be considered for visas. There is obvious merit in all member states holding to the same policies, but it will not be easy to harmonize existing arrangements and to achieve co-operation between the many police forces involved. It is already clear that

France has little confidence in some of its neighbours' ability to police the EU's frontiers effectively.

The Maastricht Treaty of 1992 further complicates national approaches. The notion of European citizenship with certain voting rights in the EU citizen's place of residence rather than country of origin will negate the traditional French linkage between citizenship and nationality. Over 1 million Portuguese, Italian and Spanish residents will be able to vote in French local elections in the near future, while non-EU immigrants will remain without a say in French politics.

France's involvement in supranational schemes like Schengen and Maastricht has provoked a sharp response from the nationalist right and from those who fear that the loss of nationally determined immigration and entry controls will lead to an important erosion of security and to a dilution of the notion of French citizenship. The election of a centre-right government in the spring of 1995, the terrorist campaign waged by the *Groupe islamique armé* in France – which involved several bombings – and against Europeans in Algeria, ever increasing support for and pressure from the *Front national* (at the 1996 celebration of the *Fête Jeanne d'Arc*, Le Pen predicted that civil war would result from the government's lack of determination in handling the immigrant question) have led to more stringent proposals to check immigration and to tighten citizenship rights. In October 1995, the National Assembly set up a *Commission d'Enquête sur l'Immigration clandestine* which included some of the most extreme right-wing deputies in the Assembly. The commission published its proposals in April 1996. They include systematic fingerprinting of non-EU nationals applying for visas to enter France for any reason (tourism, for example); giving mayors the power to grant or refuse the right to settle in *communes* and to set up a list of property owners renting accommodation to immigrants; the refusal of welfare and housing benefits to illegal immigrants (including households where there is an illegal immigrant); and extended detention powers (45 days instead of 10). Meanwhile, in March 1996, the Minister of the Interior, Jean-Louis Debré, put forward his own proposals which were broadly similar: fingerprinting foreigners; the establishment of a national computerized database to track the movements of foreigners with tourist visas; harsh penalties for abetting the entry of illegals, sheltering or employing them; and the possibility of deporting delinquent minors (including those born in France) to the country of origin of one or other of the parents.

At the time of writing, these remain proposals and will have to be debated in the National Assembly and scrutinized by the Constitutional Council to test their constitutionality. It is far from clear that the government wants to embark on a fundamental revision of an area of legislation which has been modified thirteen times in the last sixteen years. Yet there can be no doubt that some modification of the policies governing citizenship and residence will be made in order to reassure those who regard the large number of foreigners in France and the apparently limitless numbers threatening to break into the country as a significant threat to security, social stability and a French way of life.

BIBLIOGRAPHY

Readers are urged to refer to the fifth and sixth editions of *France Today*, published in 1983 and 1987 by Methuen, and to the seventh edition published in 1993 by Hodder and Stoughton. In the fifth and sixth editions the origins of post-war immigration and French immigration policy are treated in more detail than in the present edition.

Bernard, Ph., *L'Immigration*. Paris, Les Editions du Monde/Marabout, 1993. This is an excellent account of the background to immigration and the social problems immigration has provoked. Written by a journalist with *Le Monde*, it is typical of the rigorous approach adopted by that newspaper.

Cesari, J., *L'Islam en Europe*. Paris, La Documentation française, Dossiers d'Actualité mondiale, no. 746, March 1995.

Champsaur, P., *Les Etrangers en France: portrait social*. Paris, INSEE, Série Contours et Caractères, 1994. An excellent statistical survey of France's immigrant population. Living conditions are compared with those of the French.

Dupeux, G., *La Société française 1789–1970*. Paris, Armand Colin, 1975. Essential background information concerning economic and social change in France through the nineteenth and twentieth centuries.

Expert, J., *Gens de l'Est*. Paris, Editions de la Découverte, 1992.

Hargreaves, A. G., *Immigration, 'Race' and Ethnicity in Contemporary France*. London, Routledge, 1995. A detailed and up-to-date monograph devoted to immigrants in France.

Haut Conseil à l'Intégration, *La Connaissance de l'immigration et de l'intégration*. Paris, La Documentation française, November 1992. A valuable source document.

Lapeyronnie, D., *Immigrés en Europe: politiques locales d'intégration*. Paris, La Documentation française, 1992. A comparative study of integration policies and their results in the member states of the EU.

Mottin, J., *Immigration et naturalisations*. Paris, Union Nationale Interuniversitaire, 1992.

Todd, E., *Le destin des immigrés. Assimilation et ségrégation dans les démocraties occidentales*. Paris, Seuil, 1994.

Vargaftig, M. (ed.), *Télévisions d'Europe et immigration*. Paris, La Documentation française, Institut national de l'Audiovisuel/Association

Dialogue entre les Cultures, 1993. An interesting and valuable comparative approach to the depiction of immigrants through the television stations of most European countries.

Current affairs magazines regularly carry descriptive and analytical articles concerning most aspects of immigration, also specially commissioned opinion polls (particularly the *Nouvel Observateur*). The weekly *Nouvel Observateur* is on the political left; *L'Express* and *Le Point* are liberal 'centrist' weeklies with no specific political attachment; the monthly *Choc du mois* and the bi-monthly *Identité* are on the right and express *Front national* views.

Le Monde continues to provide the most accurate reporting of important issues. It has a valuable tradition of inviting specialists – lawyers, academics, doctors, community leaders – to write occasional articles.

The Economist publishes well-informed analytical articles on the European dimension of immigration.

The author is pleased to acknowledge the contribution to this essay of Madame Mavis Mercoiret, Monsieur Michel Fleury and the late Comte Alexandre de Marenches. Dr Paul Hainsworth made helpful comments on the text.

6

EDUCATION

Roger Duclaud-Williams

Introduction

There is no one best way in which to organize a discussion of the French educational system; each approach to this subject has its strengths and weaknesses. This chapter adopts an approach which concentrates on five problems which the educational system must confront. The first advantage of such an approach is that it recognizes that policy-makers behave as problem-solvers. The identification of problems helps us to understand the reasoning processes and solutions adopted by those who control education. The second advantage is that such an approach facilitates comparison. Many of the problems which French education confronts are also present elsewhere in the world and an emphasis on such problems helps us to avoid the common conception that everything which occurs in France is peculiarly French.

EDUCATION AND THE ECONOMY

All educational systems accept some responsibility for preparing young people for the world of work. If this world changes, then so too must education if it is to continue to be effective. There are several economic factors which are particularly important for education and training.

The most dramatic of the relevant changes since the mid-1970s has certainly been the emergence of a persistent problem of youth unemployment in France. Tables 6.1 and 6.2 illustrate the rise of youth unemployment and also clearly demonstrate how the less well qualified have suffered most. Unemployment of any kind was relatively unusual and often of short duration in the period between 1945 and 1973. The government response to the problem does not necessarily take an educational form. Employers may be provided with a financial incentive to take on young people and economic policies may be adopted whose object is to reduce unemployment, but there are also important educational repercussions of youth unemployment. The existence of this problem has certainly persuaded governments in France to make increased efforts to encourage more young people to stay on at school, thereby reducing the unemployment figures and enhancing the future prospects of these young people. French governments have also responded by creating, with the help of employers and trade unions, new forms of training and apprenticeship for young people who have left school but whose education ought to be continued.

Table 6.1: *Chômage des jeunes: Taux de chômage des jeunes débutants par grands niveaux de diplômes (1973–83)*

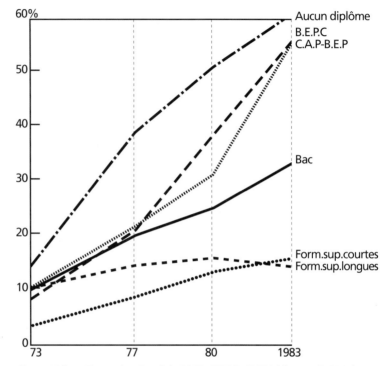

Source: Bilans Formation-Emploi INSEE, CEREQ, SIGES (devenu SPRESE).
Taken from: C. Dubar et al., *L'Autre jeunesse: Des jeunes sans diplômes dans un dispositif de socialisation*. Presses universitaires de Lille (devenues Presses universitaires du Septentrion), 1987

A second major change concerns the international division of labour. A number of countries which were once predominantly agricultural have become important industrial producers and exporters in the last twenty or thirty years. This means that the older industrial economies of Europe must face up to new competition to which they were not previously exposed. The most successful European economies have met this challenge by moving away from the production of simple goods towards the production of goods and services which involve the use of more sophisticated technologies. Because these goods are more difficult and more costly to produce they can often be sold with greater profit. This in turn requires the creation of a labour force that is more skilled, and this is where the educational system may have to adapt in training young people in new skills and in raising the level of many traditional skills.

Table 6.2: *Chômage des jeunes: Taux de chômage, en pourcentage des jeunes débutants* en 1973, 1977, 1980, 1983 selon le niveau scolaire et le sexe (Apprentissages exclus)*

	Hommes				Femmes				Ensemble			
	1973	1977	1980	1983	1973	1977	1980	1983	1973	1977	1980	1983
Sans diplômes	12	31	42	59	18	46	63	63	15	38	52	61
BEPC	5	22	29		16	20	43		11	21	37	56
CAP-BEP	6	17	21	49	10	26	42	62	8	21	32	55
Baccalauréat	9	15	19	32	10	22	28	35	10	20	25	33
Etudes supérieures courtes	3	7	12	17	4	9	13	11	4	8	13	16
Etudes supérieures longues	10	14	11		12	14	21		11	14	16	14
Ensemble	9	20	26	44	13	26	39	44	11	23	36	44

* Jeunes débutants: élèves ou étudiants sortant lors de l'année N qui se déclarent actifs occupés ou à la recherche d'un emploi en mars de l'année N + 1.

Source: Bilans Formation-Emploi INSEE, CEREQ, SIGES (devenu SPRESE), Données sociales, édition 1984 (INSEE): p. 74

Taken from: C. Dubar et al., *L'Autre jeunesse: Des jeunes sans diplômes dans un dispositif de socialisation*. Presses universitaires de Lille (devenues Presses universitaires du Septentrion), 1987

A third economic change which has important educational implications concerns the organization of work within a firm. The typical manufacturing company of the first half of the twentieth century had a small number of qualified and responsible individuals at its head and a very much larger number of less skilled and responsible operatives performing unskilled work at its base. Many industries and companies are still organized very much in this way but there is a growing sector of companies whose products and philosophy are moving in a quite new direction. These companies have found it useful to extend the responsibilities and skills of many of those employees who were previously confined to narrowly defined and relatively unskilled tasks. As this trend develops, the general level of education and skill within the workforce must be increased.

Finally, modern educational systems must prepare young people for a labour market in which they will change jobs a number of times during their career. Products become outdated, industries decline and new forms of employment replace older forms. In these circumstances people must be able to learn new skills in adult life and this is only possible when earlier education has been carried forward to a sufficiently high level.

The educational response most directly arising out of the problem of youth unemployment has been the development of a constantly changing system of traineeships, *'stages'*. These *'stages'* offer some people who have left school a combination of work experience and training on and off the job. They have developed since the late 1970s within a framework of rules which is in part legislative, and in part the result of negotiation between employers and trade unions.

The appeal of this system of traineeships lies in its ability to offer early school-leavers a second chance by linking training to work. These *'stages'* are, however, sometimes criticized because they do not always lead to a recognized qualification and because some of them are educationally of doubtful value. One should, however, not be too quick to condemn the high drop-out rates and absence of certification in these courses because they are taking on young people who, in most cases, have already failed in, or have been failed by, the mainstream school system.

Unions and employers, through their role in the organization of these traineeships, have now become important educational providers and policy-makers. They are often in agreement with one another in criticizing what they regard as the over-theoretical and bureaucratic character of school-based education and they are keen to expand both apprenticeship and the new traineeships because both offer a form of training which is more directly linked to wealth creation, and can adapt more quickly to the changing world of work.

Any consideration of the relationship between education and the economy in France must carefully assess technical education at secondary level and the way in which this education is developing. The secondary technical schools, now called *lycées professionnels*, have not been created recently in order to deal with new economic challenges. They have their origins in the inter-war period but have expanded rapidly since the Liberation. Most young people go to the *lycée professionnel* having completed four years of secondary education in a *collège*. Aged fifteen or sixteen they spend usually two or possibly three years in secondary technical education. They work towards qualifications of two kinds: the more specialized and less academic qualification is the *Certificat d'aptitude professionnelle* (CAP); the slightly less specialized, and more theoretical, qualification is called the *Brevet d'études professionnelles* (BEP). Although great efforts have been made to improve the atmosphere and working conditions in these schools in recent years, they nevertheless continue to suffer from a number of important handicaps. A large number of the pupils in a *lycée professionnel* were unable to gain admission to the general *lycées*. This means that pupils and teachers alike are conscious that, for many of them, the *lycée professionnel* is second best. A further difficulty is that many young people cannot get into the type of training in a *lycée professionnel* which they would prefer. Some forms of training are heavily over-subscribed and pupils therefore have to be turned away.

A number of changes are taking place in the *lycée professionnel* with a view to dealing with some of these problems. Every effort is being made to inform new arrivals about employment prospects, so that as many young people as possible will prepare for qualifications which give them the maximum chance of employment once they leave school. The course content is in a constant process of revision, aiming to reduce the number of CAPs, which are thought to be rather too narrow, and to increase the number and attractiveness of the BEPs, which prepare pupils better for the more fluid labour market referred to above. Periods of work experience related to the kind of courses which young people are studying have also been organized for almost all pupils in a *lycée professionnel* since 1979. But the most important reform which, it is hoped, will make these schools more attractive, has been the creation in 1986 of a new type of *baccalauréat* (*baccalauréat professionnel*) which will offer those leaving the *lycée professionnel* the possibility of continuing their studies at a higher technical school or a university. Although all of these reforms are necessary and useful, a note of caution may be sounded. There is no reason why standards and achievements in the *lycées professionnels* should not be raised considerably and more and more young people may well be encouraged to stay on the extra year required to obtain the *baccalauréat professionnel*. But most of these pupils are conscious of the fact that they have already been eliminated from the mainstream of educational provision. Their performance has been judged not promising enough to allow them to go on to the general *lycées* to prepare one of the more familiar and longer established general *baccalauréats*. In these conditions it is difficult to create the kind of enthusiasm and commitment necessary for success.

Post-war French governments have sought to expand business studies and science at both the secondary and higher levels of education and thereby to redirect educational priorities away from their traditional preoccupation with the classical languages and the humanities. In the *lycée* this re-orientation occurred in the 1960s but it was brought about not so much as a result of government policy, but more as the consequence of the numerous decisions made by pupils seeking to maximize their job prospects. What now attracts the most able pupils and enjoys the highest prestige is undoubtedly mathematics. Every pupil who has the necessary mathematical ability enters the science stream in his penultimate year. One of the principal reasons for this is that success in the competitive examinations for entry into the higher business and engineering schools (*grandes écoles*) depends to a very great degree on mathematical ability. Pupils who have not followed the science stream, and have therefore studied much less mathematics, are at a substantial disadvantage. Of course, anyone successfully passing the *baccalauréat* is entitled to a university place in France, but the schools of engineering and business studies offer to their graduates career possibilities which are considerably more attractive than those which university graduates are likely to obtain. Hence the attraction of mathematics and the science stream.

Higher education in France is then of two quite different varieties; firstly there are vocationally oriented schools which offer their graduates attractive career prospects and, secondly, the universities with many more students, and much less attractive conditions for study. The universities also experience high drop-out and failure rates, and produce graduates whose career opportunities do not compare with those from the *grandes écoles*. This two-tier system of higher education provides a very strong incentive for secondary school pupils to study those subjects which are economically most useful. At this level then, there seems no need for governments to intervene in order to encourage the study of those subjects which they regard as most important for the expansion of the national economy. What recent governments have succeeded in doing, and will continue to do for the foreseeable future, is to increase the number of places available in these *grandes écoles* so as to provide the country with a much increased supply of administrators and engineers. Table 6.3 below shows to what extent technical and vocational education has been successfully expanded in the period since 1970.

Table 6.3: *Number of students gaining technical diplomas by level*

	Total Level V (CAP + BEP)	Total Level IV BT + Bac.tech. + Bac.pro.	Total Level III BTS + DUT Short cycle two-year higher education
1970	211,845	36,022	16,945
1975	159,443	54,255	26,272
1980	313,951	67,181	37,211
1985	377,226	89,484	53,639
1990	430,886	145,085	80,502
1991	426,942	157,036	86,148

Source: OECD, *Reviews of National Policies for Education, France*, 1996: p. 67

Some critics of recent government policy on the left and the right disapprove of attempts to link education more closely to the economy. Left-wing critics argue that there is little point in improving technical education if many of those who leave school have no jobs to go to. They feel that many of the young people taken on as apprentices or trainees are poorly paid, exploited and often provided with inferior training facilities. They also argue that much that is not economically useful in education is nevertheless extremely valuable and that education and educational institutions ought to enjoy some real independence so that they may resist the demands of employers and governments who are too narrowly interested in economic success. In other words, these critics argue that there is more to life than high pay and promotion and that it is the business of the school especially to make young people aware of these other values. Of course, it is conceded, schools should prepare young people for the world of work but they should also prepare them for their role as citizens in a democracy, for leisure and for their role as family members.

Some of this stress on human values is also present in right-wing criticisms. Some on the traditional right are particularly scandalized by the neglect of subjects like philosophy, ancient languages and history, which have no obvious or immediate economic utility. They also criticize what they see as a lowering of standards and an undesirable resort to continuous assessment. It is important to be aware of these dissenting voices but we should remember that, for the time being at least, there is very widespread agreement in support of those educational reforms which aim to produce a closer relationship between the worlds of education and work. Young people are anxious to avoid unemployment and so are their parents. Employers are keen to recruit well-educated and highly motivated young people. Opposition from teachers to moves in this direction was strongly and repeatedly voiced in the 1960s and 1970s but is seldom heard today. It seems probable that the trends towards a closer relationship between education and work will continue for the foreseeable future.

OVERCENTRALIZATION AND DECENTRALIZATION

The rulers of France in the nineteenth and the first half of the twentieth century maintained strict central control over most aspects of education. This was largely because they wished to impose and encourage a sense of belonging to one nation, and because the educational system was an effective tool with which to discourage the use of regional languages and create the greatest possible degree of linguistic uniformity. The sense of national unity is now strongly developed in all French regions, with the exception of Corsica, and a once crucial spur to centralized administration therefore no longer operates. The problem of linguistic diversity has also disappeared.

There are also positive arguments in favour of greater decentralization, however, for which there is strong support in France. Many French observers of foreign educational systems, especially those familiar with English and American schools, have been struck by the contrast. They have criticized French schools for concentrating too narrowly on the academic function and undervaluing extracurricular activities and the pastoral role of the school. Jacques Chirac, elected as President in 1995, has expressed his personal admiration for the experiment currently taking place in Epinal, under local authority auspices, to redress this imbalance. In Epinal, the morning is devoted to academic study, and the whole of the afternoon is given over to sport and to expressive artistic activities of all kinds. Those who sympathize with Chirac would like to turn French schools from academic institutions into self-governing communities. As matters stand, however, one cannot expect teachers who have been posted to schools which are not of their own choosing to show any great loyalty or attachment to them. If, for example, schools could play some part in the appointment of their own teachers, then a team spirit of co-operation might be more easily developed.

This emphasis on schools as self-governing communities, rather than impersonal institutions controlled from afar, is strongly supported by many on the left and in the centre of political life. A rather different perspective, but one which is equally supportive of decentralization, appeals more to those on the right. In this line of argument the analogy between the school as a provider of education and the firm as a provider of goods and services plays an important part. The argument is that greater efficiency and responsiveness to local demand could be encouraged if head teachers and their staff enjoyed more independence in the management of their schools. The same kind of free-market logic underlies the argument that, if parents had more choice as to the schools attended by their children, schools might be encouraged to compete with one another and in the process pay more attention to parents' and perhaps even pupils' demands.

Because many of the right are strong supporters of educational decentralization, we might reasonably suppose that the victory of Chirac in the presidential election of 1995 would lead to further progress towards greater autonomy for schools and universities. Such a conclusion would be too hasty. In the first year of Chirac's presidency, his government was often divided between liberal and moderate tendencies with the former tendency showing a strong sympathy for new measures of privatization and decentralization. So far, when called upon to arbitrate between these two tendencies, Chirac has favoured the moderates and preferred to avoid any rocking of the ship of state. The obvious danger of student and teacher demonstrations, and the known moderation of the Minister of Education, François Bayrou, both reinforce the tendency to play safe and therefore to avoid any radical moves in the direction of greater decentralization.

A final element in the case for decentralization relates to the role of local authorities. Between 1981 and 1986 an attempt was made to extend the responsibilities and independence of local authorities by transferring to them functions previously exercised by departments in Paris. Many local politicians would like to see this process applied in education just as it has been already in areas such as town planning and the social services.

When we compare universities with schools we are immediately struck by the greater scale and complexity of the former. Both of these characteristics can be cited as strong arguments for permitting universities greater autonomy than schools. Students have also often demanded greater self-government and autonomy for universities. However, student opinion and student organizations are not really the strong supporters of university autonomy they appear to be.

Since 1986, local authorities have become responsible for the building of new schools and the maintenance and repair of existing ones. The *lycées* are the responsibility of regional authorities; *collèges* are the responsibility of the *départements* and primary schools are left to the *communes*. Recent legislation has also provided for local authority representation on the governing bodies (*conseils d'administration*) of schools, and authorities are permitted and encouraged to organize after-school and out-of-school activities of an educational character. Finally, in the outline law (*Loi d'orientation*) enacted in July of 1989, provision is made for secondary schools of all types to prepare what is described as a school plan (*projet d'établissement*). Each school must prepare its own and it is intended that parents, pupils and local politicians should play some part in this process alongside teachers and head teachers. The same law provides for the creation in all *lycées* of a pupil council which is elected by the pupils, meets three times a year and is consulted on school rules and regulations.

Many commentators on these developments have come to the conclusion that they do not yet amount to very much. Teachers are still posted to schools rather than recruited by them. The content of the national curriculum and the internal organization of schools are still centrally determined. A cautious beginning only has been made towards allowing parents more choice of schools for their children. There is a widespread feeling that the school plans which have been prepared are theoretical documents which are unlikely to have much impact on practice because of the inability of schools to take control of their own future. How can the widespread commitment to decentralization but the failure to do very much in this direction be explained?

Part of the explanation is that it is easy to praise decentralization in general terms but more difficult to accept that schools and universities should be allowed to do things which are controversial and to which powerful groups and interests may object. But there are more specific obstacles to the progress of decentralization. Teacher organizations, either based on particular subjects, or in the form of unions, are generally either lukewarm supporters of decentralization or outright opponents. It is not too difficult to see why this is so: trade unions are concerned to protect their members from the exercise of arbitrary power by superiors. Under present arrangements teachers' appointments and promotions are governed by rules which protect teachers' rights. If decentralization were to become a reality it would almost certainly mean that head teachers, or perhaps even local politicians, would come to possess new powers which they might exercise in unpredictable ways to the detriment of teachers' interests. A further cause for doubt about decentralization is the fear that it might lead to greater inequalities between institutions and regions. Those who fear this see existing arrangements as providing an effective guarantee that the same quality of education is available to all pupils wherever they live and regardless of the school they attend. This may be an illusion but there is still a widespread sentiment that whatever unintended inequalities are found within

Teachers try to balance the need to conform to traditional teaching ideas with that of adapting to decentralization

the existing school system these might become more acute if schools were made more self-governing.

Through much of the debate about decentralization in education runs a set of mixed and contradictory feelings about the role of the state. Some see the state as the heavy hand of distant bureaucracy stifling local initiative and presenting obstacles to genuine pupil and parent involvement. This view is hostile to the state and seeks to promote decentralization. A second group sees the state as the impartial, external arbiter whose power prevents the outbreak of local conflicts and ensures fair play and respect for the rules. This position is much more sympathetic to existing arrangements and sees more danger than advantage in the promotion of decentralization. Finally, a particularly influential group cannot quite decide whether to sympathize with the anti-state or the pro-state faction. Many who find themselves in this camp have confused and contradictory ideas about decentralization, often demonstrating support in principle but opposition in practice. With public and expert opinion divided in this way it is not surprising that reform in this area has so far proceeded with much caution and hesitation.

THE EQUALITY DEBATE

The equality debate focuses on the early years of secondary school. In France this means the *collège*, which is attended by most children between the ages of eleven and fifteen. Since the 1950s, the belief has been that there is no justification or need for different kinds of school for children of primary-school age. At the other end of the scale, arrangements for the teaching of the over-fifteens are highly differentiated, and this differentiation between general, technical and vocational education is broadly supported. The difficulty and the controversy arise over exactly at what point and in what form differentiated education ought to begin.

In 1963 the Minister of Education, Christian Fouchet, established the *collège d'enseignement secondaire* (CES). The CES was what used to be described in England as a multilateral school, catering for all abilities within a single institution but in a differentiated manner. In fact, Fouchet decided that he would recreate within the CES the three-fold division of staff, curriculum and ability level which had previously existed within separate institutions.

Between 1963 and 1977 this system was gradually established, thereby providing within a single institution what had previously been provided in three. Critics of the CES continued to argue during this period that it was not enough to bring all pupils together under one roof and that a single curriculum for all could be taught without disadvantage to the more able pupils. From the beginning of the school year in 1977 and starting with the first year of secondary education, the jump was made from streamed provision to a common syllabus and mixed-ability teaching in all the CESs (now relabelled *collèges*).

In English terminology 1977 marked the triumph of the comprehensive school in France. It is true that some pupils continued to leave the *collège* in order to pursue a technical education at the age of thirteen and that there was limited separate provision in some *collèges* for the least able pupils, but by and large the comprehensive ideal was adopted. For most pupils selection would now occur only at fifteen, at which point some would go on to the *lycée* to prepare for the *baccalauréat* and others would go into technical education.

Since 1977 there has been no major reorganization of the structure of French secondary provision but there has been some piecemeal evolution. Many teachers complained of the difficulties which they encountered in teaching the new mixed-ability classes. The number of secondary pupils who were required to repeat a year because of unsatisfactory academic performance increased. There were also complaints that some parents and schools connived to create selective streams which were contrary to the spirit of the 1977 reform. These complaints produced a state of affairs in which most people were convinced that it was impossible and undesirable to return to the streaming practised before 1977 but that, on the other hand, existing mixed-ability arrangements needed modifying in some way.

When a socialist President and government were elected in 1981 they were faced with this difficult problem. The approach they adopted is spelt out in the Legrande Report. The Legrande Report and the socialist government were very sympathetic to the comprehensive principle, but the report argued that mixed-ability teaching was not working for certain fundamental subjects. Legrande therefore recommended that separate ability groups could be constituted, if schools so desired, for mathematics, science and French but reunited for the rest of the timetable. Legrande was also successful in persuading the Minister of Education, Alain Savary, that there should be some shift of emphasis in the *collège* away from traditional academic subjects so as to allow more time and attention for the moral, aesthetic and sporting sides of the curriculum. One of the justifications for this shift was that it might provide more encouragement for less academic pupils and in this way provide them with an incentive to work harder. Legrande also hoped that each *collège* would be allowed some flexibility as to the precise form of the compromise it adopted between mixed-ability and differentiated forms of education. In practice, this autonomy has not always been realized but there is at least now some variation in organization and teaching style between different *collèges*. The most recent shift in this delicate balance between differentiated and undifferentiated provision occurred in 1994. The Minister of Education, François Bayrou, in the newly elected government of the right led by Edouard Balladur, decided to make general provision for support teaching for the weakest pupil in the *collège*. This differentiated provision was to be made available from the first year onwards. He also extended the range of optional subjects which pupils could add to their study programmes in the later years in the *collège*. Both of these changes represented small steps in the direction of greater differentiation, but it seems very unlikely that there will be any return to the rigid streaming of the period before 1977.

A pessimistic view of such developments as these is possible. The work of statisticians and sociologists of education makes it quite clear that there is still a close correlation between social origins and academic success. Table 6.4 gives some indication of the scale of these inequalities as they affect pupils in the first year of primary schooling. The sons and daughters of workers are still heavily

Table 6.4: *Taux de redoublement du cours préparatoire en 1979–80 des enfants entrés à six ans, selon l'origine socio-professionnelle (enseignement public)*

Salariés agricole	29.9
Ouvriers sans qualification	23.9
Non actifs, non déclarés	22.9
Ouvriers spécialisés	22.5
Personnels de service	21.4
Ouvriers qualifiés	14.9
Agriculteurs, exploitants	11.1
Employés	10.7
Artisans, petits commerçants	9.8
Autres catégories	5.7
Cadres moyens	4.4
Industriels, gros commerçants	3.7
Cadres supérieurs, professions libérales	2.4
Ensemble	13.8

Source: J.-M. Favret, *Consultation-réflexion sur l'école*, ministère de l'Education nationale, avril 1984: p. 144

Taken from: J. Lesourne, *Education et société. Les défils de l'an 2000*. Editions La Découverte et Journal, 1988: p. 211

under-represented in the *lycées* and universities. More seriously, the academically able child who comes from a working-class family is less likely to fulfil his or her full potential than a child of similar ability from a professional or business background. Governments have found it easier to equalize inputs into education and to standardize educational provision than to secure equality of results.

But a more optimistic interpretation of these events is also possible. Achievements might be assessed not so much in terms of equality or inequality as in terms of the numbers of pupils who achieve a particular level of qualification. Those taking this point of view feel that genuine progress has been made because, whereas in 1960, 10 per cent of each age group obtained the *baccalauréat*, today the figure has reached 50 per cent. This is a benefit which has been enjoyed by young people from all social classes even if some groups have been able to exploit the new opportunities more successfully than others. From this more optimistic perspective one may take satisfaction in the rise in the general level of education and worry less about inequalities of educational achievement between social classes. Those who take this view also argue that it is difficult to imagine a society in which family advantages or disadvantages did not have some impact on the educational and career prospects of young people. As long as family characteristics (whether biological or cultural or influenced by wealth) continue to have an impact on children, it cannot be expected that equal opportunities in schooling will produce equal results. One may also argue, in defence of existing French arrangements, that it is more important to do all that is practicable to eliminate inequalities than to ensure success in all areas. Any French observer of English education would also remark that the most prestigious French *lycées* are state schools, not fee-paying, and that at the secondary level there is no French parallel to the English public school phenomenon with its associated social and educational inequalities.

THE STATE AND PRIVATE SECTORS

An examination of this subject is important because it helps us to understand to what extent a genuine partnership between state and private interests has been created in the provision of education. In other words, it helps us to determine whether power is concentrated within the state or dispersed. The greater the role of the private sector, the more likely it is that some variety, experiment, or even choice may be introduced into the educational system. This is particularly the case in France because of the uniformity of the state sector.

Throughout the nineteenth and early twentieth centuries the most important challenge to the state's dominant position in education came from the Catholic Church, and conflict and rivalry were often acute and sometimes violent. We must remember that throughout the nineteenth century, and during the early years of the twentieth, the Catholic Church in France was a declared enemy of parliamentary democracy. Those anti-clericals who attacked the educational role of the Catholic Church did so in the name of democracy and republicanism, making the conflict more political than educational.

In the 1980s and 1990s these great questions of political principle no longer divide French Catholics from non-Catholics, but this does not mean that Church and state have been able to establish an easy relationship in the sphere of education. During his election campaign in 1981, François Mitterrand promised to create a single education system, which would include state and Catholic schools but which would be created by negotiation with the representatives of the Catholic Church. Since the Church no longer represented a threat to the democratic constitutional order, we may well ask why the new President and his allies in the socialist, communist and radical parties were intent on tightening the links between the public non-denominational and the private religious parts of the educational system.

Those who worked within and sympathized with the state educational system harboured a number of grievances against their competitors in the Catholic sector. They felt that the latter occupied a privileged financial position because it could freely attract new pupils, and then effectively oblige the state to finance expansion from public funds. Schools in the state sector could not do this. They had to obtain permission for any expansion in advance. There were also complaints because whereas parents could choose freely between the state and religious schools, they were not able to choose between different state schools. There were other objections, particularly from the teachers' trade unions. Teachers employed in the Catholic sector, for example, did not in practice enjoy the same freedom and the same degree of professional recognition as those within the state sector. Head teachers in Catholic schools were occasionally open to criticism for interfering in the private lives of those whom they employed as teachers. We must remember that these establishments were not self-supporting but received state support approximately proportional to the numbers of pupils for whom they were responsible. Many on the left felt that it was only right and proper that in return for this substantial public financial support, the Catholic schools should be bound by the same rules as the schools in the state sector.

These grievances may not seem to be of overwhelming importance, especially when one remembers that negotiations and legislation on a question of this kind were very likely to prove politically controversial and possibly damaging to a left-wing government. An explanation of the risks which a left-wing government was willing to incur in this area must take account of some less tangible considerations. Although the great issues of freedom of conscience and the legitimacy of parliamentary institutions were no longer at stake, many on the left were still emotionally affected by the memory of these conflicting principles. Tradition had outlived the reality to which it related but was still an important influence on the behaviour of those involved. A less emotional and more honourable argument in favour of legislation to create a single system by agreement with the Catholic Church, which appealed to some on the left and on the right, was that France had for long been divided by the secular/Church question and, if this difficulty could be settled amicably, it could have advantages for the nation in terms of educational co-operation between state and private sectors. This, it would seem, was the argument which principally appealed to Alain Savary, who was entrusted with implementing Mitterrand's electoral undertaking.

The one question which was never answered in the 1981 election campaign was, what would happen if it proved impossible to reach agreement with the Church about the closer relationship desired between the two sectors? Would the government press on regardless and use its majority to impose legislation in the name of the majority, or would it give way to Catholic objections, thereby effectively conceding that a minority was entitled to exercise a veto over government policy of which it strongly disapproved? The events of 1984 demonstrated that it was the second option which Mitterrand preferred. When legislation to which the Church took strong exception was in the process of being discussed in parliament, there were demonstrations in Paris culminating in late June with more than a million demonstrators present. The President concluded that it was electorally too risky to continue.

In the years from 1984 to the socialist electoral defeat of 1993, relations between the state and the Catholic education authorities remained generally amicable. When, in 1992, the Minister for Education and the representative of Catholic education signed what was known as the Lang–Cloupet agreement, most commentators concluded that every possible source of subsequent difficulty had been removed and that the left was now fully reconciled to the continued existence of an administratively separate Catholic education sector. This optimism proved misplaced. When the right returned to power in 1993, new legislation was passed permitting local authorities greater freedom than they had previously enjoyed to aid Catholic schools financially. Many on the left were incensed by what they regarded as socially unjust and a demonstration was organized in Paris in which many hundreds of thousands of teachers, parents and young people took part. The new law was in fact declared unconstitutional and therefore the demonstration was to some degree unnecessary. What the events of 1993 and 1994 show is that the 'school question' seems frequently to have been solved but that, unexpectedly, it re-emerges in a new form.

In interpreting the events of 1984 and the government's decision not to proceed with legislation, we must also ask ourselves exactly how Catholic were the Catholic schools whose character the Church had fought successfully to protect. The major difficulty which the Church faces in this area is one of recruitment. Before 1945, Catholic schools generally had no difficulty in finding the teachers they required. It was assumed that everyone who taught in a Catholic school was a practising Catholic and that the school would therefore have a markedly Catholic character. Since the Second World War it has become more and more difficult to find appropriate teachers and as a result many of those who teach in the French Catholic schools of the 1990s are indistinguishable in terms of attitude and belief from those who teach in the state sector. The progressive de-Christianization of post-war France has made it impossible to maintain fully the Catholic character of nominally Catholic institutions. In interpreting the Catholic 'victory' of 1984 we should not forget the very limited degree of educational independence which these schools enjoy. They must apply the national curriculum in exactly the same way as schools within the state sector. We might well ask ourselves how far there was any genuine independence to defend. In fact, under the terms of the Debray law of 1959, in order to obtain the public financial support which was necessary for survival, Catholic education had already given up most of the real independence it had once enjoyed – and to a right-wing government not a left-wing one. There was a large measure of hypocrisy in the left's case against the Catholic schools, just as there was a similar degree of empty rhetoric in the Catholic defence.

One of the most important areas of recent expansion in private education concerns adults as well as young people. Under the law of 16 July 1971, all companies in France employing more than ten people must devote 1.1 per cent of their wage budget to education and training. Many of the smaller employers, rather than attempt to provide training themselves, pay this levy to private organizations of various sorts who then offer courses to the private sector on a profit-making or cost-covering basis. As mentioned earlier, many new forms of traineeship have grown up since the late 1970s to cater for early school-leavers. Nor should we forget that many smaller businesses, especially retailers, offer apprenticeships to young people and are required to allow apprentices time off for study at college. Finally, although the most prestigious *grandes écoles* are state establishments, there is an increasing number of private institutions often administered and partially financed by chambers of commerce, who provide higher education for which parents are willing to pay substantially. The forms of private education referred to here often enjoy a much more genuine independence than the more politically controversial primary and secondary schools within the Catholic sector.

The question of how state education ought to respond to forms of religious practice which are relatively new in France was raised in the autumn of 1989 when three young North African girls were turned away from their *collège* in Creil because they wished to wear the Moslem head-covering in class. Exactly the same problem has re-emerged in a large number of secondary schools since the autumn of 1994 when the Minister of Education issued a circular, addressed to all head teachers, the aim of which was apparently to prevent the wearing of the headscarf in future. The controversial and heated debates to which these incidents have given rise can best be understood by contrasting the views of two opposed camps. We shall describe these as integrationist and pluralist. The solution that has so far been adopted is a compromise between these two extremes, although since the election of 1993 policy and practice have certainly moved in the integrationist direction.

The integrationist position is more popular in France than the pluralist and is most strongly defended by the teachers' unions, the parties of the right, and a large number of members of left-wing parties. The integrationists supported the exclusion of the North African girls. They felt that a strict defence of the non-denominational principle was necessary in state schools. They argued that the provision of education would be endangered if religious controversy, associated with the wearing of particular forms of dress, was allowed to enter the school. They also insisted that Moslems had no right to request exemption from aspects of the curriculum to which they took objection. Among the integrationists many on the left adopted the feminist position that the young girls in question were almost certainly being compelled to wear a headscarf and that therefore their exclusion from class could be justified as assisting their emancipation from improper parental influence. The weaker, pluralist camp was represented by the Minister of Education at the time, Lionel Jospin, some of the organizations representing the French Moslem population (although Moslems were sharply divided over this question), and representatives of other religious minorities in France, in particular Jews and Protestants. The strongest pluralist argument, and an argument often repeated by the Minister of Educa-tion, was that exclusion would probably have the result of depriving these young women of the education which was so necessary to their futures. The pluralists felt that the dangers of religious division, if particular forms of dress were accepted, were greatly exaggerated by the integrationists. They felt that French society was sufficiently mature to recognize *'le droit à la différence'*.

In practical terms the integrationists had their way because the young women in question were eventually persuaded to discard their headscarves and they were subsequently re-admitted to school. However, with respect to the new rules for dealing with similar situ-ations in future, something closer to a compromise has been reached. The *Conseil d'Etat*, the supreme French administrative tri-bunal, has ruled that the law does not permit pupils to wear ostenta-tious signs of political or religious belief; but the court declined to specify what 'ostentatious' means. It is clear, for example, that some particular forms of dress are not necessarily objectionable under this ruling. A discreet badge or form of dress giving some indication of political or religious preference might not be a proper basis for excluding a pupil from school. The question then arises of how to distinguish between 'ostentatious' and 'discreet' dress or decoration. Here the court said that it was the responsibility of the governing body of each school to lay down general rules and make particular decisions. This seems to leave the field wide open for a variety of interpretations. In practice this is probably a solution which leans more towards the integrationist than the pluralist position because experience suggests that, largely as a result of teacher influence on school governing bodies, almost any sign of religious or political belief will be locally designated 'ostentatious' and can therefore serve as a proper basis for exclusion. Nevertheless, if opinion should evolve in a more tolerant and pluralistic direction, it is possible to imagine that local decisions at the school level will relax the applica-tion of the court's ruling so as to allow the display of religious and political beliefs in school.

Neither side can claim an outright victory in this conflict although, on balance, those who feel that the obligation rests with religious minorities to accept a degree of conformity in the interests of social and national unity certainly seem to have gained the upper hand. Commentators on the position of minorities in French society often observed in the 1970s and 1980s a trend to what they regarded as a more pluralistic and tolerant approach. They argued that, whereas pre-war and nineteenth-century French society had insisted on a high degree of linguistic and religious conformity to majority practices, this was proving less and less necessary. The controversies of 1989 and 1994 over the wearing of the headscarf seem at least to have set back this trend. Many politicians are sensitive to the hostility which a vociferous minority of French voters exhibit towards Moslems, Arabs and foreigners in general. The steady support by 10–15 per cent of the electorate for the extreme right-wing and anti-immigrant *Front national* are a constant reminder to politicians of the dangers they might run with the electorate if they are perceived to be too sympathetic to immigrants and their children.

PROTESTS IN SCHOOLS AND UNIVERSITIES

Student and pupil protest has been a recurrent feature of the educational scene in France since at least 1968. The student protest movement of 1968, with widespread support from the trade union movement, came near to overthrowing the government and even perhaps the whole regime. The student unrest of November and December 1986 damaged the prestige and credibility of the newly-elected right-wing government led by Jacques Chirac and caused reform legislation relating to the universities to be abandoned. More recently we have seen a movement of protest led by younger pupils in the *lycées* in the autumn of 1990 which led to a commitment by the Minister of Education and the government to spend the equivalent of 400 million pounds sterling on improving the facilities in the *lycées*. Most recently, in the autumn of 1993, a proposal to withdraw housing benefit from some students living away from home was dropped by the government in response to student demonstrations.

In attempting to understand why protest occurs in French schools and universities it is important to take account of two rather different contributory traditions. The first is a tradition of political protest on questions of principle. The second is a tradition of protest designed to press claims on behalf of particular groups. The first kind of protest is often associated with radical critiques of contemporary society coming either from the left or the right, whilst the second is simply an instrument used in the defence of particular interests. Often these two traditional forms of protest combine in complicated ways. In 1968 both forms of protest were present but the political and revolutionary demands were very much to the fore. In 1986, on the other hand, radical critiques of contemporary society were almost entirely absent and the student protest movement concentrated very narrowly on opposing prospective legislation which was thought likely to be inimical to student interests. The 1990 pupil protests were more difficult to classify. On the one hand, these pupils were clearly not interested in revolutionary objectives, but on the other, they did not seem to have any very specific demands which they wished to press.

In trying to understand the protest phenomenon we should also take account of the important social changes of attitude and behaviour which are evident in the post-war history of the French family. Parental control is clearly now exercised with much greater restraint. Young people enjoy a degree of independence to which they did not feel entitled forty or fifty years ago. The tendency of young people to stay on much longer at school, and in higher education, also means that many who in the past would have been at work, and therefore subject to employer and market disciplines, now enjoy the free atmosphere of secondary or higher education. The institutional setting of French higher education also contributes to our understanding of protest. The French university is organized so as to accept a very large number of applicants but then to make their successful graduation very uncertain. This policy of easy entry, followed by severe selection and consequent uncertainty as to graduation, creates acute anxiety among students, and it is this anxiety which constitutes the soil in which protest movements can quickly grow.

Overcrowding and consequently deteriorating conditions for study have also contributed to arousing protest. In the five years from 1983 to 1988 the number of *lycée* classes with more than 35 pupils rose from 15.3 per cent to 38.8 per cent in the state sector and from 5.6 per cent to 14.4 per cent in the non-secular sector.

Institutions at the secondary and higher level are often rather impersonal, if only because the pressure of numbers requires teachers to define their responsibilities rather narrowly.

Yet student protest is not a uniquely French phenomenon; it is a rather common feature of educational life in many advanced industrial countries, and we should therefore not expend too much effort in trying to explain why it is present in France. What we need to ask ourselves additionally is why it is absent in some countries such as the UK.

In examining the official response to protest we need to distinguish between the short term and the long term. The official short-term response has usually been to attempt to negotiate with student leaders. Meetings and negotiations in 1986 and 1990 led to legislative and financial concessions by the government. In the longer term the government is promoting a number of measures whose object is to make student life, and life in the *lycées*, more attractive, comfortable and purposeful. We have already mentioned the new advisory councils which have been established in each *lycée*. Students already elect their representatives to university governing councils. Money has also recently been made available to pay teachers, on an hourly basis, for out-of-school activities. It is also hoped that the anxiety and uncertainty of student life can be reduced in a number of ways. If the quality of advice and information which students receive, especially when first arriving in the university, can be improved, then perhaps students can make wiser choices and avoid preparing for examinations which they have little chance of passing. It may also be possible to persuade more students to follow vocational courses which offer more secure employment prospects. The morale of students on courses of this type is usually higher than that of young people pursuing studies of a purely academic character. There are few who believe that these measures, though undoubtedly desirable, can ever turn volatile students into compliant and obedient young people. There seems every possibility that, from time to time, protest movements will re-emerge, especially where large numbers of students are crowded together and obliged to work under difficult conditions.

CONCLUSION

There is a great deal which cannot be discussed in a chapter of this length. We have said nothing about the moves to create a more united teaching profession by doing away with the existing distinction between *instituteurs* and *professeurs* through a common training. Nor have we referred to the attempts to reduce working hours in the *lycée* by removing irrelevant material from syllabuses. Radical suggestions are also under consideration for reorganizing the school year and the school week, involving perhaps the abolition of Saturday school which is at present normal in both the primary and secondary sectors. Nor have we said anything about the controversies which have affected the teaching of particular subjects: spelling and grammar with respect to the teaching of French, chronological versus thematic approaches to the teaching of history, traditional versus modern mathematics, and many others.

One theme does emerge from the above discussion, namely the shift away from a remote and rather authoritarian state towards a more extensive but more responsive one. We can find evidence for this trend in the development of the new forms of privately provided education and training. The same is true of the so far rather tentative moves towards greater decentralization. The willingness of the administration to permit parental choice in a rather larger number of localities also implies a move in the direction of greater responsiveness. Only with regard to the acceptance of cultural and religious diversity does this movement seem to be making limited progress or none at all.

Although there is undeniably a trend of development in this direction it does not go uncontested. There is still a strong temptation for politicians and religious leaders to use schools as instruments of control rather than organizations designed to serve. Teachers are often sceptical about the value of innovation in education and doubtful about the new forms of decentralization and priva-tization. It is natural that this should be so. Those in positions of authority make decisions, but the cost of implementing them and adjusting to new arrangements often falls principally on those who work at the chalk face. Educational policy is made and educational change occurs through a constant dialogue and compromise between those at the summit of the pyramid, who wish to impress and who are never short of new ideas, and those at the base, who are asked to implement these ideas and accept without compensa-tion many of the costs which change imposes. It is not surprising then that there is much resistance to change. We should not be too ready to condemn the caution or obstruction of teachers and school administrators. It is their role to try to explain to those on high the complicated realities with which they are confronted day by day, just as it is the role of those in positions of responsibility to convince the teachers and administrators at the base that some changes are necessary in order to adapt to a changing world.

This chapter has concentrated on trying to understand and explain. Little attempt has been made to evaluate the performance of the system. The information which would be necessary for such an evaluation is almost entirely lacking. We may nevertheless conclude by tentatively suggesting that the strength of the French educational system lies in the very real demands which it places on young people. Much is expected, especially from the more able pupils, and much is certainly obtained. The system is severely competitive at almost all levels. This is very praiseworthy if one adopts a narrowly academic or economic view of the educational system. However, if one takes a broader perspective which pays more attention to the human costs of existing arrangements, one is inclined to be more critical. The personal, the human and the pastoral are too often neglected. Bureaucratization and centralization too often mean that teachers and administrators refuse to accept responsibility, blaming the government or the ministry for any difficulties that arise. This stiffness and formality of approach probably imposes the greatest costs at primary level where it frequently means that young children of only seven or eight are required to repeat a year because they have not learned to read as rapidly as their classmates. Perhaps we should conclude: *'pourrait mieux faire'*.

BIBLIOGRAPHY

The best historical introduction to the French education system is certainly A. Prost, *Histoire générale de l'enseignement et de l'education en France*, vol. 4: 'L'école et la famille dans une société en mutation'. Paris, Nouvelle Librairie de France, 1981.

For discussions of the relationship between education and economic performance, see particularly:

OECD, *Youth Unemployment in France*. Paris, OECD, 1984.

OECD, *Education and the Economy in a Changing Society*. Paris, OECD, 1989.

Commissariat général du Plan, *Deuxieme chance de l'école*, vols 1 and 2. Paris, Commissariat général du Plan, 1988.

More general and recent studies include:

Corbett, A., and Moon, B. (eds), *Education in France. Continuity and Change in the Mitterrand Years 1981–1995*. London, Routledge, 1996.

Devaquet, A., *L'Amibe et l'étudiant*. Paris, Editions Odile Jacob, 1988. The first-hand account of the minister responsible for the unsuccessful attempt to reform French universities in 1986.

Haby, R., *Combat pour les jeunes Français*. Paris, Julliard, 1981. The first-hand account by the Minister of Education from 1974–78.

OECD, *Reviews of National Policies for Education, France*. Paris, 1996.

Prost, A., *Les Lycées et leurs études au seuil du 21e siècle*. Paris, La Documentation française, 1983. Accessible, moderate and full of common sense.

Raynaud, P., and Thiebaud, P., *La Fin de l'école républicaine*. Paris, Calmann-Lévy, 1990. A good example of recent conservative attitudes.

Toulemonde, B., *Petite histoire d'un grand ministère*. Paris, Albin Michel, 1988. A revealing first-hand account by a senior civil servant in the Ministry of Education.

7

RELIGION

John Flower

Introduction

Within only a few years of the new millennium, religious practice and attitudes to religion in general in France seem to be constantly under review. In part this is due to important shifts within French society as political boundaries within Europe become less significant, but even more so it has to do with immigration from and relations with former colonies, especially Algeria. There is no better precise example of the latter than the *affaire du foulard*, the refusal of a state school in the autumn of 1989 to allow Moslem girls to attend wearing their traditional veil, the *tchador* or *hidjeb*. At the time this caused widespread and heated debate. The then socialist Prime Minister, Michel Rocard, and his Minister of Education, Lionel Jospin (six years later to become presidential candidate for his party), local authorities and, in this instance, the Moroccan government eventually arrived at a compromise, but only after much publicity. But those who wished to make political as well as religious capital out of the affair did so. Some, and not only members of the Moslem communities, accused the headmaster of racism; some claimed that the girls were merely pawns of local Moslems who wished to make a political gesture; women's groups extended the debate to embrace the issue of women in society generally; some argued that since the wearing of a cross, even as an ornament, or of the Jewish cap was tolerated, why should the veil not be. Spokesmen for France's religious communities were inevitably drawn in. The Cardinal Archbishop of Paris, Jean-Marie Lustiger, was cautious, interpreting the girls' gesture as one of teenage rebellion rather than as a political statement, but he pointed at the same time to the dangers of discrimination. He also warned that in his view it would take at least thirty years for Moslems to understand and accept the notion (and law) of *laïcité* in France. The head of the Islamic Church, Sheik Tdjini Haddam, declared himself to be *'indigné par l'attitude discriminatoire'*, a view shared by the principal rabbi, Alain Goldmann:

'*Aujourd'hui ce ne sont plus les religieux qui font preuve d'intolérance, comme on le leur reproche si souvent, mais les laïques. L'école laïque doit donner l'exemple de la tolérance.*' He was also reported to have said that the wearing of the veil or cap could be educationally worthwhile: '*La confrontation des petits Français avec la "différence" [leur] apprennent à connaître et à respecter l'autre.*' Such statements as these were perhaps predictable and indeed seemingly not unreasonable, but behind the *affaire du foulard*, inevitably magnified by media attention, lay concerns which threatened to assume greater proportions. Since this initial affair there have been others and they are now almost a regular feature of the beginning of each school year. In 1993, for example, at Nantua (a town where one-third of the population is made up of immigrants) or a year later at Gousssainville (an industrial town north of Paris) pupils were excluded. Responsibility usually rests finally with the head of the school and local authorities, and the *Conseil d'Etat* appears to want to judge each case according to its specific context, but the situation is complex and always open to exploitation. There is also the matter of attendant publicity. As yet no satisfactory overall solution has been found but so entrenched are some of the positions taken that any legislation will almost inevitably be challenged. Catholicism remains, of course, the dominant practice in France, but as that of Islam grows and as the Catholic Church itself experiences internal disputes, what religious stability there is will continue to be challenged and undermined.

CATHOLICS

Recent polls have shown, almost paradoxically, that by the mid-1990s there has been a slight increase (to about 85 per cent of the population) in the number of French people baptized, even if considerably fewer (about 56 per cent) claim to be Catholic. Yet of these now under 10 per cent attend mass regularly and fulfil what is expected of them by their Church. Furthermore a more general kind of erosion, which has been in evidence for over a decade, continues. A number of newly married couples either do not bother with the religious celebration of marriage or treat it virtually only as a social event (a recent unofficial survey put this as high as 50 per cent): an increasing number of marriages of mixed religions are taking place; the divorce rate continues to grow; papal instruction concerning contraception and the use of condoms is clearly ignored; the numbers of children receiving instruction in the catechism in preparation for confirmation decreases each year; the awareness of Catholicism among the young as part of the nation's cultural heritage is also, according to a number of teachers, now alarmingly slight.

One teacher of art who showed his pupils a picture of the martyr-dom of St Sebastian, for example, commented that *'certains ont affirmé qu'il s'agissait d'un Indien victime de la conquête de l'Ouest par les Américains'*. Others have complained that to study certain aspects of works of literature such as Racine's plays or Bernanos's novels has become virtually impossible. Only among the minority group of those people whose political allegiance is to the extreme right, with its traditionalist and nationalist values, is there evidence of real increase in the practice of the Catholic faith.

Within the structure and organization of the Catholic Church the kinds of problems now in evidence for several years also continue. Despite the intended appeal of a more varied training programme, fewer young men are attracted to the priesthood. Ordinations have stabilized at around 120 each year, but on average only one new priest is ordained for every seven who die and it has been estimated that by the end of the century the number of priests in office will be the equivalent of barely more than half those presently so. The num-ber of secular priests, for long seen as a possible solution to an increasingly critical situation, is dropping at an even faster rate. More and more responsibility is assumed by deacons (*diacres*) of whom there are over 300 and who have the authority to celebrate mar-riages, baptism and extreme unction, but not mass. And as the total number of priests shrinks so the responsibilities and difficulties for those left increase. Of the 38,000 parishes in France nearly two-thirds are without their own priest. A single priest usually, and almost always in rural areas, has responsibility for several parishes and on average for 1,000 people, an increase of 100 per cent since the late 1970s. Many churches are in poor condition and threatened with demolition, and while the government continues to invest money in the restoration of those with significant historic interest, expenses of this kind more often than not have to be met by local councils or from private contributions. Many churches are nonethe-less being closed.

While he may well benefit from gifts, the priest himself remains poorly paid. His official salary is on average 4,000 francs. This is sup-plemented by the *denier du culte*, a contribution made by members of his congregation, representing (it is recommended) 1 per cent of their annual salary and of which a proportion is tax deductible, though this practice appears to be falling. The priest is also faced, often, with a physically demanding job, especially in rural areas where he may be obliged to travel as many as 5,000 km per month. A car, if he is lucky enough to have one, is a heavy drain on his slim financial resources. If security of employment, free (if sometimes poor) accommodation and no immediate family expenses do, as some willingly acknowledge, allow them to exist without real hardship, loneliness can be a problem. Years ago, a priest spoke for many when he remarked: *'La boîte de sardines mangée seul, un jour de Noël à midi, a un affreux goût de solitude.'* If today this sounds outmoded and almost caricatural, the underlying problem surrounding celibacy nonetheless remains and the growing debate over whether priests should be allowed to marry highlights an issue which is human as well as vocational.

Yet whatever the apparent disaffection among Catholics, and despite the ongoing crisis in recruitment and the problems of organization and morale, the Catholic Church still has a significant presence in French society. Catholic schools, for example, constitute almost all of the private sector; a press ranging from daily papers like *La Croix* or *Le Pèlerin* to publishing houses ensures that issues and information are permanently available. Two specific events point to this presence. The first is the building of a new cathedral, the first for over a century, at Evry to the south of Paris. Designed by Mario Botta, its chamfered drum shape is a hallmark of his buildings across the world and certainly unusual for a church. Some government money was allocated but the largest proportion of the cost has been met by private donations. The reactions have been mixed and traditionalists in particular have been scornfully dismissive, seeing it *'à mi-chemin entre la salle des fêtes et le stade coupe du monde ... tout est symbole maçonnique'*. The second event of note has been the publication of two papal encyclicals: *Veritatis splendor* (translated as *Splendeur de la vérité*) in 1993 and *Evangelicum vitae (Evangile de la vie)* in 1995. In itself the publication has nothing unusual, but after the resounding success of the new catechism in 1992 (half a million copies sold within a few weeks) each has enjoyed significant sales and has been widely debated. The first, centred on what is seen as a moral crisis, has as a form of sub-text a critique of theologians and bishops whose interpretation of *'la sainte doctrine'* is judged to have become too flexible. It is a call to order and an appeal for the Catholic Church to regain what one commentator called *'une sorte de leadership moral'*. Two years later the Pope focused on what he has termed *'la culture de la mort'* which dominates modern society – birth control, euthanasia, abortion, surrogate mothers and capital punishment. Together, these two texts have generally been considered authoritarian, dogmatic and even anti-democratic, and not sufficiently aware of what one priest called the *'enjeux existentiels pour l'homme d'aujourd'hui'*, but what is important is the fact that the discussion they have provoked illustrates, irrespective of the positions taken, the permanence of a fundamental Catholicism across the nation. As one priest in Lyon remarked in April 1995: *'Beaucoup de Français sont croyants par tradition ...'*

PROTESTANTS

By *croyants* the priest in Lyon meant *catholiques*, of course, but while statistically these remain pre-eminent it is essential not to forget that other Christian denominations have roles to play in religious matters in France. The most significant body is that of the Protestants of whom there are over 2 million; 1.3 million are said to be practising and it is claimed that numbers are increasing. Many are to be found in those areas where they withdrew in the face of Catholic persecution in the past – Alsace, the Cévennes and the southern reaches of the Rhône valley. Most belong, however informally, to the Reform Church, but there are important, more fundamentalist groups within the Lutheran tradition. In Alsace, where these proportions are reversed, there has been a move since late 1993 to bring the two movements together in a *'communion ecclésiale'*, and this spirit of dialogue (somewhat different from the climate within parts of the Catholic Church) re-emerged in May 1994 at the Protestant synod. Here much emphasis was placed on ecumenicalism; Protestants were to be encouraged to seek ways of forging links with such minority groups as the Methodists, Baptists and even Anglicans. As one leading theologian observed: *'On va vers une communion des Eglises de la Réforme.'* Nor is the Catholic Church excluded. While remaining critical of its hierarchical organization, of its *'doctrine [. . .] centralisatrice de l'ecclésiologie de communion'* and of what they see as ambiguity in its attitude towards education and a number of political issues, notably that of immigration, Protestants have appealed for dialogue. Indeed, the dominant tone of modern French Protestantism was set by Monique Veille in 1990: *'Il est souhaitable qu'un vaste public sache que l'on peut être chrétien de plusieurs manières. Il ne s'agit pas de faire de prosélytisme, mais de montrer qu'il y a une alternative possible.'* In politics and in the context of a changing Europe the Protestant Church has also shown an awareness and openness not always apparent elsewhere. In March 1995 at a conference to debate the challenges of the twenty-first century, an emphasis on increasing democracy was a frequent theme, as was a warning that France was in danger of isolating herself: *'Ce n'est pas le danger d'invasion qui nous menace, mais celui de l'enfermement. De peur de devenir une passoire, la France devient une forteresse.'*

JEWS AND THE ORTHODOX CHURCH

Together these two communities account for around a million. The Paris region accommodates most (especially the fourth *arrondissement* and the area around the Rue des Rosiers) but there are important Jewish settlements as well in Lyon, Marseille and Provence. Numbers swelled, especially during and after the Algerian war in the mid 1960s, and have continued to grow. A simple illustration of this is the fact that while in 1962 there were only three kosher butcher's shops in Paris there are now nearly a hundred. Jewish schools have developed apace with little difficulty or opposition. But anti-semitism is not dead. Acts of violence have included the bombing of restaurants, department stores and railway stations, and in September 1995 a Jewish school in Lyon miraculously escaped carnage from a time-bomb thanks to a faulty school clock – the pupils were a few minutes late in leaving their classrooms. Cemeteries too in Carpentras, Aix-en-Provence and Strasbourg have been desecrated, tombs have been opened and daubed with Nazi slogans. Traditionally, the Jewish community has shown a high degree of discipline and uniformity and a willingness as well to enter dialogue with other religions. At the third Yom Hathora held at Le Bourget in October 1993, Joseph Sitruk, Grand Rabbi of France, praised *'un épiscopat français formidable qui, depuis vingt ans, a pris des positions courageuses vis-à-vis de la communauté juive et israélienne'*. But signs of tension and a split between liberal and fundamentalist groups have appeared. In Paris in particular a new dynamism to Jewish culture and activities in the early 1990s was provided by Benny Cohen, but he was seen by some to have overstepped the mark and has been replaced by his homonym Moïse Cohen. But this debate, notionally over the role of the Paris Consistory, may well point to a more fundamental ideological division.

MOSLEMS

Active, well-organized and more numerous than the Protestants, Moslems can justifiably be considered the second most significant religious group in France. There are now approximately 4 million of them meeting in as many as 1,500 places of worship which range from a disused garage in the back streets of Marseille to the Grande Mosquée in Paris or the new equivalent in Lyon. About half this number are practising, about three-quarters of a million are of French nationality and there are increasing numbers of converts (now over 30,000), principally from Catholicism. In October 1994 Charles Pasqua, then Minister of the Interior, remarked: *'L'Islam est aujourd'hui une réalité française, parce que c'est pour une grande part une religion de Français.'* The extensions to the mosque in Paris, the construction of a new one at Evry and in particular that of the one in Lyon all suggest a climate of tolerance. Pasqua's words were reciprocated by the first imam to be appointed to the Lyon mosque, Abdel Hamid Chirane, who stated his intention in his opening address in June 1994 to encourage *'un Islam convivial, tolérant, ouvert et rassembleur'*. This move towards mutual respect and tolerance has been evident for over a decade. In the face of the growing Moslem fundamentalism throughout the world and in particular, as far as the French are concerned, in Algeria, where it is represented in its most extreme form by the violent *Groupe islamique armé* (GIA), there has been a sustained attempt to arrive at a 'French Islam'. Not, as Pasqua again said in 1994, at *'l'Islam en France'* but *'l'Islam de France'*.

An important step was taken in 1990 by the socialist government whose Minister of the Interior, Pierre Joxe, set up a *Conseil de réflexion sur l'Islam en France* (CORIF) which, while it had no legal status, was intended to establish an overview of Islamic activities in France and was to prescribe a policy for the future. Joxe's successor, Pasqua, did not dissolve the body but nonetheless refrained from organizing any meetings, and it is now defunct. This and his general policy over immigration did not seem promising, but in fact a number of measures have been taken precisely to try to develop a French Islam free, as far as is possible, from the influence of the fundamentalists, the FIS (*Front islamique du salut*) in Algeria and their mouthpiece in France the FAF (*Fraternité algérienne-française*). One move was to create, in October 1993, the *Institut de formation d'imams*. The existence of these in French soil would more easily justify any government refusal to award visas to imams from overseas, as happened, for example, earlier, in February 1993, and again a year later. Also, in the château of St Léger de Fougerat in the Nièvre, a centre for Islamic study has been set up by the *Union des organisations islamiques de France*. Teaching is in Arabic and, while the institution is said to be intolerant of fundamentalism, there have been signs that infiltration has been attempted. And this is what many French people find worrying. An imam, of whom there are about 1000 in France, is not simply a priest; he is a guide whose wisdom and authority extend beyond matters of faith. And such is the network between mainland France and North Africa that influence and directives pass easily, even if individuals are sometimes stopped. It is this kind of perceived threat which, despite a general growing tolerance, has given rise to pockets of opposition. In Toulouse, for example, the town council remains resolutely opposed to the construction of a mosque despite the presence of an important Moslem community.

At the same time, in Marseille (where there are 100,000 Moslems), the project to build a new *mosquée-cathédrale* has been revived. Its presence would give Islam greater visibility and, in the words of the Mayor, Jean-Claude Gaudin, *'[le] sortir des caves et des garages qui conforte l'imaginaire des Français et qui humilie les*

musulmans'. Plans have been drawn up and a model put on display, but whether land and finance will be found in a town and region where the influence of the *Front national* is growing must remain in some doubt.

There is also the problem of internal division within the Moslem hierarchy. The current rector of the Grande Mosquée in Paris, Dalil Boubakeur, follows the conciliatory line: *'Je voudrais que l'imam soit intégré à la société française comme le prêtre, le pasteur ou le rabbin,'* he remarked towards the end of 1993. A year later he established the *Conseil consultatif des musulmans de France* in order to create *'une structure définitivement représentative de l'Islam de France'*. But as within the Jewish (and indeed Catholic) communities such views are not always shared unquestioningly. Some members of the former CORIF are cautious, as are those of the *Fédération nationale des musulmans de France*. So far Boubakeur has managed to have his way, and in February 1996, Islam was awarded legal status in France, a change which will open the way to state funding in, for example, education. But there are those who, without going so far as to accept the tenets of fundamentalism, nonetheless see all moves of this kind as a threat to the true values of Islam. The debate is important and has a resonance well beyond the frontiers of France.

TRADITION AND PROGRESSION: DEBATE WITHIN THE CATHOLIC CHURCH

The rise of traditionalism

All of these issues and developments illustrate a religious climate in France increasingly affected by social and political ones. No less than Moslems or Jews, Catholics have been subject to a resultant tension which on occasions has threatened to become openly confrontational. Fundamentally, and certainly for the last hundred years, the Catholic Church in France has been subjected to a debate between its traditionalist and progressive members. The former, rather casually dismissed in a survey carried out by *L'Express* in December 1994, as today constituting *'une infime minorité'*, witness a tiny increase in support each year. There are various groups within the broad movement but the bulk of traditionalists are allied to the *Fraternité sacerdotale de Saint-Pie-X* (FSSPX), begun in 1969 at Ecône in Switzerland by Marcel Lefebvre. Having returned to France in 1962 to become Archbishop of Tulle, Lefebvre at once made his mark at the Second Vatican Council. He emerged as the spokesman for minority groups in opposition to the council's generally progressive tone and declared in his final intervention: *'Ce n'est pas le Saint-Esprit qui inspire le concile, mais le diable.'* Lefebvre's opposition to the directives to emerge from the council continued unabated. In 1974 in his book *Un Evêque parle* he wrote: *'nous refusons de suivre Rome dans la tendance néo-moderniste et néo-protestante clairement manifestée au cours du Vatican II et des réformes qui en sont issues'*. His own brand of traditional Catholicism – *lefebvrisme* as it has become known – supports the retention of the Tridentine Mass, is opposed to religious freedom and to links with non-Catholics and is deeply critical of all attempts to dismantle the Church's hierarchy or to rewrite its basic texts. When, for example, the new catechism was published in 1992 Lefebvre's successor in Paris, Philippe Laguérie, described it as *'une tromperie supplémentaire [...] un document foncièrement moderniste, dans la pure logique de la rupture conciliaire'* and *'un nouveau désastre pour l'Eglise'*.

Lefebvre's career was marked by a series of direct conflicts with the Vatican. In 1976, after defying the Pope's authority and ordaining priests into his movement, he was suspended *a divinis* which in principle barred him from celebrating mass, dispensing the sacrement and preaching. He refused to modify his position and in February 1977 his supporters in Paris, organized by one of his most devoted supporters, the abbé Ducaud-Bourget, defiantly occupied the Church of Saint-Nicolas du Chardonnet in the fifth *arrondissement*. Despite appeals by local people to the church and civil authorities alike no action was taken and Saint-Nicolas now regularly draws increasingly large numbers to its mass from all over Paris. It was claimed that on Palm Sunday 1995, for example, no less than 10,000 were present.

Despite the impression often given by the media, the positions apparently adopted by Lefebvre and Rome were not totally immovable. When in 1988 the former announced his intention to ordain four bishops – an action which would automatically incur excommunication – Pope John-Paul II attempted to arrive at a compromise. Lefebvre could celebrate mass in Latin but the Pope would ordain one of his nominees; Lefebvre would also have to acknowledge the authority of changes against which he had set himself in matters of religious freedom, liturgy, hierarchy and ecumenicalism. Despite a ratification of the general principles in a *'protocole de paix'*, Lefebvre was apparently not satisfied and carried out his ordinations on 30 June. Excommunication followed. Not even this, however, could deter Lefebvre from continuing to justify his position and from accusing the Vatican of misguided policies and even of having no legitimacy: *'On nous a dit excommunication, mais excommunication par qui? Par un Rome moderniste, par un Rome qui n'a plus de foi catholique [. . .] Nous sommes condamnés par des gens qui devraient être excommuniés publiquement.'* Similarly he continued to voice his resistance to all progressive measures (seen as a dilution) and ecumenicalism. On 14 November 1989 his comments at a press conference on the role of Islam in France were far from conciliatory: *'Les musulmans vont petit à petit imposer leurs lois. Le droit chrétien ne peut s'accorder avec le droit islamique. Les musulmans ne peuvent vraiment être français. Il ne faut pas leur permettre de s'organiser, ni sur le plan politique, ni sur le plan religieux.'* A year later he concluded that the Catholic Church had succumbed to *'l'anarchie totale'*.

There has been no letting up in the force of Lefebvre's message. After his death and the retirement of Ducaud-Bourget, the traditionalist cause in France has been taken on at Saint-Nicolas by Philippe Laguérie, described in one survey as the embodiment of faith and fanaticism. In 1989 he too remarked: *'Aujourd'hui le sens de la foi est le seul recours des fidèles devant l'imbroglio inimaginable d'une hiérarchie qui prêche droits de l'homme, œcuménisme, liberté religieuse, Révolution.'* Later that year he dismissed the French episcopacy as *'une bande d'assassins de la Foi'* and he has never hesitated subsequently to attribute what he and his fellow traditionalists see as a continuing and worsening state of affairs to the Second Vatican Council and its aftermath. In his editorial of the March–April 1995 issue of the Saint-Nicolas parish magazine *Le Chardonnet*, for example, he wrote:

... il faudra bien un jour, refermer la parenthèse diabolique de ce Concile qui a chanté le monde [...] qui a exalté l'homme et son culte, qui a introduit l'erreur et le poison dans le Magistère, dévasté le sanctuaire et retourné les autels, ruiné la civilisation chrétienne et réduit l'Epouse de Jésus-Christ au rang d'une secte, d'une prostituée qui cherche partout les clients que son ignominie fait fuir.

[...]

Il faudra un jour sortir de la parenthèse; et non s'y fourvoyer. Une seule solution, la papauté et donc un successeur (pas forcément le prochain...) de Jean-Paul II. Toute autre solution pour sortir de la crise nous y ferait sombrer nous aussi et j'affirme qu'elle est un manque de foi en la divinité de l'Eglise. Il faut refuser la Rome telle qu'elle est aujourd'hui [...] pour continuer à croire en Elle et ceux qui l'admettent telle qu'Elle est, prouvent par là la piètre idée qu'ils s'en font. Un vrai catholique est plus romain que cela!

Not surprisingly we find the same kind of language issuing from Ecône, from Lefebvre's successor there Franz Schmidberger (*l'esprit de Satan pénètre la société et la détruit*') and from Bernard Fallay who has now replaced him. Schmidberger and Laguérie have forecast that by the end of the century the traditionalists would constitute a kind of Catholic resistance in a country largely indifferent to the Church. In recent years another voice has been heard, no less strident in its defence of traditionalism and highly critical in particular of any move the Pope has made towards dialogue. André Cagnon, whose column is a regular feature of *Le Chardonnet*, poured scorn on John-Paul II's willingness to talk to voodoo priests in Africa: '*... il a véritablement tendu la main au diable [...] C'est bien en effet, la première fois qu'un successeur de Pierre pactise aussi ouvertement avec le diable, trahit sa mission d'enseigner toutes les nations, et ce faisant insulte notre Seigneur Jésus-Christ.*' Even more provocative were his comments on the world AIDS conference held in Paris in November 1994. Scornful of 'scientific' explanations Cagnon remonstrated: '*nul ne veut y voir la main de Dieu, le châtiment des hommes qui Le bafouent. [...] La dérive est totale. Il n'y a plus de moralité. On ne respecte plus la vie, on ne respecte plus la femme, on ne respecte plus les autres, on ne se respecte plus soi-même et la cause en est simple: on ne respecte plus Dieu [...] et le salaire du péché, c'est la mort!*'

The full extent to which sympathizers of the *Fraternité* group accept such views and just how wide the movement's appeal is are difficult to measure. Virtually every department in France, however, now has a *'lieu de culte'* where the traditional mass is celebrated. At

Barroux in Provence, for example, where the monastery is a stronghold of nationalist ideology, Sunday mass attracts an international congregation. The pronouncements of the prior, Gérard Calvet, are frequently strident. In August 1996, he declared that all true Catholics should unite in their struggle against *'les grands malfaiteurs du jour, pornocrates qui souillent les mœurs, fauteurs d'hérésies qui déforment la religion, mondialistes inconscients qui détruissent l'âme d'un peuple'*. Over 200 priests are being trained each year at Ecône, privately funded schools are growing in popularity, the *Institut universitaire Saint-Pie-X* has established a link with the Sorbonne and offers a range of courses, the movement has its own radio station and claims a subscription list of over 40,000 for its magazines *Fidelitur* and *Anti-89*. Special services and demonstrations or pilgrimages – to Chartres or to celebrate the Virgin Mary or Saint Joan – regularly attract up to 10,000 people. The post-Lefebvre status of the movement has created a form of 'schism' within the French Catholic Church, even if it is not acknowledged as such, and in fact this marginal status has caused it to have trouble in securing money (over 50 million francs) which has been bequeathed to it by the faithful.

Not all traditionalists are of a *lefevbriste* inspiration, however. Some have advocated the acceptance of papal discipline, but others have become even more entrenched in their integrism, expressing their views through such movements and magazines as *Comité chrétienté-solidarité*, *Présent* and, more recently, *Reconquête* with which Laguérie has an ongoing debate. Of much greater concern though is the band of sympathy between many traditionalists and Le Pen's *Front national* (Bernard Antony, leader of *Comité chrétienté-solidarité* is a party member in the European parliament). The traditionalist mass is regularly celebrated at major *Front national* rallies and Le Pen's comments about immigration, progressive trends within society and the erosion of national sovereignty fall on receptive ears, though it has to be said that a poll in June 1996 indicated a slight lessening of support for his political programme. Quite how the movement will develop is impossible to say. In spite of the claims of Laguérie and others it is not likely to become a major force within the Church, nor is its brand of fundamentalism likely to have the kind of impact which that exerted by certain Moslem groups has. But it does appear to be becoming more strident, more critical of the church authorities and of individuals like Lustiger. One spokesman accused the Church, in March 1995, of lacking all direction, of being *'l'église du vide'*; another in September 1995 criticized the episcopacy of being *'plus soucieux d'agitation sociale et écologique que d'évangélisation'*. And in September 1996, the Pope's visit to France was heralded by Laguérie as *'un voyage qui réactive tous les démons de la gauche endormie et oisive'*. Until or unless the rift with the Vatican is healed it seems destined to pursue its somewhat marginal position. But it is not without influence and there is no doubt that the traditionalist voice will continue to be heard.

The progressive legacy

Until January 1995 and what became known as the *affaire Gaillot*, issues at the heart of progressive trends within the Church had been largely overshadowed by the debate around traditionalism. Certainly the legacy of progressive measures whose roots lay in the earlier years of the twentieth century has remained healthy. The *Mission de France* continues its work in industrialized regions, the *Action catholique ouvrière* and the *Jeunesse catholique ouvrière* have sustained their membership and attract thousands to their annual rallies. At the heart of their preoccupations is a concern for adaptation and dialogue. André Lacraupe, head of the *Mission de France* since 1988, summed up their position thus: *'L'Eglise n'est l'Eglise que dans l'ouverture et le dialogue que si elle aide les chrétiens et les non-chrétiens à vivre au cœur des défis quotidiens: l'éthique, la santé, les droits de l'homme, les choix économiques.'* Such sentiments hardly find favour with the traditionalists!

In October 1994, the weekly magazine *Témoignage chrétien*, for long a vehicle for progressive ideas, organized a conference significantly entitled *'Que sont devenus les chrétiens de gauche?'* This, to be sure, was about the mass of ordinary people whose itinerary could be traced through the MRP, *mendésisme*, creation of the CDFT in 1964 and so on. And with the presidential election only a year away and the candidature of Jacques Delors still a possibility the debate was timely. But one of the main conclusions to emerge was that Christian and humanist values had become so intertwined that dialogue was the norm and the need for militant groups in particular who would corner the Church and exert pressure had significantly lessened. To a degree such a conclusion is justified. There have been a number of developments in recent years which suggest that the Church is sensitive to a modern climate and that the spirit of the Second Vatican Council lives on, even if the consequences are not always met with approval. Perhaps the most visible sign has been the rewriting (since 1985) of the catechism in an attempt to produce an *'exposé complet et organique de la foi chrétienne'* (whatever the traditionalists might think) dealing not only with matters of faith and exegesis of the Bible, but with moral and social issues as well. The question of religious instruction to which pupils have a right has also been examined. The government's decision to allow schools to move religious instruction to Saturday morning may be a recognition of the value attributed to the weekend, but has resulted in a drop of about 25 per cent in attendance, and while it was tolerated by the Church it drew criticism from Joseph Duval, the former head of the episcopal assembly, and from Lustiger, who sees it as interference with the *'équilibre culturel et spirituel du pays'*. Structurally too there have been attempts to meet criticisms that the Church is still too distant. Training centres like the *Centres d'intelligence de la foi* (CIF) have been established and part-time study at the *Ecole cathé-drale (Notre-Dame) institut catholique* is possible. Elected diocesan synods composed of clerics and lay members of the Church have been created across France in an attempt to register local opinion in a spirit of *'co-responsabilité'* and to make recommendations to the national episcopal assembly.

Inevitably, however, just as traditionalists consider the Church to be betraying its true values, there are those who remain critical of an institution which they see as remaining fundamentally conservative and out of touch. The lay movement *Jeunes Chrétiens service* or the group in Lyon centred around the periodical *Golias* frequently voice criticism of papal policies and of their implementation by the French Church as well as of individuals. An issue of *Golias* was devoted to

From Le Monde, *15–16 January 1995*

Lustiger in 1991, entitled *Les Dix Ans du Cardinal Lustiger à Paris*, in which he was accused of authoritarian behaviour, conservatism and patronage. A year earlier the review had produced a survey of all French bishops, *Trombinoscope pour épiscopes*. In it each of them was rated, on a scale of 1–5 mitres, for their openness. Lustiger then, classified as *'imprévisible'* and in fact *'inclassable'* was awarded three. Many (29) were awarded none or only one mitre. Only seven were defined as *'Conciliaires "battants" '* (*'On peut les considérer comme l'aile marchante de l'épiscopat')* and of those only five were awarded the maximum five mitres. One was Jacques Gaillot, then Bishop of Evreux (since 1982) and already a constant source of embarrassment for his episcopal superiors. In November 1988 Gaillot had caused a fundamental disturbance at the episcopal assembly by commenting that *'L'Evangile est une parole parmi d'autres, une parole contestable, et nous ne devons pas chercher à l'imposer.'* In favour of the ordination of married men and women and of the re-admittance to the priesthood of those who had left to marry, tolerant of homosexuals and in favour of contraception (*'Si le préservatif peut sauver des vies, alors utilisons-le'*, *Lui*, January 1989), and active on behalf of the homeless, Gaillot was perceived, not unreasonably, as difficult. He has been openly sympathetic to communists, to the Palestine Liberation Organization, and has even advocated tolerance towards Islamic fundamentalism. In 1994, in his book *Coup de gueule contre l'exclusion*, he condemned Pasqua's policies over immigration and accused the Church of not taking a more positive stance: *'Ce n'est pas Charles Pasqua que l'on devrait plaindre, mais les innombrables victimes de cet arsenal répressif.'* And unlike so many of his colleagues, Gaillot has always been skilful at using the media to get his opinions across to as large an audience as possible. Gaillot was warned on several occasions about the dangers of not conforming to the policies of the episcopal majority: Lustiger was known in private to have expressed his exasperation and a decision had been taken late in 1994 to ask Gaillot to leave his post. Eventually, however, and, as several commentators pointed out, with a timing which could hardly have been more ill-judged, he was removed from office on 13 January 1995 by a decree from the Vatican at the moment when the Pope was visiting the Philippines and remonstrating with the local population about the rights of man. Gaillot, it was claimed, *'ne s'est pas montré apte à exercer le ministère d'unité qui est le premier devoir d'un évêque'*. Reaction in France was marked. Thousands expressed sympathy for Gaillot, protested to their bishops and signed petitions. Within the Catholic Church and indeed in others there has been criticism. The Moslem and Jewish communities argued that they would have dealt with a similar problem through internal tribunals. Jacques Stewart, head of the Protestant community, made the same point and commented: *'La sanction qui frappe Mgr Gaillot fait tort à toutes les Eglises. Le Vatican se prive d'un ministère qui pouvait certes choquer, mais qui était un signe de liberté évangélique.'* The *Mission de France* declared itself to be *'stupéfait et alterré'*, while a priest in Caen, in a direct message, wrote: *'Jusqu'où ira la hiérarchie contre celles et ceux qui sont espoir pour les pauvres. On aurait pu penser que l'épuration était un temps révolu. On ne les laissera pas faire de toi un martyr. Une fois de plus, Rome s'est laissé influencer par les intégristes.'* His replacement at Evreux, Jacques David, Bishop of La Rochelle and himself a liberal, called Gaillot's dismissal *'un échec douloureux'* and has declared his intention to *'(s)inscrire dans sa continuité'*.

There were, of course, some who approved the papal decision, notably the traditionalists (*'intégristes'*). For Laguérie the *'infâme évêque d'Evreux'* with his *'flegme bouddhique et sa morgue mielleuse'* should never have been nominated, and inevitably a comparison between his fate and that of Lefebvre has been made. The difference is that however problematic Gaillot may have been and however uncomfortable his presence and remarks, he has done nothing to contradict the dogma of the Church. Moreover, since he remains a bishop he is, in a paradoxical way, at liberty to continue to act and speak with authority on an even larger stage than before. (It was popularly reported that Gaillot had been given the diocese of Partenia in Mauritania. In fact it is a non-existent diocese in the ancient province of Maurétanie in Algeria.) Some have suggested he is not unwilling to be seen as a martyr, an image which his slight, even frail physique, soft voice and deceptively ingenuous attitude sometimes support, and he has increasingly associated himself with the *exclus* in modern French society.

There is no doubt either that those who wish to make capital out of this will do so. In March and June 1996, for example, he was active in supporting the occupation of churches in the eleventh and eighteenth *arrondissements* of Paris by groups (mainly Africans) who do not have immigration papers. But rather more significantly, the *affaire Gaillot* underlines the way in which Rome has seemingly acted with a kind of distant and, worse still, reactionary authority. Some have argued that this is only to be expected as the end of a papacy draws near and may, if only subconsciously, have been exacerbated by the approaching millennium. In many ways, as a specific incident, like the excommunication of Lefebvre, it will pass into history and remain only meaningful for those close to and convinced by Gaillot's rhetoric. But the gap between the latter and the central authority of the Church in France is narrower than that separating the traditionalists. However intransigent the Pope may seem on certain issues, the progressive spirit, set in motion by John XXIII, remains. Gaillot has tested it to the full and has suffered the consequences but his views will come increasingly to the fore. It is their reception and the manner in which they are balanced against official directives which will be the test for those responsible for the French Catholic Church over the next few years.

CONCLUSION

In April 1995, Joseph Duval, then head of the episcopal assembly and usually a retiring and somewhat cautious figure, was moved to voice his disquiet at the negative press he claimed his Church received, especially over the AIDS issue and the question of homosexuality amongst priests. His statement seems to have been triggered by the release of Antonia Bird's controversial film *Priest*. Like Scorsese's *The Last Temptation of Christ*, which had appeared on French cinema screens in the autumn of 1988, or Jacques Duquesne's biography, *Jesus* (1994), *Priest* provoked much discussion and, amongst Catholics, considerable outrage. Duval reminded his fellow countrymen that while opposed to artificial birth control, in the face of AIDS some compromise had to be admitted. He recalled the statement which had been issued by the episcopacy in 1993, *'Sida: éduquer, accompagner'*, and in which the use of contraceptives was deemed permissible but to be seen as *'une toute première étape de responsabilisation'*. It was not just a question of preventing conception but of transmitting a terminal disease, a view not so far removed from that of the Protestants, whose position Stewart summarized in the words: *'Vous ne devez pas donner la mort. Vous devez aussi vous protéger.'* And on 12 February 1996, after what *Le Monde*'s editorial called *'le coupable retard'*, the Catholic episcopacy issued a statement, *La Société en question*, in which they finally recognized that the use of condoms could be condoned since they prevented the spread of the virus. Welcoming the decision, Marc Gentilini, president of the *Comité catholique des médecins français*, remarked: *'Sur le plan moral, l'Eglise catholique romaine peut être contre le préservatif en tant que moyen de contraception empêchant la transmission de la vie; elle ne peut pas être contre le préservatif, moyen de prévention empêchant la transmission de la mort.'* But while a form of compromise in this matter may have been reached, over celibacy there was none; the papal ruling on *'la discipline du célibat'* was absolute whatever dissidents like Gaillot might propose. A similarly firm line has been adopted by Lustiger over experiments on and with human embryos and over abortion. The *loi Weil* legalizing abortion in certain circumstances was passed twenty years ago. The episcopal assembly considered that such had been its relaxation that over 160,000 abortions were now being performed each year and in January 1995 issued a statement which was posted in every church: *'La mise à mort d'êtres humains innocents et dans leur plus grande fragilité est, et demeure, une blessure mortelle, une blessure physique, morale et spirituelle, de notre humanité [. . .] Aimer la vie et la défendre en toutes circonstances est pour nous un engagement absolu.'* Such words were, of course, an instant foretaste of John-Paul II's encyclical *Evangilicum vitae* which appeared two months later.

The official bodies through which all directives from Rome are channelled have a difficult if not impossible task. Castigated by the traditionalists for betraying the Church's true values and of being in league not only with the political left but with the Devil as well, and by progressive Catholics for being timid and conservative, they have to struggle on as best they can. In this struggle two key figures have emerged. The first is Jean-Marie Lustiger, Cardinal Archbishop of Paris and since March 1996 a member of the *Académie française*. A man of deep faith, he is ideologically close to John-Paul II with whom he is said to enjoy a warm relationship. He has a particular responsibility for links across Europe and has tended to recommend the appointment of bishops sympathetic to it. He is said to be authoritarian and rather old-fashioned in some respects. He condemns the way in which, in his view, television has contributed to a sub-culture of anarchy, disrespect and violence, yet he is astute enough to use it when it can be to his advantage. Of Jewish origins (he was baptized in 1940), he knew as a child what it was to experience hatred and persecution and he is not without his opponents today. Criticism of him, especially from the right, is often tinged with racism or anti-Semitism, a tone set by Lefebvre's reaction on his appointment to Notre-Dame in 1981: *'On peut être surpris de penser que se trouve à la tête du plus grand diocèse de France quelqu'un qui n'est pas d'origine vraiment française.'* The second figure is Pierre Eyt, former director of the *Institut catholique* in Paris and since 1989 Archbishop of Bordeaux; he is close to Lustiger (according to the traditionalists his *'cheval de bataille'*) and noted for his openness and ecumenical instincts. He too is said to enjoy the Pope's confidence. In November 1994 he was nominated cardinal and was soon giving a series of high-profile interviews. In these his qualities re-emerged, as well as an anti-materialism and anti-consumerism. In *L'Humanité* (5 January 1995), for example, he remarked: *'Il est sûr qu'une société où la souveraineté de l'argent et de l'Audimat – qui sont d'ailleurs deux aspects de la même réalité – est la principale source de légitimité est une société qui ne peut pas durer.'* And in the same interview: *'Il y a des moments où l'on peut se sentir proche, par exemple, des analyses de Proudhon sur l'argent et la société, et personnellement, je n'ai jamais été tellement à distance de certaines analyses de Marx sur le travail, l'argent, l'aliénation des personnes et de la société qui sont aujourd'hui déstructurées'* – words which the traditionalists were not slow to pounce on.

Just where Lustiger and Eyt will lead the French Church, or indeed go themselves over the next few years, is not easy to predict. Some commentators estimate that Lustiger is bound for Rome (some have even suggested that he could eventually become Pope) and Eyt, in turn, for Paris. For the present, however, they remain significant voices as they try to maintain the delicate balance between orthodoxy as it emanates from Rome and the conditions prevailing in France. But how much attention is paid to them? Do they have meaningful roles for many beyond their immediate constituency? While they may be in general dismissed by the traditionalists, there is a sense that they are not vitally central to many, especially the young, amongst whom there are signs of what the review *Prier* defined over a decade ago as a *'spiritualité populaire'*. One of the under-secretaries to the episcopal assembly remarked in 1994 that while a high percentage of young people admitted to a 'belief in God' (*croyants par tradition'* perhaps) they resisted both dogma and institutionalization: *'ils ne peuvent s'habituer à un discours qui serait une sorte de préfabriqué chrétien spirituel'*. Evidence supports this. Movements which are fundamentally Catholic like the scouts are growing, but the religious element is played down. More significant still is the role played by ecumenical centres, especially the one at Taizé near Cluny which attracted over 25,000 between Easter and Whitsun 1995. Deeply committed to pacifism and strongly European, the community has organized, in each of the last seventeen years, an annual gathering in a major city. For August 1997 a *'journée mondiale de la jeunesse'* in Paris has been announced by the Pope; it may well be attended by up to a million young people. In 1995 a parliamentary inquiry into sects identified 172, which are followed by 160,000 people; in addition it claimed that well over half as many again expressed sympathy for them. These sects vary considerably. Hermit groups – especially of Catholic women – in remote areas of the southern Rhône valley have formed; others belonging to the *'renouveau charismatique'*, who believe that the Holy Spirit manifests itself by signs (for example exorcism, the gift of tongues or of prophecy), are also illustrations of a search for an alternative. Even more so is the growth of Buddhism, officially recognized in France in 1986 and now practised in nearly 200 centres including the largest temple in Europe at Plaige in Burgundy and the influential Kagyu Dzong centre in Paris. While a figure of

150,000 converts to Buddhism may be exaggerated there is no doubt of the religion's growing popularity.

As the end of the twentieth century approaches, France, like all developed European countries, is host to an increasingly racially mixed and complex society, and it seems certain, even within the relatively narrow context of religion, that new pressures from extreme groups will increase. While the abduction and eventual murder by the GIA in the spring of 1996 of seven Trappist monks in Algeria was condemned by the orthodox Moslem church, the growth of Islamic fundamentalism and its politicization are very real. And what the French bishops see as the fragmentation of society in metropolitan France, accelerated by the development of nationalist ideology around Le Pen's *Front national*, has prompted them to speak out. In September 1996, Marcel Herriot, Bishop of Verdun, remarked in a radio broadcast: *'les thèses de Monsieur Le Pen sont absolument et radicalement incompatibles avec l'Evangile de Jésus-Christ'*, a view echoed by the Pope, who referred to them, during his visit the same month, as *'un courant dangereux'*. The Pope also spoke in favour of dialogue with *'compatriotes qui appartiennent à d'autres traditions religieuses ou à d'autres familles d'esprit'* in order to create *'une harmonieuse cohésion de la société française dans son ensemble'*. These messages were repeated at length in the *Lettre aux catholiques de France sur la proposition de la Foi dans la société actuelle*, issued by the episcopal assembly in November 1996. Wholesale approval of such ideas was unlikely, and in the December issue of *Le Chardonnet* Laguérie dismissed the *Lettre* as *'une belle hypocrisie et une minable supercherie'* and instructed his parishioners not to read it. As the political climate increasingly bears upon the religious state of the country, values and perceptions are changing. Whether faith will have any formative role to play on a large scale as the end of the millennium approaches seems unlikely, but there appears little doubt that the need for some kind of spiritual guidance and comfort for young and old alike is being expressed, albeit in a number of different guises.

BIBLIOGRAPHY

General background information for the history of the Catholic Church in France in the early part of the twentieth century will be found in:

Dansette, A., and Rémond, R. (eds), *Histoire du catholicisme en France*, vol. 3. Paris, Spes, 1962.

Rémond, R., *L'Anticléricalisme en France de 1815 à nos jours*. Paris, Fayard, 1976. Good on the period from the Second Vatican Council to the early 1970s.

Chapters in earlier editions of *France Today* provide information on the period from the early 1950s.

Books dealing with specific issues include:

Aziz, P., *Le Paradoxe de Roubaix*. Paris, Plon, 1995. An interesting assessment of some of the problems created by cultural implantation.

Donegani, J-M., *La Liberté de choisir*. Paris, Presses de la Fondation nationale des Sciences politiques, 1994. On the various religious and political groupings within contemporary French Catholicism.

Gaspard, F., and Khosrokhavar, F., *Le Foulard et la République*. Paris, La Découverte, 1995. Wide-ranging in its discussion but somewhat superficial.

Gilson, G., *Les Prêtres*. Paris, Desclée de Brouwer, 1990.

Hazard, M. J. (ed.), *Printemps d'église: aujourd'hui, les laïcs*. Paris, Desclée de Brouwer, 1987. On the resurgence of lay movements.

Kepel, G., *Les Banlieues de l'Islam: naissance d'une religion en France*. Paris, Seuil, 1987.

Mehl, R., *Le Protestantisme français dans la société actuelle*. Paris, Labor et Fides, 1982. Sympathetic and wide-ranging. Deals with internal disputes.

'Religions et société en France'. In *Problèmes politiques et sociaux*, no. 518, September 1985. Paris, La Documentation française. Now dated but an interesting summary of information about all religions and sects.

The following reviews also contain important and interesting material:

L'Actualité religieuse dans le monde, no. 55, 15 April 1988. On the traditionalist movement.

Certitudes, no. 16, April 1995. Integrist in inspiration. Attack on the *diabolisation* of the media. (Service Certitudes, 5 rue de Navarre, 75005 Paris.)

L'Express. On the presence of Islam (19 May 1989); 'Le Besoin de Dieu' (15–21 December 1994) which looks at all aspects of modern developments in France and elsewhere and includes an interview with Eyt.

Les Cahiers de l'Express: 'L'Eglise en question', December 1994. Series of articles, mainly from *L'Express* (1962–94), on all aspects of the Catholic Church, its development and activities.

L'Evénement du jeudi. On the Jewish community (19–25 April 1990); Supplement on *laïcité* (12–18 July 1990).

Le Figaro magazine 'La France de 1995 est-elle encore chrétienne?' (1 April 1995). General survey. Not overly sympathetic to dissident groups. Conservative in tone.

Golias 'Trombinoscopes pour épiscopes' (June–July 1990). Pen portraits of all French bishops; not all of them flattering, some amusing. (*Golias*, four main issues per year, is available from BP 4304, F-69615, Villeurbanne Cedex).

Histoire 'Chrétiens, juifs et musulmans en France' (July–August 1990).

Le Point 'Il existe un bouddhisme français' (4 December 1993).

Le Nouvel Observateur (29 July–4 August 1988). On Lefebvre and the
traditionalist movement.

Télérama 'Comment peut-on être Catholique aujourd'hui?' (no. 2412, 3 April
1996).

The official 'handbook' of the Catholic Church in France is *L'Eglise catholique
en France*. Information–Communication, 106 rue du Bac, 75341, Paris Cedex
07.

8

THE PRESS

Ray Davison

Introduction

Two important pieces of legislation, enacted in the early 1990s, will intensify the economic difficulties facing the French press, as it heads towards the millennium, in what is likely to be an increasingly convergent and competitive Europe. Whatever the arguments about their inherent, respective merits, *la loi Evin* and *la loi Sapin* (*Evin et Sapin* as they now tend to be called) are exerting further downward pressure on the already struggling advertising markets of the French press. Media analysts will certainly want to note that in 1994, for the first time, the press share of the total advertising receipts of the media in general dropped below 50 per cent.

Evin, which came onto the statute books in 1991, in a period of recession, has caused the greater controversy. The law introduces regulations relating to the consumption of alcohol and tobacco in a number of contexts, including, in particular, the domain of advertising and sponsorship. Henceforth, only specialist magazines can advertise tobacco, whilst the advertising of alcohol is subject to restrictions and conditions concerning health warnings, timing and so forth. *Sapin*, introduced two years later in March 1993, seeks to introduce some degree of transparency and equity in the purchasing of advertising space across the media and the country during election campaigns. Newspaper groups must now follow strict rules of practice (or face penalties) when negotiating electoral advertising terms and contracts with their purchasers or clients. They must declare fixed prices and stick to them and have in place proper invoicing and accounting procedures (to avoid clandestine deals). The widespread practice of 'brokering', or using large negotiating agencies, has been terminated by the law, leading to accusations that the free market in advertising space is now severely impeded. Both laws have been the subject of considerable controversy and counter-lobbying, especially *Evin*, and neither can be said to be very secure, given the magnitude of the forces ranged against them.

These laws should not occlude the fact that the period since 1991 has also contained one very bright spot: the birth in 1994, against the odds, of a new Parisian daily or, more precisely, a new Parisian daily seemingly capable of sustained, continuous existence, *InfoMatin*. Unlike its would-be pre-emptive competitor *Le Jour*, which broke, as it were, on 25 March 1993 as an *Ile-de-France* daily, only to set or fade away some eight months later; unlike *Paris 24 hr*, another ill-starred venture from the capital, which lasted only eight weeks, with sales of a mere 6,000 daily, despite its bold intention to displace *InfoMatin*; unlike so many other initiatives of a similar kind (*Le Français*, 25 October 1994 to 6 June 1995 and *La Truffe*, six weeks in 1991, *Aujourd'hui*, launched briefly as a rival to *InfoMatin* on 5 January 1994 by *Le Parisien*), *InfoMatin* appeared to have found itself a niche and an audience in the market. With sales ranging from 60,000 to 80,000, *InfoMatin* seemed, as far as one could tell, to be a solid part of what must be described, for all their fragility and lack of substantial readership, as Paris's impressively diverse range of daily papers. However, early in 1996, because of its failure to increase its sales, *InfoMatin* went into liquidation, and so this latest new Parisian daily went the way of so many others, despite its very auspicious beginning.

All things considered, the French press still faces the challenges of the final years of the decade in a beleaguered state. Pierre Albert, one of France's leading anatomists of the world's and his own country's press, continues to look despondently at the present state of the French press, hesitating between the choice of *'une crise'* or *'une maladie de langueur'* as the more appropriate term to describe it. The note of optimism struck by Jean-Marie Dupont in his widely discussed article in *Le Monde* (28 April 1989) appears not to have been fulfilled and the general consensus among media specialists continues to place the accent on, at best, a kind of stagnant stability, prefacing further decline and even entropy. France is still well down in the world tables of newspapers consumed per thousand inhabitants with, now, a figure of 156 (it was 178 in 1992). Although her position in the tables has marginally improved to 24th in 1995 (from 30th in 1992), despite the continuing fall in consumption, France is still well behind the leaders Norway (610) and Japan (575), first and third respectively, but she is also behind her major European competitors, Switzerland (592), Britain (362) and Germany (335). France does, however, maintain her lead over Italy (113), Spain (105), Greece (83) and Portugal (80).

The scale of this decline in consumption from the turn of the century is dramatic. In 1914, France with the United States headed the world tables with a rate of 344 papers sold per thousand population. It then possessed 80 Parisian dailies producing 5.5 million copies, and 242 provincial dailies with a combined print run of 4 million. By 1988, there were just eleven Parisian and 65 provincial dailies with a combined production of 10 million copies, despite an increased population of 56 million. Today there are just over 70 daily papers with combined sales of under ten million. Because of these figures, the sense that the glorious years are over and that, in the 350-year history of the French press, the golden age has long since vanished, is not the least significant of the problems affecting the industry.

This general pattern of declining titles and circulation since 1914 has, it is true, been interrupted on occasions. The immediate post-Second World War years, 1945–46, which witnessed the vigorous relaunching of the industry, produced a boom in circulation to 15 million and a consumption rate of 370 per thousand for a population of 41 million – there were then 28 Parisian and 175 provincial dailies. However, these figures have not been matched in the years subsequent to 1946 and both titles and circulation have declined annually since that date, although there were intermittent booms between 1962 and 1973; the Events of May 1968 augmented sales to a record post-Second World War level of 13 million. The latest figures record further successive years of declining titles and circulation with total sales now below 10 million (just below 3 million for the national dailies and under 7 million for the regional dailies, excluding the free newspapers).

Such statistics tend to mask the even more dramatic decline of the Parisian daily papers. In 1939, the circulation of the provincial dailies equalled that of the Parisian ones for the first time in the history of the French press (6 million each). By 1945 the figure for the Parisian papers was 4.606 million with 26 titles and for the regional dailies 7.532 million with 153 titles. The latest statistics record 2.741 million and twelve titles for the Parisian dailies (including the specialist ones) and 7.010 million and 62 titles for the provincial ones. The French provincial press has thus outstripped in importance the contracting Parisian dailies and indeed it now controls over 70 per cent of that market. It is the Rennes-based provincial daily *Ouest-France* which is now France's most popular paper and it is the only daily to achieve sales in excess of 500,000 (768,102 in 1995), making it the fifteenth best-selling press publication in France. The preponderance of the regional press over the national dailies can be explained largely by economic reasons. The cost of processing regional news is significantly lower than at the national or international level. Production and distribution costs are much higher in Paris than in the provinces. With over 20 million readers and sales of 6–7 million, the regional press is a big force to be reckoned with in the advertising world and the national dailies find themselves constantly squeezed for advertising revenue by this regional preponderance.

Furthermore, it should not be forgotten that the percentage share of the press market held by daily papers is also declining: for example in 1965, daily papers constituted 57.3 per cent of the total press market. By 1988 the figures had reduced to 41.2 per cent and the latest figures confirm this trend. This is not to overlook the relative strength of the periodical press in France which continues to thrive. Over 90 per cent of French people take some kind of active interest in the French press and the penetration levels are much higher in France than in Germany and Britain. Female readers are a significant force in the periodical press market. The prosperity and dynamism of this section of the French press will be examined later.

This history of decline threatens pluralism and diversity in a country which has been anxious, particularly since 1945, to restrict both press monopoly and over-concentration of press ownership, especially in the area of the dailies. The latest issue of *Francoscopie* estimates that, within the last ten years, the number of readers of a daily newspaper in France has dropped by a massive 25 per cent. Although there is some evidence that the proportion of readers of a daily paper is stabilizing, the actual number of regular daily readers is still in decline. One in four households buys a daily paper in France, compared to one in two in England, but only one person in ten reads a national daily in France. Regular readers have a definite profile (they are 60 per cent male, 47 per cent resident in Paris – where only 19 per cent of the population lives – 38 per cent highly educated and they are predominantly in the 40–50 age group). The average French reader spends 36 minutes reading the paper (and 3 hours 39 minutes watching the television). French media critics have created the term *'démassification'* to describe the phenomenon whereby French newspaper readers seem to be becoming more and more interested in local diversification and specialist material when it comes to their press reading.

Explanations for these falling circulation figures and the declining range of titles, especially in the vital area of the national dailies, are plentiful among media specialists but not always convergent. They range from the rudimentary to the sophisticated. For example, some commentators point to the high cost of French newspapers in the post-war period and regret the absence in France of the cheaper tabloids available in Britain (they do not appear to regret the absence of the particular modes of journalism practised by such tabloids). Admittedly, since 1975, the price of French daily papers, which until 1982 was fixed by the government, has increased at twice the rate of the general cost of living, whilst the percentage of the French family budget allocated to newspapers has remained static. In 1996, a

Parisian daily costs between 5 and 7 francs (*InfoMatin* was exceptionally low-priced at 3.80 francs). The regional dailies are cheaper (about 4 to 4.50 francs) and their circulation has not declined so much. However, it is interesting to note that, despite price deregulation in 1982, there has been no attempt at a price war.

More sophisticated explanations tend to concentrate on the history of the French press and its complacent relationship with French political life in the inter-war years and especially during the period of the Vichy regime and collaboration. According to this thesis, daily papers, and notably the Parisian dailies, became publicly discredited through collusion with the bankrupt politics of the Third Republic and the Nazi propaganda machine. Cut off from Paris, the regional dailies were spared some of this opprobrium and have not declined to the same extent. Such an explanation may have some cogency for it is certainly true that the French do not appear to like or to trust their journalists very much at all; surveys frequently point out that the French distrust what they read in the papers and that they treat the whole press medium with touching suspicion. Yet it is also true that the French distrust the written word much less than the language of radio or television journalists who are nevertheless absorbing a growing proportion of the leisure time activities of the French, compared to the journalists on the daily papers.

While no clear or single explanation exists, it may be possible to define further the features of this undoubted decline and to comment more precisely upon its possible causes. For this purpose an overall analysis of the main characteristics of the press as an industry in France today, together with a profile of its general daily and periodical production, is necessary.

THE FRENCH PRESS AS AN INDUSTRY

The economic and industrial situation of the French press embodies areas of weakness which may offer some parallel explanation of the decline of circulation and titles. The press had a turnover in France of 60,000 million francs in 1995, well behind Britain and Germany. This figure represents about 1 per cent of PIB (GDP) and makes the press industry between the twelfth and seventeenth largest sector of the French economy.

It has been argued, perhaps paradoxically, that the relative weakness of the French press industry's financial base compared to, say, Britain and Germany is linked to the many direct and indirect state subventions to the industry. France protects its newspaper industry more generously than any other European country apart from Italy. State subventions, amounting to some 12 per cent of the industry's turnover, were designed along with a whole series of judicial regulations in 1945 to resist the tendency to economic concentration and monopoly and thus to protect pluralism and diversity of informational viewpoints. With the general movement of capital concentration in Europe in the post-war period and especially over the last fifteen years, the industrial and financial base of the French press has perhaps found itself weakened by such protectionist policies, and thus outstripped on the capital front by more powerful European conglomerates. For example, the turnover of the German Bertelsmann group has frequently equalled, over the last few years, the total turnover of the French press. Such an argument is often linked to another factor tending to check development of concentration: the previously mentioned relative strength of France's regional newspapers. Paris simply does not dominate France in terms of papers in the same way that London dominates Britain, and the emergence of large powerful groupings may well have been further checked by this fact. With European and global competition for markets intensifying all the time, the diminutive stature, in relative terms, of the top French press financial groupings will certainly put the industry's growth at a disadvantage. Slowness in both modernization and diversification is also adding to the industry's problems as is the historical separation of the various components of the media industry, preventing the rapid rise of multi-media conglomerates.

Be that as it may, the French press currently employs more than 150,000 people, almost half of them journalists. The numerical strength of the journalistic staff has actually increased by 50 per cent over every decade of the post-war period and the largest growth area has been the increasing number of female journalists in the profession. The development of television and radio has also provided the industry with a rising number of cross-media journalists. The industry now generates some 3,000 publications, providing 8.25 million copies, of which some 7.03 million are sold. The rather large margin of unsold copies in France is linked to distribution problems, for household deliveries and subscriptions are relatively undeveloped compared to sales at kiosks.

A further important dimension of the industry is its paper consumption. It uses 1.3 million tons of paper annually, France being twelfth in the world tables of paper consumed per inhabitant for press purposes. Sixty-four per cent of the paper for newspapers is imported and 45 per cent is magazine-quality paper.

The profit margins of the French press generally are also depressed relative to the larger European groups. Worker–management relations, the already cited slowness in adapting to technical advances, rigidity of practice in production leading to increased costs are among the reasons most often given to explain this low level of profitability.

A kiosk does brisk trade in Aix-en-Provence

Such phenomena render the French industry increasingly vulnerable to competitive advances from Britain and Germany after Maastricht. A single European currency and the convergence criteria which will preface its implementation will further exacerbate the industrial problems of the French press.

If under-capitalization and depressed profit margins have obstructed the growth of the French press industry, developments in the advertising world have also contributed to its enfeebled state. Although the advertising market in France, as in many places in the world, is expanding – indeed its rate of expansion is faster than in other countries – this is because the present size of the industry itself is quite small. France in 1995 devoted only 1.25 per cent of GDP to the advertising industry compared, for example, with the United States' 2.4 per cent and Finland's 1.7 per cent. Advertising expenditure per head of population was 81 US dollars, placing France fourteenth in the world (the United States is naturally in first place with 424 US dollars per head and Britain ninth with 145 US dollars per head). In terms of the world market in advertising, France has a 4 per cent share (the United States has over 50 per cent, Europe generally 25 per cent). Competition for advertising revenue in France tends to be extremely fierce because of the restricted scale of the market in general. At the same time, however, the French press is becoming increasingly reliant on advertising revenue, as opposed to sales, for its viability. In 1975, for example, 36.8 per cent of its revenue came from advertising; by 1988 this had risen to 43.2 per cent and, by the 1990s, to 46 per cent (this should be compared to the figures of 70 per cent in the United States and 65 per cent in Britain). Simultaneously, however, the market share of advertising revenue held by the press has been falling, partly because of declining sales, partly because of the growing stake of television in the advertising world since deregulation in 1981. In 1967, 78.8 per cent of advertising expenditure in France was directed at the written press with 15 per cent going to radio and 3.5 per cent to television. By 1987, the television share had risen to 22 per cent whilst the press received 57 per cent and radio 7.5 per cent. In 1995, the television share had risen to 32.4 per cent while the press share was down to 48.1 per cent. Of course, everywhere in Europe television is making inroads into the advertising revenue market, although the rate of progress is by no means as swift as many anticipated. Nevertheless, in the last thirty years the French press has lost some 20 per cent of its advertising market whilst in Switzerland, the Netherlands and Germany the press maintains much higher shares of the market (between 69 and 75 per cent).

This decline in advertising revenue is particularly marked in respect of the daily press, which has seen its share dwindle from 30.5 per cent in 1975 to 20 per cent in 1992, whilst in the same period the periodical press share has remained stable. The growth of *la presse gratuite* since 1960 and the erosion of the small ads market by the ever-expanding number of *Minitel* terminals have also added to the financial difficulties of the big dailies in terms of advertising revenue.

The press industry today is largely composed of fourteen groups whose annual turnover exceeds 1,000 million francs. The main group is Hachette Filipacchi Presse (it absorbed the Groupe Filipacchi in 1993 and moved to new headquarters in Levallois in June 1994). The group was founded in 1829 as a publishing business. Its annual turnover has augmented from 7.8 thousand million francs in 1981 to 30,000 million francs in 1994, some two-fifths of this increase coming from expansion abroad. This is a multi-media consortium which in 1986 made an unsuccessful bid for TF1. About a third of its activities relate to the press proper. It has a one-third stake in the Parisian daily, *Le Parisien*, and controls the provincial dailies, *Dernières Nouvelles d'Alsace*, *Le Provençal* and *L'Echo républicain*. It also owns nine weeklies, including the Sunday papers *France-Dimanche* and *Le Journal du Dimanche*, as well as the very popular *Télé 7 jours*, *TV hebdo*, *Elle*, *Ici Paris* and *Le Journal de Mickey*. Sixteen monthly magazines are also under the group's control including *Max*, *Onze*, *Parents*, *Vitae*, *Fortune* and *Première*. It was this group which envisaged launching a new national daily in the 1980s, but it abandoned the project in 1987. Fearful of *InfoMatin*, the group tried to pre-empt its launch with a new daily, *Aujourd'hui*, but, as we have seen, it did not last long.

The second largest group is the Groupe Hersant, controlling some 22 per cent of the regional and 33 per cent of the Parisian dailies and with an estimated turnover in 1995 of over 12,000 million francs. The group was established in 1950 with *L'Auto journal*. From this small beginning the group has grown spectacularly by taking stakes first in the regional press (*Le Havre libre*, *La Liberté du Morbihan*, *L'Eclair* and finally, in 1972, *Paris-Normandie*). Then, in the 1970s, the group took control of *Le Figaro* (1975), *France-Soir* (from Hachette in 1976) and *L'Aurore* (1978, and absorbed by *Le Figaro* in 1979). This sudden expansion of the group in the 1970s led to the accusation in 1978 that it had breached the Liberation monopoly laws but nothing came of the case against it. In 1983 the group expanded again, taking control of *Le Dauphiné libéré* and *Le Progrès de Lyon* in 1985 and *L'Union de Reims* in 1986. The laws of 15 August and 27 November 1986 prohibited a single press group from controlling more than 30 per cent of total circulation, so the group's further expansion cannot be so spectacular. However, it did purchase from Hachette in 1992 the regional dailies *Le Maine libre*, *Le Courrier de l'Ouest* and *Liberté Dimanche*. Hersant controls some twelve magazines including *Le Figaro magazine* and the French racing weekly *Paris-Turf*. Hersant too, like Hachette, has talked of launching a new daily, *Paris-Star*, but it has not yet twinkled.

Other large groupings with some of their better known titles include:

- Editions Mondiales (turnover 4,500 million francs): *TéléPoche*, *Intimité*, *Nous deux*, *Bonnes soirées*, *Caméra vidéo*, *Auto-plus*
- Ouest-France (turnover 1,333 million francs) controls the regional daily *Ouest-France*, France's best-selling paper, *La Presse de la Manche*, and the large group of free papers called 'Le Carrilon'.
- CEP Communication (turnover 2,720 million francs). Created in 1988, this group controls some 70 specialist publications and also owns *L'Express*, *Lire* and *Biba*.
- Prisma Presse (turnover 2,670 million francs) is the French arm of the German group, Grüner und Jahr, and its titles include some of the most popular magazines such as *Géo*, *Télé-loisirs*, *Femme actuelle* and *Cuisine nouvelles*.
- Editions Amaury (turnover 2,100 million francs) controls *Le Parisien*.
- Bayard-Presse (turnover 2,014 million francs) owns the Catholic papers *La Croix*, *Le Pèlerin magazine* and a whole range of periodical titles.

Two smaller but self-evidently important groupings should also be mentioned: the Groupe de presses communistes and the Groupe Le

Monde. The Groupe de presses communistes is directly controlled by the French Communist Party and is responsible for the three communist dailies *L'Humanité*, *L'Echo du Centre* (Limoges) and *La Marseillaise*; it also owns the weeklies *L'Humanité-Dimanche Liberté* (Lille), previously a daily, *La Terre* and *Regards*, the new weekly which has replaced *Révolution*, which closed down in March 1995, and numerous other locally based militant papers. The Groupe Le Monde produces *Le Monde*, *Le Monde de l'éducation*, *Le Monde diplomatique*, *Le Monde des philatélistes*, *Le Monde des débats* and *Sélection hebdomadaire* and many other satellite publications which are coming under the axe of the new editor (see below). Such groupings, as already indicated, are not on the scale of their German and British counterparts but that does not reduce the ferocity of the competition for market share in all domains. New titles, especially in the magazine press, come and quite often go and shifting arrangements and alliances between groups make their precise description uncertain. It should be said that the growth rates of these larger groupings seem sound and healthy, notwithstanding the problems outlined above. However, the relationship between capital infrastructure and a varied and reliable news service is never far from the minds of press analysts who fear that further contractions of pluralism will result from inter-group competition.

This press profile would not be complete without mentioning that the development of large capital groupings has also created the conditions for the growth of a multitude of press agencies in France. Despite the increasing numbers of journalists, the actual gathering and supplying of news is more and more channelled through agency services, again leading to fears of excessive uniformity and repetition in the selection and presentation of news items. The use of specialist foreign correspondence in international news reporting is declining (*Le Monde* is a notable exception to this and the benefits are all too evident in the brilliance of detail and penetration of its foreign coverage). The international agencies, Associated Press, Reuters, Tass and the French-based *Agence France Presse* (created in 1945 as the successor to *Agence Havas*, the first international news agency established in France in 1832) are increasingly strengthening their grip on world news information processing. National and local news coverage, however, is also rapidly being sucked into agency systems, undermining the role of locally based individual reporters. At the last count there were some hundred such agencies. News as an industry in the intensely competitive capital markets is running the risk of becoming a processed and packaged commodity. Thus pluralism and diversity are threatened not just in terms of the shrinking number of titles but also in terms of the systems of news dissemination which are growing up as a response to economic developments. This does not augur well for the French press as it confronts the problem of loss of readership.

A SURVEY OF THE FRENCH PRESS

This survey will concentrate on three key areas: the Parisian dailies, the regional dailies and the periodical press.

The Parisian dailies

There are now just ten general daily newspapers which are Paris-based, together with one specialist sporting daily, *L'Equipe*, one racing daily, *Paris-Turf*, and two specialist financial dailies, *Les Echos* and *La Tribune Desfossés* (the result of an amalgamation of *La Tribune de l'expansion* and *La Cote Desfossés* in 1992. *Le Temps de la finance* has ceased publication since the last survey in 1993). The combined circulation of the Parisian dailies is now just under 3 million and it has declined yearly since the peak post-war figure in 1968 of just over 5 million. A substantial proportion of all sales is in the Paris region which, curiously, has the least active readership levels of all the regions of France. Many titles have disappeared: *Le Quotidien du peuple*, launched in 1975, ceased publication in 1980. *Rouge* lasted only three years and was withdrawn in 1979. *J'informe*, a centre-right daily, appeared for just a few months in 1977. A similar fate was reserved for *Combat socialiste*, 1981, *Paris ce soir*, 1984, *Forum international*, 1980 (a financial daily) and *Le Sport*, 1988. Three of the most important casualties were the popular *Paris-Presse* in 1970, *Paris-Jour* in 1972 and, of course, *L'Aurore* in 1980. With the falling sales of *France-Soir* since 1967, it is the *Parisien libéré*, now called *Le Parisien*, which strives to be France's most popular daily. The paper experienced industrial and disputed-ownership problems in the late 1970s during its modernization programme. It has now re-established itself as a centre to centre-left paper with a circulation of 400,000, making it the second largest-selling paper in France.

▼ Le Figaro

This is France's oldest daily newspaper. It was founded in 1826, became a daily in 1866 and calls itself *'le premier quotidien national français'*, although over 50 per cent of its sales are in the Paris area. It has a circulation of over 400,000 and, since 1975, has been the flagship of the Groupe Hersant. Its finances are relatively healthy – its economic strength derives partly from its successful weekend supplements, *Le Figaro magazine*, *Madame Figaro* and *TV magazine*, totalling some 500 pages and sold as a package for 20 francs on a Sunday. *Le Figaro* is printed in the larger format and includes three other supplements: *Le Figaro économie* (daily), *Figaroscope* (Wednesday) and *Le Figaro littéraire* (Monday). It is basically a conservative paper, which savaged the French socialist President over the *Rainbow Warrier*, immigration policy and law and order issues. During the Mitterrand/Chirac period of *'cohabitation'* in the late 1980s, the paper responded in a very supinely conservative way in support of Chirac's government. After Mitterrand's re-election in 1988, it somewhat softened its opposition to the socialists and to government policy. Since then the paper has taken a broad approach to political analysis, confining its more conservative and, some would say, simplistic voice to a single and sometimes amusing page called *Opinion*. Under its new editor, Oliver Giesbert, transferred from *Le Nouvel Observateur*, the paper increasingly resembles the British *Daily Telegraph* or the American publication, the *Herald Tribune*. Its economic pages are readable and informative, as is its literary supplement, and the paper certainly appeals to the French people's sense of their own pragmatism. *Le Figaro* is probably not quite as good as it was under its post-war editor, Pierre Brisson, who died in 1964. Nevertheless, it is a quality paper with a touch of cultural distinction which speaks for the right-wing intelligentsia of France. *Le Figaro* also strives to be useful by providing sources of practical information in its well-documented *'pages pratiques'* and its jobs and holiday advertisements. As it approaches the millennium, *Le Figaro* aims to be the voice of the modern, pragmatic France and its leading non-class-based family paper.

▼ Le Parisien (libéré)

This is the only French newspaper which remotely resembles a popular national daily. It was founded in 1945, and by 1975 its circulation of 785,000 made it France's leading daily. Its long-time owner, Emilien Amaury, killed in a riding accident in 1977, had built up the paper on strong anti-communist lines and engaged it in continuous populist and sensationalist polemics against immigrants, delinquents and left-wing activists. It repeatedly called for the reintroduction of the death penalty. It never wished, however, to sink to the level of the *Sun*, nor did it adopt the tabloid format. A long industrial dispute, including an all-out strike between 1975 and 1977 over Amaury's decision to modernize the paper's production methods, led to a boycott by distributors, and this halved its circulation. Neither were the paper's finances helped by family squabbles about political direction after Amaury's death. Finally, Hachette took a 50 per cent stake in the paper in 1983 and helped resolve the difficulties. Since then, sales have increased to 405,000 in 1989, and it has a target figure of half a million. The paper introduced colour in 1985 and dropped *'libéré'* from its title in 1986. Paradoxically, *Le Parisien* has become increasingly liberal since that date and tries now to be informative and balanced, although it is still a right-wing paper. It does not offer in-depth analysis but specializes in short, punchy reporting aimed at swift readability. It is abundantly illustrated, uses quite a lot of cartoons and graphics and has the sort of sporting, games and advice pages associated with the popular press. Since 1989, the paper has strengthened its position and created regional editions helping it to 'deparisianize' its identity as the daily of Paris. The paper tried unsuccessfully to kill off *InfoMatin* before its launch with the short-lived *Aujourd'hui* in January 1994.

▼ Le Monde

Arguably the best newspaper in the world, *Le Monde* impresses by the range and depth of its news coverage, by the brilliance of its foreign affairs columns and the intelligence of its approach to reliable and informed journalism. It achieved circulation figures of 362,048 and 302,203 in 1993 and 1994 from 110,000 in 1946 and 200,000 in 1957. It manages a high level of sales abroad (17.09 per cent compared with 3.68 per cent for *Le Figaro*). Its coverage of developments in the Soviet Union was in a class of its own and the paper generally lives up to its name by providing insights into political realities which sometimes challenge the reader's grasp of geography. Regular exposure to the paper's concentrated text, until recently unadorned by any diverting photographs or graphics, would ensure a well-informed and comprehensive grasp of world political events. However, *Le Monde* with its *'belle écriture'* is an austere paper, not meant for the faint-hearted, and swift readability is not one of its attributes.

Le Monde first appeared on 18 December 1944 and saw itself as the successor to the pre-war daily, *Le Temps* (1861–1942). Its founder and editor until 1969 was Hubert Beuve–Méry, who had worked for *Le Temps* and had a distinguished record in the Resistance movement. Politically the paper is centre-left: in the 1950s it supported Mendès-France, questioned the return to power of de Gaulle and condemned torture in Algeria. In 1974 and 1981, the paper backed the Mitterrand presidential campaigns, and it also celebrated the liberation of South Vietnam. The paper was widely read by young students during May 1968 and it maintains an enlightened and progressive line on matters relating to world famine, debt and conservation, thus guaranteeing it a continuing audience among educated youth. Its independence of judgment and depth of analysis often give its journalists considerable influence over economic and political affairs, causing displeasure to professional politicians on all sides. *Le Monde* sometimes trebles its circulation to over a million when important matters are under debate in France (it did so during the second round of the last presidential election), and the opinions of its political analyst are deservedly well respected.

Over the last ten years *Le Monde* has had to face the challenges of modernization, European-scale competition and finding a replacement for Beuve-Méry – editors are elected by the journalists themselves at *Le Monde*. The retirement of Jaques Fauvet in 1982 (Méry's successor) brought financial difficulties which the new editor, André Fontaine, had to address with his famous rescue package in 1985. This involved selling the paper's premises in the rue des Italiens and restructuring its capital base with a novel organizational format and increased outside shareholdings. Its total market value is divided into 1,240 share parts distributed among the founders' group, the journalists' trust, a new readers' trust, a management trust and a white-and-blue-collar workers' trust. *Le Monde entreprise*, set up in 1985 to promote the paper, is also a shareholder.

The paper has now put most of its difficulties behind it. It has a new headquarters in the rue Falguière, a new modern printworks at Ivry and is fully equipped with new technology. It faces the future with considerable confidence, aiming to be the fourth strongest French daily after *Ouest-France*, *Le Figaro* and *Le Parisien*. André Fontaine left the paper in 1991, creating another editorial and financial crisis. Jacques Lesourne briefly tried to steer the paper out of trouble but it was its present editor, Jean-Marie Colombani, who, in 1994, put the paper back to its formidable best, although it has abandoned some of its supplements in favour of a weekly magazine. *Le Monde* does justice to the complexity of events, providing consistent informed coverage of European affairs. There is also *Le Monde hebdomaire*, a selection of articles designed for the overseas market, published in French and English.

▼ **France-Soir**

Under the editorship of Pierre Lazareff, this was once France's strongest daily paper, achieving high circulation levels in the 1950s and 1960s. Its slogan, *'Faites comme tout le monde, lisez France-Soir'*, underlined its aspiration to be a readable, somewhat dramatic popular daily. It is now part of the Groupe Hersant but still faces an uncertain future. Although one of Paris's big dailies in terms of circulation (213,000 in 1994), its readership is seemingly set in irreversible decline. The paper is also in deficit. Its political affiliations are still insistently conservative, although its political coverage has generally been reduced. It delights in eye-catching scoop headlines involving scandals, frauds or national disasters and, since 1988, it has appeared with front-page colour. It is now really a morning newspaper (there is some talk of changing its title to *France-Matin*).

France-Soir appears to have lost its circulation battle with *Le Parisien* and *Libération* which are eclipsing it in the use of *faits divers*. It does have the advantage of swift readability: the latest estimate of average reading time is three minutes. *France-Soir* was founded after the Liberation in 1944 and was successor to the Resistance journal, *Défense de la France*. Since July 1994, Hersant has directly managed the paper himself after entrusting it, for a short while, to his son. This is unlikely to prevent its sale.

▼ Libération

Established, with the help of Jean-Paul Sartre, in 1973, as a political left-wing daily, part-successor to the Maoist *La Cause du peuple*, *Libération* was split by internal divisions in 1981 and ceased publication in February that year. It reappeared in May 1981, under the editorship of Serge July, with a much more moderate but basically left political stance. Its circulation then grew from 70,000 to 165,000 in 1986, and 180,000 in 1989, but is now down to 173,000. The paper is now a long way from its roots in 1968 student sensibility and from its preoccupation with left-wing intellectual and ideological issues. In the 1980s, it established itself as a quality paper with a serious and professional approach to analysis of political, cultural and international events. It maintained a degree of non-conformism and freshness in its reporting, and its leader-writers were always interesting. More recently, the paper has appeared to lose some of its vitality and to be unable to adapt to historical change. Despite attempts to create regional editions and to relaunch itself as the citizen's paper of France, the paper is vulnerable to *InfoMatin* and may have to alter its format to survive.

▼ InfoMatin

Launched on 10 January 1994, this was the first Parisian daily over the last two decades to make a successful entry into the market. Despite the ill-starred pre-emptive strike by competitors with *Le Jour* and abortive destabilizing missiles after its launch from *Paris 24 hr* and *Aujourd'hui* (see earlier comments), *InfoMatin* survived with a circulation of about 80,000 and a low price of 3.80 francs. The paper had the smallest format of all the dailies, measuring a mere 235 by 320 millimetres, making it suitable for easy reading on public transport. It offered a 20–24-page concise synopsis of the news with plenty of colour and photographs to accompany it. The second page of the paper *'Arrêt sur images'* focused attention on an important historical event (such as Hiroshima in the 7 August 1995 edition) by the use of photograph with accompanying statement. News items followed under a variety of headings, embracing both national and international events. There was a regular *'Espace du lecteur'* for letters, comic strips, television and sports pages. The emphasis was on brevity, diversity and liveliness. The paper was practical, readable and informative and should have presented a challenge to the less skeletally verbal of its rivals. Unfortunately it was not to be.

▼ L'Humanité

Established by Jean Jaurès in 1904 as the paper of the Section française de l'internationale ouvrière (SFIO), *L'Humanité* was the first French newspaper of the socialist movement and of the working class. It quickly established itself as a paper of working-class militancy and peace. Since 1920, it has been the organ of the Parti communiste française (PCF). Between 1939, when it was banned, and 1944, the paper operated clandestinely. It reached a peak circulation in 1946 with a readership of 400,000. Between then and now its circulation has declined regularly to below 100,000 with 14 per cent of its sales abroad. Its annual losses are covered by receipts from the world-famous *fête annuelle de l'Huma*. It has repeatedly embarked on modernization strategies to check falling sales. It became a tabloid in 1985 and acquired new headquarters in the Parisian suburb of Saint-Denis in 1989. The paper is designed to arm party members all over France with the ideologies and political weapons which they need and to brief them on official party policy lines. Developments in the former Soviet Union have put severe pressure on its ideological perspectives and the future of the party itself is the subject of much recent debate. Always interesting and always doctrinaire, *L'Humanité* gave exceptional coverage to South Africa and to Nelson Mandela. Its cultural pages are among the best available in the daily press. Since 1993, the paper has been exposing very powerfully the impact of social cuts caused by free-market ideology and its circulation has begun to rise again.

▼ La Croix

Another Parisian daily with a circulation of just over 100,000 is *La Croix*, a Catholic evening paper founded in 1883. Its readers pay mainly by subscription (some 80 per cent) and four-fifths of them live in the provinces. It is the only national Catholic daily and is part of the leading religious press group, Bayard Presse. It enjoys a reputation for serious, reliable and concise journalism and has a discreet mission to promote Christian values. It has a good letters page and often pursues detailed debates on current political issues. It, naturally, also has a profound interest in matters of personal freedom concerning abortion and contraception, although it is arguably too close to the Vatican for modern French tastes. The paper's sales are declining and it is in deficit, subsidized by Bayard Presse's other more successful publications.

▼ Le Quotidien

Born in 1974 as *Le Quotidien de Paris*, with two-thirds of its editorial team former journalists on *Combat*, *Le Quotidien* is now a struggling anti-socialist paper with a small circulation of some 50,000. The paper changed its format and title in March 1994 and reduced its selling price from 6 to 4 francs. It then ceased publication in September 1994 and reappeared with new financial backing in 1995. It has appeared irregularly since then and its future is unclear.

▼ Other Parisian newspapers

The remaining Parisian dailies are all specialist papers. *Présent* is an ultra right-wing Catholic daily appearing five times a week. It operated, until recently, on a subscription-only basis but, under the slogan *'Dieu, famille, patrie'*, it is beginning to appear in the newsagents. Its present circulation is about 50,000. *L'Equipe* is the leading sporting paper of France. It has an 87.57 per cent male readership and a circulation of some 300,000, 40 per cent of it in the Paris region. *Paris-Turf*, the racing daily, sells about 126,000 copies. The specialist economic dailies – *Les Echos, le quotidien de l'économie*, founded in 1908, and *La Tribune Desfossés*, have circulation figures of 99,700 and 70,000 respectively. No specialist economic paper in France yet matches the British *Financial Times* with its circulation of almost 300,000. The Pearson group, which owns the *Financial Times*, acquired *Les Echos* in 1988 and it has now established itself as the best financial daily in France. *Impact Médecin* (established 1991, circulation 60,000) and *Quotidien du médecin* (90,000) are the medical dailies of France.

The regional dailies

The regional daily papers of France are generally prosperous and much stronger than their Parisian equivalents. Modernization programmes have advanced quite swiftly and the whole regional industry has a certain all-pervasive dynamism. Until 1939 when, with a combined copy total of 6 million, it equalled the production of the Parisian press, the regional press was treated with some contempt and as inferior-level journalism by the French intelligentsia. The regional press now accounts for some 70 per cent of the market in dailies, where its supremacy is unchallengeable, selling nearly 7 million copies daily compared to sales of just under 3 million for the national dailies. Since 1976 it has been the regional daily *Ouest-France* which has been France's best-selling daily paper (at the time, it toppled *France-Soir*). Most of the regional dailies have different editions according to their distribution zones, and at present the regional dailies generate some 400 different editions in about 250 different localities. In 1914, there were 242 regional dailies, in 1946 175 and in 1996 just 62. Even though globally its readership is declining, with an estimated audience still of some 20 million people, the regional press can compete well with television for advertising receipts. The free press, with a combined run in 1995 of some 18,000 million, now takes 20 per cent of the advertising revenue of the press. Nowadays, 75 per cent of the free papers are controlled, directly or indirectly, by *la presse payante*. The largest free press groups, in order of importance, are: Comareg (Havas), Spir Communication (90 per cent owned by *Ouest-France*), S3G (Groupe Sud-Ouest), Groupe Hersant (8 per cent of the free press) and Hachette Filipacchi Presse.

The greatest strength of the regional dailies is, of course, their local news component, which takes up some 50 per cent of their space. French people read their local papers seriously and with greater commitment and continuity than the national ones. The regional dailies in general tend to avoid precise political affiliations, even during election periods. They try to balance their coverage of the different political groupings or attempt to avoid politicizing issues altogether. Where a paper has a monopoly or quasi-monopoly, political neutrality is seen as essential to secure the continuing loyalty of all readers.

Space does not allow for detailed examination of all the regional dailies but a synoptic view of the principal ones in each region follows. The geographical areas listed take into account the spheres of interest of the various papers.

▼ Northern region (Pas de Calais, Somme, Aisne, Oise Nord)

With the switch of the PCF daily *Liberté* to a weekly and the swallowing up of *Nord Matin* by *Nord-Eclair* and of *Nord Littoral* by *La Voix du Nord*, this area now possesses only two dailies, *La Voix du Nord* and *Nord-Eclair*. *La Voix du Nord* (346,343 copies) is in a crushing position of domination and could eventually achieve monopoly status. It is one of the best-selling French daily papers. Politically of moderate right-wing persuasion, the paper also gives good space to rival parties. Its Saturday editions consist of plentiful advertising and minimum editorial content. It set up, in the late 1980s, *La Voix de l'Aisne* to avoid the charge of being too Lille-based. The paper is tightening its grip on the area with investment in a radio station, *RVN*, and in *Nortel*. It has a rising turnover and a much weaker rival in the Hersant-based *Nord-Eclair* (91,390 copies), a left-leaning paper selling in both France and Belgium and having the best home-delivery service of any French newspaper.

▼ Normandy (Manche, Calvados, Orne, Eure)

Paris Normandie (102,436 copies), established in 1944 and now the flagship, in this area, of the Groupe Hersant, runs twelve different editions from its base in Rouen. Some of its pages are the same as other regional dailies from the Groupe Hersant in the area, such as the politically moderate *Le Havre presse* (15,445 copies) and the left-inclined *Le Havre libre* (23,743 copies). *La Presse de la Manche* (26,000 copies), now controlled by *Ouest-France*, operates in Cherbourg and *L'Echo républicain* (32,000 copies), 40 per cent owned by Hachette Filipacchi Presse, in Chartres. The circulation of regional dailies in this area is depressed by a very strong and flourishing weekly press involving some 30 titles.

▼ **Brittany**

This is the home of the Rennes-based *Ouest-France*, sometimes described as *'le plus impressionnant menhir de la presse quotidienne française'*. It was founded in 1944 and, since 1975, is France's leading daily with a circulation of some 790,133 in 1994. It produces 38 local editions. It has quite strong sections on farming and fishing and fairly lengthy sports pages. Political news is concisely and responsibly presented. The paper is the successor of the 1899 Catholic paper, *L'Ouest-Eclair*, launched at the time of the Dreyfus appeal hearing. *Ouest-France* does not yet have a monopoly. The Morlaix-based *Le Télégramme de Brest et de l'Ouest* (187,641 copies), dominant in the department of Finistère, is an independent paper which used to be radical socialist but is now rather *'chiraquien'*; *Liberté du Morbihan* (7,011 copies, Groupe Hersant) operates in Lorient, whilst *Presse océan* (78,000 copies) and *L'Eclair* (12,524 copies), both owned by Groupe Hersant, share the market in Nantes and are virtually the same paper nowadays.

▼ **Eastern region (Alsace-Lorraine)**

The regional dailies in this area are all bilingual (written in French and German) and benefit from a very well-developed home-delivery service, although their circulation is declining. They appear on Sundays but not Mondays and have very extensive coverage of economic matters. *L'Alsace* (117,200 copies) is a bulky but excellent 40–48 page paper with a good strong team of journalists. It has operated since 1944 and has a high level of penetration in a restricted area (some 70 per cent of households). *Dernières Nouvelles d'Alsace* (211,419 copies) was part of the Hachette group but has been with Groupe Hersant since 1993. It dominates in the *Haut* and *Bas Rhin* with some 28 editions. This is a good quality daily enjoying a peace treaty with *L'Alsace*. The Catholic daily, *Le Nouvel Alsacien*, collapsed in 1988. *L'Est républicain* (214,965 copies) produces a Sunday edition with a very high level of sales (350,000 copies). Its regional news coverage is excellent but its national reporting is sketchy. It competes in Lorraine with the Metz-based *Le Républicain lorrain* (183,835 copies) which partly owns it.

The other dailies in the region are: *La Liberté de l'Est* (29,682 copies), which produces four editions, appears every day of the week and is firmly on the left; *L'Est-Eclair* (30,096 copies), based in Troyes; *La Haute-Marne libérée* (15,065 copies), which operates on a subscription basis (72 per cent) and has its own radio station; *Libération Champagne* (10,939 copies), a socialist paper; *L'Union* (134,275 copies), part of the Groupe Hersant since 1988 and dominant in Champagne; *L'Ardennais* (15,000 copies), originally a socialist paper but now politically neutral if not neutered, also under the Groupe Hersant.

▼ **South west**

In Aquitaine, the Sud-Ouest group virtually has a monopoly in the five departments. As well as producing the Bordeaux-based *Sud-Ouest* (349,544 copies), the third strongest of the regional dailies, the group controls the radical socialist *La Charente libre*, (38,733 copies), the Périgueux daily *La Dordogne libre* (5,136 copies), the cheapest of all the dailies at 2.70 francs, and very readable with it, *Sud-Ouest la France*, known since 1992 as *La Charente Maritime* (11,500 copies), *La République des Pyrénées* (28,496 copies) and *L'Eclair des Pyrénées*. *Sud-Ouest* itself averages about 30 pages with little or no colour. It is clearly written, readable and a reasonably good paper. It has twenty local editions and also produces a Sunday edition *Sud-Ouest Dimanche* as well as the *Dossiers du quotidien*, special numbers treating in detail regional issues such as the tourist industry in Aquitaine. The group has had a fair amount of industrial problems of late with the Confédération générale du travail (CGT).

▼ **Midi, Pyrénées, Languedoc**

Two dailies compete for readers – the radical and dominant *La Dépêche du Midi* (213,500 copies) based in Toulouse and the free paper *Le Journal de Toulouse* (45,800 copies). *La Dépêche du Midi* specializes in sharply focused interventions into local political debates and has a loyal readership because of this. The paper has a controlling interest in *La Nouvelle République des Pyrénées* (15,617 copies) and a 40 per cent stake in *Le Petit bleu de l'Agenais* (12,408 copies). The popular but somewhat ailing *Midi-Libre* (207,508 copies) dominates the five departments of Languedoc–Roussillon and it appears to have beaten off a challenge from *Nîmes-Matin*, launched in 1989 by Hachette as a centre-right daily but now defunct. *Midi-Libre* also now owns *L'Indépendant* (70,000 copies), one of the oldest French regional papers, founded in Perpignan in 1846.

▼ **South east**

The Marseille-based papers dominate in the Alpes de Haute-Provence, Vaucluse and Var. *Le Provençal* (144,962 copies) is the paper previously owned by the socialist, Gaston Deferre, who died in 1986. It is now part of the Hachette group and is a long way from its political roots. The paper produces an evening edition, *Le Soir* (11,572 copies) and a satellite *Var matin* (72,502 copies) in Toulon. *La Marseillaise* (139,000 copies), the more important of the two remaining PCF regional dailies, appears to be declining both in circulation and in terms of its share of the advertising market. *Le Méridional–La France* (61,216 copies) is the voice of the right in the region. *Nice-Matin* (245,358 copies) is in the dominant position in the Alpes-Maritimes. This is a quality paper with a sound financial base and a staunchly conservative stand. Lack of competition is making the paper slightly colourless in approach but it faces a change of ownership in the not too distant future. *Vaucluse-Matin* (11,000 copies), part of the Hersant group of *Le Dauphiné libéré*, also now runs three editions in this area.

▼ Rhône-Alpes

This area provided the battleground for a well-documented struggle in 1979 between the Hersant-owned *Le Dauphiné libéré* and *Le Progrès de Lyon*. Both papers are now under the control of Groupe Hersant. *Le Dauphiné libéré* (279,000 copies) has a monopoly in Grenoble, *Le Progrès* (441,711 copies) dominates in the Rhône and in the Ain. *Le Progrès* is now really a press group in itself: it controls the daily *L'Espoir* and several weeklies, giving Groupe Hersant a powerful position in the Lyon area and re-awakening governmental fears of press monopolies. *Lyon libération*, the Lyon edition of *Libération*, is now defunct. It was created in 1986 to rival the *Lyon Figaro* (20,000 copies), itself created a week earlier by Groupe Hersant.

▼ Le Massif Central

The Limoges-based *Le Populaire du Centre* (53,342 copies) was launched by the Socialist Party in 1905. It is now part of the Groupe Centre-France, which owns *La Montagne* (232,371 copies), based in Clermont-Ferrand and one of France's finest and oldest regional dailies, dating from 1919. *La Montagne* was fiercely anti-Vichy and is proud of its history. The group also produces, in Nevers, *Le Journal du Centre* (35,000 copies) and the Bourges-based *Le Berry républicain* (36,000 copies). Groupe Hersant is represented in the region by *Centre presse* (23,000 copies), which has a monopoly in Poitiers. *L'Echo du Centre* (36,000 copies) is the interesting PCF daily for the Limousin. *L'Eveil de la Haute-Loire* (13,772 copies) is the daily for the Puy-de-Dôme but it always contains two pages of national news.

▼ Val-de-Loire

La République du Centre (57,592 copies), the daily paper of Orléans, remains famous for being the only paper in the world to have published colour photographs of man's first steps on the moon, 20 July 1969. It has centre-right leanings nowadays, although its founder, Roger Secrétain, was part of the liberal left. *La République* has to compete with the dominant *La Nouvelle République* (262,190 copies). This paper, created in clandestinity in 1944, is dynamic and growing. It has a virtual monopoly in the Touraine. The staff own 35 per cent of the shares of the paper, which is very prosperous. *Le Courrier de l'Ouest* (104,391 copies), part of the Amaury group, dominates Maine et Loire from Anger. It publishes seven editions and also controls Radio Anger 101. *La Maine libre* (52,361 copies) is also part of the Amaury group and sells principally in the Sarthe.

▼ **Burgundy–Franche-Comté**

Two daily papers compete for readership in the Côte d'Or: *Le Bien public* (founded in 1868, 62,358 copies), 42 per cent owned by the Luxembourg TV company RTL and very much the mouthpiece of the Union pour la démocratie française (UDF) and the Rassemblement pour la République (RPR); and *Les Dépêches du Centre-Est* (19,000 copies), a daily of the centre-left. *Le Journal de Saône-et-Loire* (55,000 copies), previously called *Le Courrier de Saône-et-Loire* is now partly associated with the Groupe Hersant, although not owned by it, and operates in that area. *L'Yonne républicaine* (39,641 copies) has a departmental monopoly in Auxerre. It is a left-wing paper with a mainly conservative readership. It contains good coverage of the local political scene, usually giving a lot of space to prominent political activists and notables of all persuasions.

The periodical press

The periodical press in France is much more extensive and important than in other parts of Europe and is the most dynamic and flourishing sector of the press industry, producing a vast and varied range of titles. It is also the sector most open to change and innovation and, as a consequence of this, it is quite impossible to pin down and classify its protean activities. In 1995, in France, of the 28 publications selling more than 500,000 copies, only one, *Ouest-France*, was a daily paper (768,102 copies); of the remaining 27, fourteen were weeklies, twelve were monthlies and one, trimestriel, the top-selling *Bonheur* (3,292,934 copies), which even outsells *Télé 7 jours*. Furthermore, the periodical press now accounts for 60 per cent of the industry's turnover and 54.4 per cent of total circulation.

One of the reasons usually given to explain the vigour of the periodical press is the absence in France of anything remotely resembling the British Sunday papers. This would certainly account for the success of publications with the news magazine format such as *L'Express* and *Le Nouvel Observateur*, modelled on the American publication *Time*. There also seems to be a view in France that a weekly or fortnightly news magazine allows for a more mature and considered assimilation of events than the hustle and bustle of the daily paper. There may thus be a certain intellectual snobbery surrounding the periodical press when it comes to news coverage.

France now possesses over 300 regional weekly papers and 27 monthlies. Although this figure is a far cry from the several thousand titles recorded in 1914, or even the 900 listed for 1939, it is still a large number. Just 22 of these regional weeklies appear on a Sunday but the combined total number of copies printed, even including the Parisian Sunday papers, amounts to only 4 million. Thus, whatever else the French may do on a Sunday, they do not appear to spend much of it reading newspapers and certainly appear to prefer magazines.

▼ **Weeklies dealing with general news coverage**

The Sunday press in France is represented by *Le Journal du Dimanche*. Founded in 1944, the paper was originally conceived as the Sunday edition of *France-Soir*. When *France-Soir* was sold to the Groupe Hersant in 1977, the *Journal du Dimanche* remained with Hachette. It has a circulation of over 342,512 and tries to combine a degree of serious reporting with the general characteristics of the popular press – eye-catching headlines, details from the glamorous world of show business, lots of photographs and so on. In a certain sense it enjoys a virtual monopoly, for its only rivals are *L'Humanité-Dimanche* (193,400 copies sold in 1994, 80,000 of which were distributed by militants) and the sensationalist *France-Dimanche*, a kind of French equivalent to the *Sunday Sport*, but far less offensive. *France-Dimanche* is famous for its bizarre and extravagant headlines about the British Royal Family (among other things), and has a special place in the hearts and minds of the French. It sells about 659,830 copies and is nineteenth in the list of the 28 best-selling press productions in France, outselling all the dailies apart from *Ouest-France* and all the weekly news magazines apart from *Paris Match*. It was founded after the Second World War with a mission to cheer up the French after the terrible experience of the Occupation. It has a rival in another sensationalist weekly, *Ici Paris* (422,466 copies), which specializes in the private and exotic lives of film stars.

▼ **The main news magazines**

France now boasts four weekly news magazines modelled on the American publication, *Time* (1984 witnessed the death of both the right-wing *Magazine hebdo* and the left-wing *Nouvelles*). The first

weekly to adopt the *Time* format was *L'Express* in 1964. Created in
1953 by Jean-Jacques Servan-Schreiber and François Giroud, *L'Ex-press* supported the socialist, Mendès-France, in the early days and
took a vigorous anti-colonialist line during the Algerian war. It aban-
doned its crusading style in 1964 and appeared in its new format,
claiming to be a news magazine aiming at an objectivity which
quickly revealed itself to be Gaullist (it was then that Jean Daniel left
it to establish *Le Nouvel Observateur*). In 1995 it sold 567,359
copies per week, making it the leading informational weekly (over
70 per cent of its sales are by subscription) and 25th of the 28 leading press publications. In 1977–78, Servan-Schreiber yielded control
of the magazine to James Goldsmith, who swung the magazine
behind Chirac. Goldsmith departed in 1988.

Le Point (302,514 copies) is also on the right and was itself a
breakaway formation from *L'Express* in 1972. Originally financed by
Hachette, it then belonged to the Société Gaumont. It specializes in
easy-to-read, sensible journalism and is attractively laid out. It has
actually been a successful publication, although its circulation was
static until 1994. It was then relaunched in a new format with an
international edition and it achieved a dramatic 20 per cent increase
in its sales. Both *L'Express* and *Le Point* are now part of the same
group under Françoise Sampermans (Express group).

Le Nouvel Observateur (416,726 copies) was launched in 1964
by a breakaway group from *L'Express* as a left-wing news magazine,
when the original publication, *France Observateur*, founded in 1950
as a voice of the non-communist left, was virtually bankrupt. The
renewed strength of the Socialist Party helped the magazine's sales
to climb from 340,000 in 1976 to 385,000 in 1981 and, after a brief
lapse in 1985, its circulation figures are still increasing. This is the
news magazine of the intellectual left and was even Jean-Paul Sartre's
favourite weekly. It is a substantial magazine and much harder to
read than *L'Express* or *Le Point*. It lost its editor, Giesbert, to *Le
Figaro* in 1988. The publication is sometimes accused of radical chic
and even of left snobbery but, politically, it is tougher and more
stimulating than the *New Statesman*, to which it is sometimes compared. It has also created *Télé-obs*, a 64-page supplement to its
already rich cultural commentaries.

L'Evénement du jeudi (210,682 copies) – since 1991 simply
called *l'Evénement* – was founded in 1984, and readership shareholdings constituted a novel part of its launch capital. Its editor,
Jean-François Khan, used to write for *Nouvelles littéraires* and
wanted to create a high-quality weekly with a progressive approach.
It contains excellent sections on literature and culture and its editor
writes equally illuminatingly on domestic and international political
issues. It is not as infested with advertising as *Le Point* and its sales

are increasing, despite its high cost of 30 francs. It is now partly owned by the Hachette group.

▼ Other important weeklies covering current events

Paris Match, established in 1949 and reaching its zenith in 1960 with a circulation of 1.5 million, is no longer commanding the attention of its readership, despite repeated efforts to renew its appeal. It has, however, recovered from the dip to 58,000 in 1975 and sold 828,596 copies in 1995, making it thirteenth of the 28 best-sellers. Over the years, the magazine has done some excellent photo reportage on events in Iran, Haiti and more recently Ruanda. Its coverage of events, in general, is vivid but a bit sensationalist, although invariably claiming to be revelatory. It has the usual panoply of headings of general interest – arts, television, health, diet, problems. Its crosswords have a popular appeal. *Paris Match*'s readership is slowly being taken over by the growing world of TV magazines. *VSD* (*Vendredi-Samedi-Dimanche*) has recovered some of its lost circulation and now sells 293,996 copies but cannot match its peak year in 1986 of 335,000. *VSD* no longer practises the dramatic photo-journalism of its earlier years and concentrates now on the lives of the famous, particularly television personalities and high media profile politicians.

Mention should also be made of the weeklies produced by the political parties, although their circulation rates are generally below 30,000. *National hebdo*, established in 1980, is the organ of the *Front national* and, since 1988, has been available in the kiosks. It achieved high sales of 80,000 in 1994. *La Lettre de la nation* (RPR), *Vendredi* (PS), *Regards*, the successor to *Révolution* (PCF), are of interest to the party faithful. *La vie ouvrière* (1909) is produced by the CGT and provides a weekly insight into the world of trade unionism. Also in this category are a wide range of weeklies from a number of religious groupings, including *Tribune juive*, *La France catholique* and *Témoignage chrétien*. *Le Pèlerin magazine*, with an estimated readership of 649,186 in 1995 and a lifeline stretching back to 1916, is the dominant Catholic weekly. Seventy-five per cent of its readers are practising Catholics. It is often compared unfavourably to the more progressive *La Vie*, another Catholic weekly, edited by Georges Hourdin. *La Vie* has 239,508 subscriptions and gives a serious account of weekly news items from a Catholic viewpoint.

The satirical press is still championed by the distinguished weekly, *Le Canard enchaîné*. Established in 1916 as *Le Canard déchaîné* by Maurice Maréchal, *Le Canard* was originally intended to be a French news-sheet with a mission to demystify, for the common soldier, official government propaganda about the First World

War. It is now something of a French institution and has never actually been banned by the government for all its satirical verve and impertinence. It is run as a co-operative, refuses advertising and has as its slogan: *'La liberté de la presse ne s'use que si l'on ne s'en sert pas.'* *Le Canard* combines serious, investigative, polemical journalism with bald and sometimes strained humour about the shortcomings of governments and politicians of all parties. Its language is full of puns and gnomic references which are not that easy to decode for the non-native. It is financially successful and sold 408,792 copies in 1995 to an estimated 2.5 million readers. *Le Canard* also produces quarterly *dossiers* which often sell spectacularly well: for example, the ones on Chabon-Delmas's tax returns and Giscard's present of diamonds from Bokassa were best-sellers.

Minute la France, originally called *Minute* (established 1962), tries to satirize the French right, but from an ultra-right perspective. Ferociously anti-Gaullist in its early days, its closest political ally nowadays is Le Pen. It faces competition from the *Front national*'s own paper, *National hebdo*. Both papers attack what they consider to be the complacency of the parliamentary right on matters of race and immigration. Both favour the restoration of the death sentence. The left counterbalance to these weeklies is *L'Idiot international*. Originally sponsored by Sartre and Beauvoir in the early 1970s, the paper, named after Dostoevsky's Myshkin, was relaunched in 1988 to be *'informé, indépendant, talentueux, insolent, digne et drôle'*. It often gets taken to court for libel when its outraged innocence gets out of control. Its appearance is sometimes erratic these days.

▼ Television and radio weeklies

This is a readily expanding and flourishing part of the press industry. *Télé 7 jours*, owned by Hachette, is France's second best-selling paper, with a circulation of just under 3 million. *Télé-Star* (1,995,640 copies) takes third place; *Télé Z*, fourth (1,871,477 copies); *Télé Loisirs*, sixth (1,480,288 copies); *TéléPoche* (Editions Mondiales), seventh (1,446,996 copies); *Télérama*, twenty-first (587,138 copies). Despite the supplement provided by Groupe Hersant, called *TV magazine*, in *Le Figaro* and *France-Soir* (an estimated 4 million people read the supplement, making it the most read of all such magazines) and the rival Hachette-based *TV hebdo*, distributed in fourteen regional dailies of the group to 2.5 million readers, television magazines still manage to achieve combined circulation figures of over 15 million copies per week. This market appears to appeal to everyone.

▼ Women's weeklies

With the loss of both *Marie France*, which went into liquidation in December 1993 after a long and unsuccessful struggle against falling advertising revenue, and *Femmes d'aujourd'hui*, which closed in

1990, this area of the periodical market is proving to be very competitive. It is still a dynamic and growing market with plenty of advertising receipts for those magazines with the highest circulation. At the last count, some eleven women's weeklies were in circulation, together with 30 monthly and twelve bimonthly magazines. Their combined annual sales topped 420 million. Top of the list for sales and the fourth best-seller in France is *Femme actuelle*, with a circulation of 1,780,660. Prisma-owned *Femme actuelle*, like its British and Spanish counterparts *Best* and *Mía*, aims to be both popular and practical. It easily outsells *Maxi* (779,811 copies) *Madame Figaro* (572,916 copies), *Nous deux* (487,755 copies), the Hachette-based *Elle* (347,703 copies) and *Intimité* (330,000 copies). Several other women's weeklies sell over 200,000 copies, such as *Voici*, *Bonne soirée* and *Jours de France*. The dynamism of these weeklies is all the more remarkable given the strength of the women's monthlies, like the Prisma-owned *Prima* (the eighth best-selling press publication throughout the whole of France, with a circulation of 1,174,863, and the number one women's monthly), *Modes et travaux* (880,576 copies), *Avantages* (626,683 copies), *Marie-Claire* (560,782 copies) and *Cosmopolitan* (272,791 copies).

▼ **The economic and financial press**

This sector is less thriving than the British and Italian equivalents. The French, traditionally, have suffered from an underdeveloped financial culture and it is certainly significant that the strongest group in this field, the Groupe des Echos, is owned by the English group, Pearson (see earlier section on the dailies). Now that the dailies are producing their own economic supplements, many analysts are predicting a degree of growth in this market, although it is doubtful that France will ever produce anything like *Business Week*. The most important weeklies are: *La Vie française* (established 1945, circulation 80,973); *Investir magazine*, formerly *Investir* (166,115 copies); *Le Nouvel Economiste* (1975, 92,000 copies); and *Business bourse* (1987, 40,000 copies). The more notable financial monthlies include: *La Revenue française* (84,000 copies); *Science et vie économie*, closed in 1992; and *Enjeux–les échos*, previously called *Dynasteurs* (113,313 copies). The new Axel group monthly called *Capital* (launched in 1991, and now with a circulation of 339,025) has displaced *L'Expansion* (153,000 copies) from its dominant position in the financial press market. The Gulf War and the financial implications of its aftermath are leading to important changes in this field. Hachette has virtually pulled out of this market and LVMH (Hennessy-Vuitton) are getting a firm grip on it. Europeanization of the press is likely to occur more swiftly in this key sector of the industry, especially if we move to a single currency.

▼ The arts

This is an area where profound changes have occurred over the last twenty-five years. *Arts lettres et spectacles* disappeared as a separate paper in 1967; *Le Figaro littéraire* was withdrawn in 1971, *Les Lettres françaises* in 1972, *Nouvelles littéraires* in 1984. As a consequence of this, the dailies have strengthened their arts coverage. The best-selling publication in this section is now the monthly magazine *Lire* (part of the Express group, with a circulation of 112,431). Formerly edited by Bernard Pivot of *Apostrophe* fame, it is now edited by Pierre Assouline. The magazine no longer has, therefore, the very successful *Carnets de Pivot*, which have been replaced by Assouline's *Pour commencer* and the *Critiques* sections, which present a survey of new works considered worthy of reference. It also has a section where readers can test their cultural knowledge or ignorance, and all for 30 francs! *Lire* outstrips in circulation, but not in quality, the 30-page *La Quinzaine littéraire* (33,000 copies), which is part of French literary life, and the monthly *Magazine littéraire* (55,688 copies), which is able to list every month 100 new titles in a highly readable way. The cinema world is covered by: *Cahiers du cinéma* (30,017 copies); *Le Mensuel du cinéma*, previously called *La Revue du cinéma* (62,000 copies); and *Positif* (10,000 copies). More like books than periodicals, are France's '*grandes revues*'. With a specialist readership and in competition with the wider circulating monthlies, these publications face an uphill struggle. The most important ones are *La Nouvelle revue des deux mondes*, *La Nouvelle revue française*, *Esprit*, *Les Temps modernes*, which recently celebrated its fiftieth birthday with a special edition, *Etudes* and *Europe*.

To conclude our survey, mention should be made of some of the other developing sections of this buoyant periodical press market. These include a thriving sports sector, a widely read '*presse du cœur*', the professional and technical press, a varied youth and children's section and the substantial area usually called '*la presse administrative*' (official publications, including the redoubtable *Journal officiel de la république*).

GENERAL CONCLUSION

The strengths and weaknesses of the French press, revealed by this current survey and by its economic and industrial profile, give no greater confidence about its future than our previous analysis in 1993. The possibility of a single currency in Europe and further economic pressure on the public sector, and therefore on subsidies, caused by the convergence criteria and the Maastricht Treaty make it difficult to predict that the industry generally will emerge from its present stagnation and imbalances. French press groups will remain highly vulnerable to rival European enterprises on a grander scale, although state protection, intervention and regulation are likely to stay to guarantee pluralism and variety of some kind. The development of the multi-media phenomenon means that newspapers will have to compete for the loyalty of their readers in an increasingly competitive and diversified media environment which will transcend national boundaries. The French press faces the millennium with a host of formidable challenges to its long history.

BIBLIOGRAPHY

Albert, P., *La Presse française*. Paris, La Documentation française, 1990. Contains full bibliography.

Albert, P., *La Presse*. Paris, PUF, 1991.

Albert, P., *Lexique de la presse écrite*. Paris, Dalloz, 1989.

Balle, F., *Médias et sociétés*. Paris, Montchrestien, 7th edition, 1994.

Bellanger, C. (ed.), *Histoire générale de la presse française*. 5 volumes. Paris, PUF, 1969–76.

Bonvoisin, S. M., and Maignien, M., *La Presse féminine*. Paris, PUF, 1986.

Cayrol, R., *Les Médias-presse écrite, radio, télévision*. Paris, PUF, 1991. Contains a full bibliography.

Charon, J. M., *La Presse en France de 1945 à nos jours*. Paris, Seuil, 1991.

Charon, J. M. (ed.), *L'Etat des médias*. Paris, La Découverte (Médiapouvoirs), CFPJ, 1991.

Dupont, J. M., *Le Monde*, 28 April 1989.

Guéry, L., *Quotidien régional, mon journal*. Paris, CFPJ, 1987.

Guide de la presse 1995. Paris, Alphom, 1995.

Guillaume, Y., *La Presse en France*. Paris, La Découverte, 1990.

Martin, M., *Histoire et médias – journalisme et journalistes français*. Paris, Albin Michel, 1991.

Média-Sid. Paris, La Documentation française, 1974.

Mermet, G., *Francoscopie 1995*. Paris, Larousse, 1995.

Quid 1996. Paris, Laffont, 1996.

Terrou, F., *Annuaire statistique*. Paris, UNESCO, 1981.

Todorov, P., *La Presse française à l'heure de l'Europe*. Paris, La Documentation française, 1990.

9

THE BROADCASTING MEDIA

Geoffrey Hare

Introduction

The common use of the term 'le PAF' (*le paysage audiovisuel français*) suggests the French conceive of broadcasting and the new electronic means of communication as separate from the written press, whereas the British tend to lump press and broadcasting together as 'the media'. The French have also sought to combine reform of broadcasting with more general technological modernization. The 1980s in particular saw wholesale changes in the PAF: an enormous increase in the number of radio and television stations and the birth of independent broadcasting, independent both in the sense of relative freedom from government interference and in terms of the creation, for the first time, of a privately owned and financed sector. A combination of ideological and political change inside France, technological developments, and economic pressures (all of these forcing a European dimension onto public and private sector decision-making) transformed the traditional system of a tightly government-controlled national monopoly into a more open, deregulated, market-oriented system. The 1990s have seen the consolidation of the new PAF, and the beginnings of the digital era.

Whereas at the beginning of the 1980s there were only three television channels, all in the state sector, and the few pirate radios challenging the state monopoly were being jammed and pursued through the courts, by the mid-1990s the French had access to 25 television channels: six national terrestrial or off-air channels, additional French 'thematic' channels and a range of European stations on the now rapidly growing city cable networks or via direct broadcast by satellite, and in a few places, a private, local television station. As for radio, the cosy competition of a handful of national stations run by Radio France and the French-language commercial stations broadcasting from across the eastern and southern frontiers, was, again in the early 1980s, rudely disturbed by the creation of some 1800 independent local and nationally networked FM stations, offering a range of programmes, even if they predominantly broad-cast pop music.

The increased supply of media outlets (both television and radio) is unequally distributed, with the privileged city dwellers having a far greater choice of programme than the inhabitants of less well-favoured rural areas. This is related to the deregulation of broadcast-ing: the traditional hegemony of the state sector was shattered during the 1980s, leaving the market open to private enterprise. This explosion of *'libéralisme'*, triggered, paradoxically, by the socialist governments of the 1980s, was boosted by the right-wing govern-ments of 1986–88 and 1993–95, and France's biggest names in industry and finance have not been slow to invest. The independent television companies were, in 1995, part owned by Bouygues (the leading company in the construction industry) (TF1), the public utili-ties company Lyonnaise des Eaux and the CLT (*Compagnie Luxem-bourgeoise de Télédiffusion*) (M6), and the advertising agency Havas and La Générale des Eaux (Canal Plus). The publisher Hachette, the newspaper magnate Robert Hersant, Jérôme Seydoux's Chargeurs group (owner of Pathé Cinéma), not forgetting foreign media inter-ests such as the companies of Robert Maxwell and Silvio Berlusconi, had previously invested in French television, but the 1990s saw a greater concentration of ownership leaving a smaller number of owners. Limits on monopoly ownership of national stations were loosened by the Balladur government in 1994. A single, private shareholder can now hold up to 49 per cent of capital. One imme-diate result was that the founder of Canal Plus, André Rousselet, was squeezed out.

The state's interest in the media has been diverted into huge investment in new technologies: cable, satellite, high-definition tele-vision, videotex (*le Minitel*), and the information superhighway. However, changes of political direction, conflicts between economic and cultural objectives, and a reining-in of the over-ambitious plans of the early 1980s delayed the hoped-for comprehensive, integrated planning of national communications that may still emerge out of the French state's approach to the *inforoutes*. In the meantime, pri-vate enterprise has begun investing hugely in the sector.

In the 1990s a political consensus about the new balance between public and private-sector broadcasting seems to have been achieved, as much through exhaustion in the face of such rapid and often unco-ordinated reforms as through real agreement. However, this consensus may prove precarious if, despite the amount of public and private money poured into broadcasting, the quality and range of choice of programmes does not continue the improvement which viewers had perceived during the 1980s. A 1989 opinion poll summed up French views of their television as: *'en progrès, mais peut mieux faire . . .'*. A 1995 poll suggested the credibility of television news had fallen to an all-time low, whereas radio retained more of the listeners' trust.

This chapter will discuss issues of broadcasting regulation and policy-making within their political context, in particular during the Fifth Republic; will describe the institutions of radio and television in the 1990s; will look at the importance of the audience in the new market system, and will finally glimpse the future through charting the progress of new technological developments.

REGULATION AND THE POLITICS OF BROADCASTING

The frequency of changes to the statutes and regulatory framework of the French broadcasting system (seven major reforms since 1959) shows how much radio and television have been a political football and how the broadcasters have not enjoyed a consensus in public opinion about their position within French society and institutions. Most governments since the Second World War, believing firmly in the power of the media to influence the electorate, have aimed to manipulate broadcasters, accepting, like President de Gaulle, himself a past master at communicating through television, that the written press was beyond their control. De Gaulle's successor, President Pompidou, even went so far as to say that broadcasters could not be as independent as newspaper journalists, and should never forget they were *'la voix de la France'*. However, after the election of François Mitterrand as President in 1981, the various forms of *direct* state control of radio and television gave way to a system overseen by a regulatory authority. The existence of this buffer organization designed, according to the socialists, to 'cut the umbilical cord' between government and the media, did not prevent Mitterrand and his ministers from putting heavy political pressure on the regulators at different times.

The state monopoly of broadcasting dated from decrees by the Vichy government in 1941 and 1942. From 1944 to 1949 *Radiodiffusion française* and from 1949 to 1959 *Radiotélévision française* (RTF) were as much an arm of government as was the Department of Post and Telecommunications. RTF's status as part of the civil service changed in 1959 as it became an autonomous public body with its own budget, but still under the authority of the Minister of Information. The huge sway exercised by government over the broadcasters, with rumours of direct telephone lines between them, is illustrated by the appearance of the Minister of Information, Alain Peyrefitte, one evening in the mid-1960s on the television news to announce how he, the Minister, had decided that the format of the television news programmes and the approach of the news broadcasters were going to be modified. In the 1960s, television was sarcastically referred to as *'le gouvernement dans la salle à manger'*. Successive changes of statute, while giving the appearance of distancing broadcasters from government, did not have a significant effect on the subservience of hand-picked media managers and presenters, nor did they break the habit of successive incoming governments changing the Directors of News and Current Affairs. In 1964 the RTF became the ORTF (*Office de Radiodiffusion-Télévision française*), managed by a Director General responsible to a board of directors, but still under the 'tutelage' of the Minister of Information.

The Events of May 1968 shook the state broadcasting system, with many broadcasters joining the strikes against their masters in the *Maison de l'ORTF* and the stifling bureaucracy they associated with the Gaullist régime, but their protest ended in dismissal for the ringleaders. A brief interlude of more liberal treatment by the Chaban–Delmas government (1969–72) was followed by another crackdown, and further changes by President Giscard d'Estaing in 1974–75, involving the splitting up of the constituent parts of the ORTF into three service bodies – *Société française de Production* (SFP) for production, *Télédiffusion de France* (TDF) for transmission, and *Institut national de l'Audiovisuel* (INA) for archives and training – and four programming networks (three television channels and Radio France). Government retained political control of broadcasting budgets and appointments to key posts, so that a form of self-censorship generally ensured compliant news coverage, even of such potential scandals as President Giscard's evasiveness over a personal gift of diamonds from the African dictator Bokassa.

There were great hopes for a more independent system of broadcasting when Mitterrand and the socialists came to power in 1981. They had consistently criticized their predecessors for their confiscation of freedoms, especially that of freedom of expression through the broadcasting media. The two most important innovations in their 1982 reforms were the creation of a broadcasting regulatory body, the *Haute Autorité de la Communication audiovisuelle*, meant to be independent of government, and the end of the state monopoly of the airwaves (*'la communication audiovisuelle est libre'*), thus opening up the possibility of commercial broadcasting.

The buffer institution proved not to be as independent as promised. The government opted, controversially, for retaining political control of the system of appointment of the nine members of the *Haute Autorité*: three being nominated by the President of the Republic (Mitterrand), three by the President of the National Assembly (inevitably a government supporter), and three by the President of the Senate (in the 1980s a right-winger). The length of mandate, nine years and irrevocable, which in principle gave its members great independence, would also conveniently prolong the influence of the initial nominees beyond the five-year term of the National Assembly and the seven-year term of the presidency. Government also retained control of budgets, and made decisions on cable, satellite and new channels. Although the *Haute Autorité*'s first president, Michèle Cotta, a former radio and television journalist, worked hard to establish the independence of the body, it was undermined by government interference and lack of support. A further erosion of its authority was the political decision to set up two new commercial television channels and the award of the franchises simply by presidential dictat in 1986, one to a known supporter of the Socialist Party, Jérôme Seydoux (in alliance with the Italian Silvio Berlusconi).

The suspicion of lack of independence in the institutions created by the socialists served as a justification for the Chirac government to dismantle the 1982 reforms in 1986. Claiming too that the freeing of the airwaves from state regulation had not gone far enough, they privatized the highest-audience channel, TF1. Their reform created a new regulatory body, the *Commission nationale de la Communication et des Libertés* (CNCL), with greater powers to police its decisions, but whose thirteen-strong membership was predominantly and obviously politically right-wing, a feature that discredited it with public opinion. Government pressure led the CNCL to revoke the contracts awarded by the socialists to the franchise holders of the two new commercial television channels, and it was widely seen as no coincidence that the CNCL chose government sympathizers as the new directors of the television channels and as holders of the franchises for the commercial channels, in particular the right-wing press magnate Hersant. Finally, as part of their wider view of the media, the CNCL's regulatory powers were extended beyond broadcasting to include the telecommunications sector.

It was no surprise of course, in such a climate of politicization of broadcasting, that the newly elected socialist government of 1988 should decide to embark on a further media reform (*la loi du 17 janvier 1989*), transforming the regulatory body, its membership and its powers yet again. Now called the *Conseil supérieur de l'Audiovisuel* (CSA), it is composed of nine members, nominated for six years by the same method as used for the *Haute Autorité*. Its responsibilities included appointing (and sacking) the directors of the public service broadcasting channels, advising government on the *cahiers des charges* (the contractual obligations of the broadcasting franchise holders) in both the public and private sectors, and overseeing respect of these contracts in terms of pluralism and fairness of political expression, of quotas of foreign programmes, of standards of public decency, etc., attributing franchises for commercial radio and television, licensing cable networks, and applying the advertising code of practice. The CSA has powers of sanction through fines and suspension of franchises.

While the continued existence of the regulatory authority does give greater independence from government in the day-to-day running of the broadcasting media, and seen in the longer-term perspective there has been a gradual freeing of broadcasting and greater professionalization, the temptation to interfere in broadcasting affairs remains part of French political culture on both left and right. The socialist government pressured a CSA appointment as head of *France-Télévision* to resign in 1991, whereupon the CSA tamely replaced him with Hervé Bourges, seemingly more acceptable to the left. Then, under the Balladur government in 1993, new appointments as heads of *France-Télévision* (J.-P. Elkabbach) and of the new fifth channel (J.-M. Cavada) were seen as conveniently sympathetic to the right, while one of President Mitterrand's last acts was to appoint Bourges as President of the CSA. The French media are now at least run by broadcasting professionals rather than by politicians or civil servants, but government still manages one way or another to influence key appointments so that the professionals are ideologically sympathetic. Interference or self-censorship in programme-making may not be as rife as in the 1960s, but a major television retrospective of ten years of Mitterrand's presidency screened in 1991 blithely avoided mentioning the embarrassing sinking of the Greenpeace boat Rainbow Warrior in 1985. The climate has nonetheless changed: there is no going back on the existence of a broadcasting regulatory body, whose powers have furthermore increased with each reform, and the idea has been definitively accepted that a buffer authority has to exist between government and the media and that ministers are not solely responsible for decision-making on behalf of the state.

With a new regulatory body in place, what sort of regulation was considered necessary as commercial competition intensified? Controlled deregulation was the watchword at first, but controls on licensing, on quotas, and on advertising were gradually relaxed through the 1980s and 1990s, as technological change and internationalization of markets eroded government capacity to regulate in national terms (as will be seen). The automatic renewal of TF1's licence for a further ten years in 1996 raised the suspicion that the regulators are now too soft on the big commercial operators. The major preoccupations of the regulators in the late 1990s are:

■ • the information superhighway, relations between cable television companies and telephone companies, cohabitation between a regulated national system and an often deregulated international system emerging from the increasing number of satellites and the arrival of new technologies;

- ■ • the French *'exception culturelle'* and national identity;
- ■ • quotas of French-made programmes and French music;
- ■ • and violence on television (much more than sex, which is nonetheless rather more explicit than on British television).

RADIO NETWORKS

Chronologically, the first beneficiary of the freeing of the airwaves was radio broadcasting. The traditional pattern of radio broadcasting was that local radio was practically non-existent, and that the state maintained a near-monopoly of national radio. Before 1981, five 'generalist' radios, each with a similar diet of programmes, shared the national audience. Four commercial radios called *périphériques* (since they transmitted from outside France) had the lion's share of listeners on long wave. They were RTL (Luxembourg), Europe 1 (near Saarbrücken, Germany), RMC (Monte-Carlo), and the small Sud Radio (Andorra). Radio France's equivalent public service radio station, France-Inter, basically devoted its programmes to what was seen as a homogeneous national audience, albeit with different needs at different times of the day.

The only other radio stations of note were Radio France's two low-audience, high-culture stations, France-Culture (programming music and drama and a lot of high-level discussion) and France-Musique (concentrating on classical music). Local radio was limited to a few minutes per day of opting-out of the national network by the fifteen regional stations of Radio France. There was little real choice of programme therefore, and a limited choice of programme supplier: state control of broadcasting was not really challenged by the existence of the *périphériques*, since the latter were indirectly controlled through state-dominated holding companies like Havas and the SOFIRAD.

In the 1980s, political change and technological innovations resulted in a radical shift, bringing increased competition by the opening up of radio broadcasting to the private sector, displacement of the centre of gravity of radio output to the FM waveband (offering better sound quality), multiplication of the supply of programmes, segmentation of the listening audience through *'radio thématique'* formats, introduction of round-the-clock broadcasting, and transformation of radio listening into an individualized activity on personal stereos or the car radio, where everyone has their own receiver and is able to listen to their chosen station.

Indeed, the challenge to the state broadcasting monopoly had come most noticeably in radio. Since about 1973, a growing number of illegal pirate radio stations on the FM waveband had been jammed and raided by the state authorities. Many were run by broadcasting fanatics who simply wanted to exercise their freedom of expression over the airwaves. Others set up pirate stations for political reasons or to publicize causes. Others wished to break the state monopoly in order to set up commercial radio stations and make money.

In 1981, faced by an explosion of *radios libres*, the socialist government proceeded to legalize and regulate the situation on the FM band. To avoid political or commercial monopolies, the new *radios locales privées* (RLP) were very tightly regulated. They had to operate as non-profit-making associations, could not therefore take paid advertising, could not set up networks of transmitters, and could not be run by town councils. Anarchy nonetheless continued to reign, as the licensing authority took an inordinately long time to draw up its list of authorized stations, since there were far more applications than frequencies available on the FM band. Some stations cynically ignored the agreed transmission strength or allocated frequency. Others, finding financial support from the *fonds de soutien à l'expression radiophonique* inadequate, resorted to more or less open advertising or sponsorship. Pressure and confusion built up and the *Haute Autorité*'s jurisdiction was undermined, until Mitterrand gave the go-ahead in 1984 for radios to operate as private companies and take advertising income. The deregulation of radio was extended when the state gave up its interest in the *périphériques*: Europe 1 was sold off to Matra-Hachette in 1986 and RTL gained its independence of the state when Havas was privatized in 1987. RMC, increasingly in deficit, failed for a fourth time to find a private buyer in 1996.

Inexpensive FM broadcasting technology had changed radio broadcasting out of all recognition. The RLP audience grew rapidly, rising to over a third of the listening public by 1988, and continues to bite into the *périphérique* audience. The *périphériques* themselves had to seek FM licences to remain competitive. Another technological development was to complete the change. The launch, mainly for business and military communications purposes, of French telecommunications satellites allowed the RLP to set up national FM networks – groups of radios transmitting the same programme in different towns – using a satellite relay. Originally networks were banned, but gradually local stations were either bought up or given the franchise to broadcast programmes produced by a central programme provider, and the state found it could not resist this evolution. Since the 1986 law, eight major RLP networks have established themselves.

Public service radio meanwhile attempted to halt the drop in audience figures in this climate of increased competition. Long-term planning at Radio France was not helped by five (often politically motivated) changes of Director General during the 1980s, although

J. Maheu subsequently brought stability. Radio France too has opted as much as possible for FM frequencies and new local stations, of which there are now 39, covering 50 per cent of France. Seeing the potential for thematic stations with the success of Radio-Bleue for the over-50s, Radio France also established the increasingly successful 24-hour rolling-news station, France-Info. Another innovation is the experiment of two up-market cultural and music programmes (Victor and Hector) broadcast to a European-wide audience in digital stereo sound via satellite.

However, the audience for its national flagship station France-Inter fluctuated from 13.5 per cent of total radio audience in 1983 to 17.3 per cent by the end of 1986 (which, for the first time in many years, put them ahead of Europe 1), to 11.5 per cent in 1996, a figure partly compensated for by the 10 per cent (and still rising) national share now enjoyed by France-Info (whose listening figures had shot up during the Gulf War in 1991–92). Totting up audiences across all its stations, Radio France can still claim in the late 1990s to be *'le premier réseau de France'*, with a quarter of the national audience.

After a decade of rapid change in French radio, the position in the 1990s is that, of the 1800 or so independent radio stations in France, some 1,000 are attached to networks and about 300 are non-commercial or community radios. The 1980s saw the gradual triumph of market forces and fragmentation of the audience. In programming terms this means the triumph of formatting, targeting a particular segment of the total listening public for sale to advertisers, and offering a very specific type of programme. The format dominating the networks is 'music-and-news', with NRJ, Fun-Radio, and Skyrock aiming at the 15–25-year-olds, and Europe 2, RFM, Chérie-FM, and the re-targeted Nostalgie at the 25–50-year-olds, leaving the over-50s mainly to the *périphériques*. Little by little music radio has been eating away at news radio, and in 1996 the advertising income of the new FM radios overtook that of the *périphériques*, although youth radio felt threatened by the *amendement Pelchat* enforcing a 40 per cent quota of French music from 1996.

Market forces have also favoured concentration of ownership and groupings of radios into advertising networks, mainly to the advantage of the *périphériques*. While their dominance over the commercial radio scene was threatened in the mid-1980s, the *périphériques* have found ways of using their financial resources to recapture the younger end of the market for their basket of audiences to sell to advertisers. Whether by taking over FM networks (RTL owns Fun-Radio, RMC owns Nostalgie, and Europe 1 owns Skyrock and RFM), or by acting as programme supplier to independent local radios (as Europe 2 does), they are maintaining a strong presence. RTL still remains the leading audience station (18 per cent market share and over 8 million listeners). As Europe 1 fell below the symbolic 10 per cent of audience in 1996, the one newcomer really challenging the *périphériques* is J.-P. Baudecroux's NRJ, now the third highest audience station, with 10–11 per cent of audience share, and ownership of a second network, Chérie-FM. The new regulatory framework is nonetheless providing some protection to local commercial independent radios (*radios de proximité*) and non-commercial *radios associatives*. However, the range of community radio in Paris (Radio Notre-Dame, Fréquence Protestante, Radio Shalom, Fréquence Gaie, Beur FM, etc.) is in no way mirrored in the provinces, where the networks dominate.

Radio listening as a whole has been consolidated in the 1990s (at about 78 per cent of the population), after the shock of increased television competition in the mid-1980s. As advertising revenue tightened in the early 1990s, one or two networks failed financially and others merged, leading to somewhat increased concentration of ownership – occasionally at the expense of diversity of programmes (for example the demise of *Féminin pluriel* in the Paris region). However, under the emerging authority of the CSA, and with increasing attractiveness of radio to advertisers, a more stable situation is being imposed. Major technological innovations on the horizon, such as Radio Data Systems (RDS) and Digital Audio Broadcasting (DAB) offering CD-quality sound, ten times more frequencies, and pay-radio, may disrupt the status quo.

TELEVISION CHANNELS AND PROGRAMMING

The commercial channels (*les télévisions privées*)

▼ **TF1**

TF1, the continuation of France's first television channel, inaugurated in 1935, was privatized in 1987, and bought by a consortium headed by the industrialist Francis Bouygues. It quickly used its new financial muscle to attract many stars from its rival channels in a ratings war. The newsreader Christine Ockrent went back to Antenne 2 after a year or so, complaining of *'la dictature de l'Audimat'* at TF1, that is, a programming policy too dependent on audience ratings.

Popular programmes have included such different offerings as the documentary programme *Cinq colonnes à la une*, major political interview or discussion programmes such as *7 sur 7* (with Anne Sinclair), *Intervilles* (a domestic French version of *Jeux sans frontières* with Guy Lux and Léon Zitrone), the detective series *Navarro*, children's programmes like *Le Manège enchanté* (now succeeded by the forgettable *Club Dorothée*), the evening programme *Journal télévisé*, consistently the highest in audience ratings, imported soaps like *Dallas*, and a series of American-style game shows such as *La Roue de la fortune*. Since privatization it has a *Télé-shopping* programme and a number of low-quality early evening American-style, French-made series such as *Hélène et les garçons*. There was controversy over the continued use of their main news anchorman, Patrick Poivre d'Arvor, after his conviction, fine and fifteen-month suspended jail sentence for involvement in a political corruption scandal in 1995. The prosecution claimed a corrupt businessman had sought to use the broadcaster to promote the political career of the Mayor of Lyon, Michel Noir, via privileged access to television coverage, in exchange for travel and other favours. More recently the poor taste of sensationalist programmes such as *Osons!* has been condemned in the press as '*télé-nausée*' or '*télé-poubelle*' and in the courts for '*provocation à la haine raciale*'. In 1995 TF1's taste for cheap imports led to its failure to respect the 40 per cent quota of European-made programmes.

▼ Canal Plus

Canal Plus, France's first subscription channel, began broadcasting in 1984 under the direction of André Rousselet of Havas, a personal friend of President Mitterrand. After a hesitant start, it benefited from various concessions, even being allowed to carry advertising. Now, with subscribers in over 4 million homes, and financially the most dynamic of the private channels, it has set up its own production company, and is seeking to expand into channels on French cable and satellite networks, and pay-television channels abroad, notably Germany, Belgium and Spain. Its programmes are mainly encrypted and visible only to subscribers. It specializes in sports coverage and recently released cinema films (one film new to television per day, with several repeats). Its most successful regular shows are *Nulle part ailleurs* (a magazine programme with Antoine de Caunes) and *Les Guignols de l'info* (satirical puppets).

▼ M6

The sixth channel was originally dedicated to programmes for young people as a mainly music channel. As M6, while retaining a lot of music videos (*Boulevard des clips*) and aiming some programmes at the 15–25-year-olds, it has pretensions to be a general audience channel, albeit a low budget one, therefore carrying no sport, no *variétés*, nor game shows. It regularly shows soft-porn films, but its main audience successes are with imported series like *The Cosby Show* or *La Petite Maison dans la prairie*, and short, focused magazine programmes (*Culture Pub*, *Culture Rock*, *Capital*).

▼ La Cinq

The original franchise for the fifth channel was re-attributed to Hersant and Berlusconi in 1986 as La Cinq, before Hachette bought the major share in 1990. It aimed at a mass, general audience, broadcasting 24 hours a day. Unable to achieve financial stability, it experimented with various programming policies, bringing it into conflict with the regulatory bodies, which sanctioned La Cinq for over-programming of American television films, for not respecting European production quotas, and for showing soft-porn material too early in the evening. Abandoning Hersant's stress on news coverage, Hachette tried to turn La Cinq into a family channel, but was unable to increase audiences and advertising revenue sufficiently quickly to avoid going bankrupt at the end of 1991. The vacant channel was re-allocated to a public service channel, Arte, in 1992.

The public service channels (*la télévision publique*)

Following the creation of new commercial channels, the diminished state sector was in danger of becoming the poor relation in France's television service. In the face of intense competition from TF1 and M6, public service television is still trying to come to terms with its new role and identity. The key media debate, which used to be on television's relation to government, is, in the 1990s, on the issue of whether, and how, public-sector television should differentiate itself from commercial television, in its financing and its programming policy. As a first step, in 1989, the two main public service off-air national television channels became part of a single programming company, France-Télévision, with a single Director General, as a preliminary to more complementarity, but, apart from sharing a sports service, they do not harmonize programming as closely as BBC television. The French public service model of broadcasting, because of its long association with the exercise of state power, also lacks the historic prestige of its British counterpart, and it remains an open question as to whether the public service channels should strive for excellence in the types of programmes that private channels are reluctant to produce, pursue a mass audience and therefore programme a lot of light entertainment, or indeed whether there is a third way as *'une télévision commerciale d'Etat'*.

▼ France 2

France 2, originally the second channel, born in 1964, becoming Antenne 2 in 1974, remains a general public channel, *'une chaîne populaire de qualité'*, catering for a mass audience, in direct competition with its main commercial rival TF1. Its best known and long-running programmes over the years have included *Les Dossiers de l'écran* (serious treatment of issues) and the game show *Des chiffres et des lettres*, the book programme *Apostrophes* (Bernard Pivot), *Dimanche Martin* (a variety show starring Jacques Martin), its current affairs programmes such as *Heure de vérité* (featuring the premier French political commentator Alain Duhamel) and *20 heures* news, turning successive presenters, such as *'la reine Christine'* (Ockrent) and, in the 1990s, Bruno Masure, into household names, and, shared with France 3, its unrivalled coverage of the *Tour de France* cycle race.

▼ France 3

France 3, the third channel, was born in 1972, and took on a regional vocation as FR3 in 1975, but most of its programming (including national news) is networked to the nation from its headquarters in Paris, with twice-daily local news programmes in each region. It has tended to adopt a strategy complementary to France 2 and TF1 in terms of differentiated programming, as *'une télévision de découverte et de différence'*. Originally its local news bulletins were used by the Gaullist régime to put across a version of local news more politically acceptable than that offered by the regional newspapers. Its news coverage is now highly regarded. The networked programmes were, and many still are, of a rather high cultural model, with a high reputation for documentary magazines: *Thalassa*, and *La Marche du siècle*. Of note too are its morning children's programmes *Les Minikeums*, regional cookery in *La Cuisine des mousquetaires*, the quiz show *Questions pour un champion*, and the evening cinema film. The channel has been described as *'la chaîne de la France profonde'*.

▼ Arte

Arte was founded in 1986 as La SEPT (*Société européenne de programmes de télévision*), with entirely public sector capital, with a vocation to become an upmarket European-wide 'cultural channel' and to help create a Franco-German bilingual satellite broadcasting channel, to be relayed on European cable networks. Since 1992 it has broadcast, evenings only, in France on the fifth channel, and in Germany on cable, to a minority middle-class audience. Its German-language programmes are subtitled in French and vice versa. It has few live shows because of the intrusiveness of linguistic interpreting. Its programmes include documentaries, discussion programmes and films, with one evening a week organized around a theme.

▼ La Cinquième

La Cinquième, the newest publicly financed channel, was born from a project for *'une chaîne du savoir, de la formation, et de l'emploi'*, with a mission to *'mettre la connaissance à portée de*

Publicity material for Arte, the new Franco–German cultural television channel

tous'. It began broadcasting in December 1994. It uses the old fifth channel from 6.15 a.m. to 7 p.m. when Arte takes over. Its most popular programmes are documentaries on animals or history (*Le Sens de l'histoire*), its foreign language news with Alex Taylor, and *reportages*. It aims to be *'populaire et généraliste'*, and is less innovative educationally than connoisseurs of Open University programmes might have hoped, although it quickly stopped programming game/quiz shows and does offer material aimed at schools, and at minorities.

An advert for the new educational television channel La Cinquième

Si votre fils
qui ne sait pas où est
la salle de bain vous
raconte l'histoire du savon
à travers les âges,
réjouissez-vous, c'est
La Cinquième.

Les écrans du savoir, tous les jours de 9h45 à 12h00

La Cinquieme
On en apprend tous les jours

▼ **RFO**

Having split from Radio France in 1982, RFO manages public service radio and television broadcasting to French overseas territories.

▼ **Programming policy**

On the national general public channels, drama series and films make up the biggest single category of programme (35 per cent), with quiz and game shows, *'variétés'* and the evening news programme being important prime-time shows, along with the new vogue for 'reality shows'. The programming schedules are more tightly regulated in France than EU rules demand. One justification is the protection of the French cinema industry. Examples of the type of regulation are that, excluding Canal Plus, the main channels cannot show more than 192 cinema films per year, of which no more than 104 may be in evening prime time. The films must be at least eighteen months old, 60 per cent must be European productions, of which two-thirds must be French. A major rationale behind these restrictions is the defence of French culture and identity in the face of imports of American programmes. There are regulations on the maximum amount of advertising per hour (12 minutes, with a daily average of no more than 6 minutes for TF1 and France 2). There has even been debate on whether, on aesthetic and moral grounds, films should be interrupted by advertising: TF1 is allowed one advertising break, France 2 none.

Production of programmes

The introduction of market forces into television has had the effect of more clearly demarcating the roles of programme producer and programme provider. Programme production has long been a weakness in French television. Alongside the traditional state programming monopoly, there also existed, until 1986, a production monopoly. Channels (programme providers) were obliged to use the SFP (*Société française de Production*) for all their French-made documentary, entertainment and drama productions. As an attempt to stimulate French programme production, channels may now have recourse to independent programme makers, and, with constant deficits, the SFP, never in a very healthy financial position since it became autonomous in 1974, seems likely to be sold off to the private sector. As in other countries, since a crucial part of their schedules are films, the French networks are increasingly financing co-productions with European partners, both cinema films and films specifically for television. However, the language and cultural problems of producing for a market wider than the national one conflict with the defence of French cultural identity, as enshrined in the programming quotas relating to *'œuvres d'expression originale française'*. As the audiovisual industry becomes more multi-media, programme production is becoming confused, for big players like TF1, with the ownership of performing rights. Programme providers need cinema or television films to exploit through a series of distribution outlets: cinema, video, terrestrial television, pay-per-view television, and they are just as likely to buy up performing rights or rights to major sporting events as invest in new productions.

THE AUDIENCE AND THE ECONOMICS OF BROADCASTING

A mass television audience emerged only in the 1970s in France. From only 6 million television sets in 1965, the number grew to nearly 21 million by 1982, by which time over 90 per cent of homes had sets. In the late-1990s, with a set in 96 per cent of homes, most French people can receive at least five off-air channels, and viewers watch on average at least three hours per day. The availability, free at point of consumption, of five off-air channels, plus an off-air subscription channel (169 francs a month), seemed at first to satisfy most viewers, who felt less need to invest in either a cable link (600 francs for the installation and, in Paris, 145 francs for the basic monthly subscription, or 240 francs for additional premium channels) or a DBS (Direct Broadcast by Satellite) receiving dish plus decoder. More recently, consumption has increased. Domestic spending on television increased by 2.9 times between 1980 and 1993, to the detriment of going to the cinema.

The emergence of a commercial sector has changed the media culture and changed the relationship with this mass audience. The viewer is seen as a consumer and programmes as commodities. Channels are placing enormous faith in the measurement of audience figures, for example via the Audimat, in order to sell advertising space. The consequences are a *'chasse aux vedettes'* and consequent public criticism of inflated salaries for star presenters, a suspicion of standardization of programme formats as programmers seek the lowest common denominator, and a reliance on tried-and-tested and often cheap American serials or Japanese-made cartoons. A constant danger is the blurring of the line between programmes and advertising, especially through the use of sponsorship of programmes or prizes.

Before privatization, TF1 and France 2 had similar numbers of viewers. Subsequently, TF1 became the clear market leader in terms of audience share, but was not as clearly ahead in 1996 as earlier: TF1 had 37 per cent of audience, followed by France 2 at 24 per cent. Since the disappearance of La Cinq, France 3 has recovered to 17–18 per cent, with M6 rising to 12 per cent. Arte attracts only 3 per cent, while the market share of La Cinquième (at low audience times) is 4–5 per cent. TF1 is therefore able to demand a higher price for its advertising space, especially in evening prime time (8 p.m. to 10.30 p.m.), but less so in access prime time (6–8 p.m.), with the consequence that it has managed to operate at a reasonable profit (600 million francs in 1995). M6 is increasingly financially sound, operating on low costs, and Canal Plus, with its main source of income from subscriptions, declared higher profits than TF1 for 1995 at 5 per cent of audience share, whereas La Cinq had been operating an unsustainable loss at 10 per cent. Its bankruptcy confirmed the predictions of those saying that too many channels were fishing in too small a pool of advertising demand for all to be able to survive.

The public service sector is not spared in the new competitive culture: one of the first tasks of the new director of France-Télévision was to seek to balance the books. In 1991 he received a promise of a one billion franc subsidy to cover accumulated deficits, in exchange for a 20 per cent reduction of staff numbers. The number of employees in the public sector was estimated in 1990 as two to three times higher than those in the private sector. France 3 in particular has traditionally had high staff costs. In addition to income from the annual television licence fee (*la redevance*), state channels have been taking paid advertising since 1968. This was not popular at the time with the written press (heavily dependent on advertising revenue), although now some of the larger newspaper companies have diversified into broadcasting. Other more ideological objections to paid advertising on public service television are surfacing again, supported ironically by the commercial stations, who see their salvation in reserving the whole of the television advertising cake for themselves. France 2 was obliged by government to find 45 per cent of its income from advertising in the 1990s. As a result it was pulled in the direction of competing for audience with TF1 to the detriment of its public service role and quality of programmes. In 1996, France 2's Director General J.-P. Elkabbach was a spectacular victim of his strategy of cutting documentaries in favour of programming music, entertainment and game shows. Having failed to raise audience ratings by more than a couple of percentage points, he was sacked when it was revealed he was paying exorbitant sums to young, big-name stars operating through their own private production companies (Jean-Luc Delarue, Nagui, Arthur). The fear remains that if, in an environment of expanding supply of channels, France 2 starts to lose its audience share, it will not only lose advertising income, but there may be pressure to cut its public subsidy further, thus setting in motion a spiral of decline for public service television. La Cinquième and Arte may also come under pressure if their audience numbers do not take off. France 3, however, has increased its income from commercial sources in the 1990s, while still getting 76 per cent of its income from licence fee and state subsidy. It has therefore not been under the same pressure to lower its standards as France 2 and its audience share rose appreciably in the 1990s from 11 to 18 per cent, proving that tabloid television is not an inevitable route. The CSA reassuringly chose the head of France 3, Gouyou-Beauchamp, to replace Elkabbach as head of France-Télévision.

NEW BROADCASTING TECHNOLOGIES AND THE COMMUNICATIONS REVOLUTION

The television audience is in the process of being fragmented and the economics of broadcasting redefined not only through the creation of commercial television, but also as a result of the introduction of new broadcasting technologies in the 1980s. A second communications revolution in the late 1990s combines changes in computing, telecommunications and broadcasting, which converge in the new digital communications media. Technological innovations in micro-electronics and telecommunications (broadband cable and satellite) have radically improved the transmission of information in the form of data, graphics, sound and vision, so that the same communications system may carry, for example, telephone, fax, videotex and computer data, as well as broadcasting signals. Modernizing national communications systems using telematics (a combination of telecommunications and micro-computer technology) offered advanced economies like France in the 1980s an opportunity to modernize broadcasting and to plan for what has been called the wired or interactive society. Such projects seemed all the more essential since communications policy has become of strategic importance in an EU haunted by the prospect of growing American and Japanese domination of European information technology sectors. Telecommunications in particular is a sector where EU countries are best placed to retain a competitive position. In this context, France-Télécom had ambitions to retain France's technological lead by developing its own series of telecommunications satellites and by providing a national broadband cable Integrated Services Digital Network (ISDN, or RNIS in French) to cater for all such data, voice and image transmission in the same digital form along the same cables, just as in the 1970s it had made its considerable reputation as the DGT (*Direction générale des Télécommunications*) by developing (and exporting) French telephone systems technology.

In the 1980s, French governments became acutely aware of threats to national sovereignty coming from two sides of the cultural industries sector. Firstly, the United States and Japan had not only established an unassailable lead in computing software and hardware, but by the mid-1980s Japan had also acquired a dominant world position in the field of audiovisual equipment (television sets, video recorders, hi-fi) and seemed about to attack the market for satellite reception equipment and high definition television (HDTV). Secondly, the United States had the world's most powerful programme production industry, and was seeking overseas markets for programmes (like *Dallas*) which had achieved profitability on the home market and so, as exports, could undercut European products.

French broadcasting policy was made in the context of these industrial and cultural challenges to national independence. The problem was how to reconcile on the one hand the promotion of French industrial competitiveness in terms of equipping the nation with the most modern broadcasting and communications infrastructure (thereby creating a large market for programmes) with, on the other hand, the aim of protecting French cultural identity by preventing foreign programmes flooding onto French screens. The task was not made easier by the growing adoption of economic liberalism in the world economy, which eventually seduced Mitterrand's socialists almost as much as the French right.

Initial developments in deregulating and expanding the supply of television in France, however, relied on traditional off-air or terrestrial broadcasting technology. The fourth, fifth and sixth channels were transmitted, like the first three channels, by Télédiffusion de France (TDF), the state-owned transmission company, as off-air channels, *'chaînes hertziennes'* (conventional ground-based transmitters, hertzian wave signals, and individual receiving aerials). This expansion of the supply of television programmes seemed bound to slow down consumer investment in new cable and satellite broadcasting technologies. The one technological novelty was Canal Plus's mode of financing as subscription television. It relies on encryption (scrambling) of the signal, requiring a special black-box decoder to view the picture. The renting of the decoder allows the collection of the subscription fee. Pursuing encrypted television technology was seen as developing a French high-tech product for export.

Pay-television is also the clearest indication of a new philosophy of broadcasting, and takes it into the marketplace. It is claimed that by creating a direct contractual link between viewer and broadcaster, viewers have an ability to express their preference for the type of programme they want in a way that, in a competitive environment, programme providers will act upon. It creates a 'market for programmes'.

Cable

A second new technology used to create a market for television programmes was in local cable television networks. With the exceptions of a nationally funded experiment in cabling in Biarritz and networks in five or six frontier towns, such as Metz, where far-sighted mayors had invested in them, cable television was almost unknown in France. In 1982 only 0.6 per cent of homes were cabled, and with 1970s copper co-axial cable technology at that. Belgium, on the other hand, had cabled as many as 90 per cent of homes. New fibre-optic cable technology, capable of sending a choice of over 100 different programmes to a user, in conjunction with micro-computer technology, was also able to offer interactive, two-way communications. In the framework of the strategic industrial aims mentioned above, an ambitious national cable plan was consequently set up in 1982, with the objective of cabling 6 million homes (nearly one-third of all households) by 1992.

It was a strategy that had industrial, cultural and political attractions to the Mitterrand government. It was ideologically attractive, since it offered not just a passive reception of television programmes, but allowed more choice and active involvement for the citizen. It was given added legitimacy through the socialists' emphasis on political, administrative and economic decentralization, intended to be 'la grande affaire du septennat': setting up of cabling systems was to be dependent on unique co-operation between France-Télécom and local authorities, newly empowered to decide their own local economic and political futures by the loi Defferre.

Economically, cable television was intended to be the incentive to set up France-Télécom's modern, national communications system, which would be made financially viable by a host of other interactive personal and commercial electronic data interchange services, such as tele-banking and tele-shopping, the electronic office, consultation of remote databases, and the videophone. In terms of economic and industrial strategy, demand for new French high-tech products at home and abroad (France had a lead in fibre-optic technology) was intended to counter American and Japanese competition, open up new markets for French electronics and telecommunications industries and therefore safeguard jobs.

The ambitious cable plan proved far less attractive to local authorities than central government had hoped. Despite state investment, the cabling of towns was three years behind schedule by 1990, by which time the demand for cable subscriptions had reached only a quarter of a million. The plan had suffered from the economic downturn of 1983, incoherence of policy by the socialists, changes of government and personal rivalries.

First of all, in simultaneously pursuing the *Minitel* videotex (viewdata) system, developed by the DGT using existing telephone lines, French governments separated the telematics market from the cable television market. *Minitel*, not a market-led project, but imposed by state planning, has become much more than a computerized telephone book, and has successfully created and satisfied a mass market for interactive information and communication services, with over 6 million terminals in use in the 1990s.

As regards broadcasting policy, successive decisions seemed alternately to favour either cable or satellite technology, or over-ambitiously to try to promote both. The cable plan was further undermined in 1984–85 by Mitterrand's decision to offer viewers three new off-air stations, two of which were free at point of consumption, which inevitably satisfied much of the demand for a wider choice of television.

Domestic programme production did not meet the cultural challenge of cable. Potential cable operators demanded foreign stations such as MTV on their networks to help the financial attractiveness of cable. So conflict emerged between supporters of a more liberal regulatory régime and those, putting cultural imperatives first, favouring the protection of cultural sovereignty through import quotas on foreign programmes and banning foreign stations.

Further erosion of the initial strategy came in 1984 when, for reasons of commercial viability, government allowed new cable systems the option of using a mix of the cheaper co-axial technology and fibre-optic cable, therefore ruling out full interactivity. Chirac went further along the deregulation route by handing over responsibility to private enterprise, ending France-Télécom's installation monopoly, and allowing private firms such as Lyonnaise des Eaux not only to construct city cable networks, but also to act as cable operators and even programme providers. This has given new impetus to cable. Many towns and cities have since invested in such market-led cable television networks. From 56 authorized sites in 1988, 282 networks were in service by 1994. By 1996 cable covered a potential 6.7 million homes, with almost 2 million actual subscribers over the 547 licensed networks (a penetration rate approaching 30 per cent). The largest new system, Paris Câble, offers 25 channels in all, including five foreign-language stations, the six national off-air channels, plus TV5 and RTL TV in French, the news channels LCI and Euronews, two premium film channels, a children's channel (Canal J), 1960s life-style programming on Canal Jimmy, a documentary channel (Planète), a local channel (Paris Première, owned by Lyonnaise communications), two music channels (MTV and Euromusique), two sports channels, and wide-screen options. The major difference between the type of programmes offered via the new media and those on conventional television is the number of thematically focused channels. This serving of specialized audiences is sometimes called 'narrowcasting'.

Local television

Some 40 local channels were being broadcast on city cable networks in 1996. A related development is the birth of local off-air commercial stations broadcasting for a few hours a day (for example Télé-Toulouse from 1988 and Télé Lyon Métropole), not forgetting local channels in the overseas *départements*. Limited local advertising revenue will, however, continue to restrict such developments, whereas nationwide audiences for focused channels catering for special interest groups or professional groups seem more promising.

Satellite

The other major new area of competition to terrestrial television, and indeed to cable, is direct broadcasting by satellite (DBS). Since the satellite footprint spills over national frontiers, national control of broadcasting is eroded, not to say destroyed, by foreign satellites. The state monopoly over television could not be pursued into the era of DBS. At best, regulation can be negotiated at European level. Its limitation for the viewer is that a fixed receiving dish can receive programmes usually from only one satellite system. However, satellite broadcasting can be seen as complementary to cable, since cable systems are used to distribute broadcasts emanating from several different satellites.

An early and successful attempt to use satellite broadcasting to promote the French language and culture in the world is TV5. Since 1985, this state-subsidized channel has been broadcasting via satellite, mainly to Europe, North America and North Africa, as an international collaborative project showing compilations from French, Belgian, Swiss and Quebec television. Its prime purpose is cultural rather than commercial: an arm of French cultural defence against the threat of American television programmes broadcast from 'Coca-Cola satellites'. It carries no advertising, and is mainly aimed at cable systems – it reaches over 21 million homes across Europe – but may be received as DBS.

TV5 is carried on a European satellite, Eutelsat, which is not exclusively French. Maintaining a national satellite construction, launching and management capacity is not only of industrial importance, but is also an element of national sovereignty, both for military purposes and because satellite technology is crucial to the strategic sector of telecommunications. Consequently, satellite television has been used by France in a context wider than broadcasting, not only, like TV5, for cultural policy or for industrial reasons, but also as part of European policy and to cement Franco-German relations.

Once France had been allocated a satellite position to cover western Europe by an international telecommunications agreement in 1977, TDF was given the go-ahead for a DBS project, in collaboration with West Germany. A five-channel French satellite (TDF1) and a German satellite were to be launched by the European rocket Ariane. The project was linked to the European cultural channel, La SEPT. A complication was competition (economic and cultural) from the American-built and Luxembourg-owned satellite Astra.

Another strategic European aspect of the project was the adoption of the European D2 MAC Packet transmission standard as a transitional stage towards HDTV, which France and the EC saw as a way of maintaining a competitive European manufacturing presence for the home electronics market in the face of Japanese and American competition.

The typically French, state-led technological *grand projet* was to suffer setbacks: multiplying terrestrial television stations in 1985 reduced the potential market for DBS; failure of the Ariane launch in 1985 put the project well behind schedule; early doubts were expressed by the DGT about obsolescent technology (the DGT favoured their own, low-powered Telecom satellites); the franchises for the satellite channels were re-allocated twice as governments came and went before broadcasting began in 1989; and international competition increased (potential operators, including Sky, were more attracted to Astra, launched in 1988, with 16 channels and lighter regulation).

In 1991 serious technical failures reduced the satellite's transmission capacity. Doubts about TDF1's commercial and technological viability caused other channels to pull out in favour of cable or other satellites. The final problem posed to the French government and the European Commission was that American advances in HDTV broadcasting using digital data compression made the European D2 MAC standard obsolete. In 1992 the *Cour des comptes* called the TDF1/TDF2 project *'un échec coûteux'*.

In the late-1990s French DBS television looks set to make a significant leap forward as private investment in digital television begins. Digital television will allow existing numbers of satellite channels to be multiplied almost ten-fold at lower cost and various forms of pay-television to operate using encryption technology: subscription channels, premium channels, pay-per-view, video-on-demand, and so on. Each programme provider, like BSkyB in Britain, will seek to offer a basket of channels. The main competitors on the French market are inevitably Canalsatellite, owned by Canal Plus, which has now plumped for the Astra satellite, and, on Eutelsat, TPS (a grouping of TF1, the CLT, M6, and France-Télévision that also aims to use the Lyonnaise des Eaux cable networks for distribution) and AB Sat (linked to the Dorothée empire). Each package of thematic channels will be separately marketed in competition with each other. Canalsatellite had begun operating a DBS service using old analog technology on France-Télécom satellites in 1992 and attracted 320,000 subscribers in four years, still well behind the UK, where the number of DBS dishes had reached 2.8 million by 1994.

In the 1990s, policy makers accepted that private enterprise could best be left to take the lead in digital television, and that cable and satellite reception are complementary and can carry the same channels to different geographical audiences. Since the TDF HDTV project was more technology-led than demand-led, there were always going to be unresolved problems regarding programmes and audience. The various commercial companies involved in television production and distribution seem by the late-1990s to have assembled enough French channels to make cable and satellite television attractive. The projected expansion of French digital channels now means there will probably be sufficient DBS supply to be able to compete with the dozens of non-French satellite channels already accessible from French territory. France may have lost the D2 MAC technology battle, but it has done the necessary to retain cultural sovereignty.

Video

Video cassettes are a further means of television programme distribution. The home video market has not developed in France as quickly as in the UK. Development was deliberately slowed down in the early 1980s when a special tax on video recorders was introduced in addition to other hindrances, such as routing all VCR imports through a small customs post in Poitiers, partly because the home manufacturers were not ready to compete with Japanese machines, and also to protect the other new French television media from competition. Chirac ended the tax in 1986 as another step in the direction of letting market forces prevail. By 1993, this market had become significant, with video recorders to be found in 62 per cent of French homes, and sales of 38 million pre-recorded and 93 million blank cassettes per year, plus 86 million pre-recorded cassettes hired annually. Sale and hire of videos is now far ahead of spending on cinema and equals that of television subscriptions (Canal Plus and cable) and the cost of the licence fee. Home consumption of the moving image has become a function of individual consumers' means and tastes, selecting from a variety of media.

CONCLUSION

New technologies, deregulation, market forces, globalization, sovereignty and cultural identity are key words in the media policy sector in France in the 1990s. The multiplication of television channels and radio stations seems to herald a new age of consumer choice in broadcasting, although commercial pressures are for a standardized, mass-market product in terms of programme. Into what was traditionally a state and public service monopoly until the 1980s have come major commercial firms and intensified competition for audiences and for advertising revenue. There has been a consequent erosion of the boundaries between broadcasting and such sectors as press and publishing, advertising, and micro-electronics: for example the publishing giants Hersant and Hachette maintain interests in French radio; the advertising firm Havas most notably has developed multi-media interests; the French electronics firm Thomson is exploiting new, potentially lucrative, but high-risk markets tied to the development of new products such as HDTV sets or fibre-optic cabling; important income for Aérospatiale and Arianespace derives from the launching of telecommunications satellites used for broadcasting. Neither the French state nor private enterprise can any longer consider broadcasting policy as an autonomous sector of decision making and investment. If a strength of French media policy has been their attempt to conceive it in a wider economic and technological context, it is only by policy makers accepting certain realities of the market that its implementation in the 1990s is becoming more coherent than in the 1980s.

Broadcasting is not only enmeshed into broader economic and industrial issues, it has also developed an irrevocably cross-national and European dimension. Canal Plus has been particularly successful in investing across the EU, while foreign firms attempting to buy into the French broadcasting market have not all been as successful as CLT.

In an era of global telecommunications, the new broadcasting media erode national cultural and economic sovereignty. As a reaction, concerns have arisen in France to protect French language and culture and therefore the national programme-making industry. The Balladur government was successful in 1994 in excluding broadcasting and cinema products from the worldwide GATT agreement on free trade. The Minister of Culture, J. Toubon, had argued for the necessary defence of French and European cultural interests against imports of American television programmes and films, the second highest American export earner in Europe. French multi-media groups have been built up in order to resist perceived threats from international (usually 'Anglo-Saxon') media conglomerates. The French state has helped Canal Plus's cross-national development and supported Hachette's (thwarted) ambitions to become a multi-media company of international proportions in publishing, radio and television. In the context of broadcasting's links with strategic issues of industrial and technological independence, France, as in other areas of policy, has seen its salvation, more enthusiastically than Britain, as lying in European co-operation, not only with Arte and TV5. Successive governments have supported the European Commission's desire to harmonize technical norms in order to compete against Japanese and American competition in the electronics industry, as well as the programme-making industry, hence the nationalized consumer electronics firm Thomson's involvement with Philips in the European HDTV standard in the Eureka programme, and support for the MEDIA 92 programme to help European television and cinema production. The French state is now taking a keen interest in promoting and attempting to control the implementation of an infrastructure to support a French information superhighway, through which broadcasting, telecommunications and computing will converge in the very different communications systems of the future. Completion of the national grid is due in 2015.

In the Fifth Republic, as political communication from de Gaulle to Chirac has accorded a privileged role to the medium of television, the French political class has traditionally been very sensitive to the media as a policy area. Under the impact of recent technological change and related economic, cultural and political issues, broadcasting is increasing in commercial and political significance. At the same time, the ability of the French state to control it has been diminishing, as a result of technological developments, but also through adoption, for ideological reasons, of greater deregulation and a free-market approach. In the light of these political, industrial, technological and cultural implications for French national identity, broadcasting is unlikely to fade as a controversial issue in France.

BIBLIOGRAPHY

Important specialist periodicals are *Dossiers de l'audiovisuel*, *Médiaspouvoirs*, and *La Lettre du CSA*. Relevant articles also appear in *European Journal of Communication*, *French Cultural Studies* and *Modern and Contemporary France*.

Important primary information is to be found in official reports and government publications, such as the Moinot (1981), Bredin (1985), Hoss (1989), Campet

(1994) and Théry (1994) reports and the annual report of the CSA, all published by the La Documentation française.

Albert, P., *Les Médias dans le monde*. Paris, Ellipses, 1994. A good short introduction, especially on France, covering press agencies, media in the industrialized world, the written press, radio and television.

Bamberger, M., *La Radio en France et en Europe*. Que sais-je? vol. 3218. Paris, PUF, 1997. Cross-national comparisons.

Barbrook, R., *Media Freedom*. London, Pluto Press, 1995. Well-informed, thematic treatment of French broadcasting history and recent changes to the PAF.

Bertrand, C.-J. (ed.), *Médias. Introduction à la presse, la radio et la télévision*. Paris, Ellipses, 1995. A good university media studies textbook, focusing on France.

Bourdon, J., *Haute fidélité. Pouvoir et télévision 1935–1994*. Paris, Seuil, 1994. Very good source book on policy making and relations of broadcasters and politics.

Brochand, C., *Economie de la télévision française*. Paris, Nathan, 1996. Detailed study.

Cayrol, R., *Les médias. Presse écrite, radio, télévision*. Paris, PUF (Thémis, science politique), 1991. Excellent source book.

Charon, J.-M. (ed.), *L'Etat des médias*. Paris, La Découverte-Mediaspouvoirs-CFPJ, 1991. Mosaic multi-authored study, with extensive bibliographies.

Les Chiffres clés de la radio. France 1996. Paris, INA-CSA (La Documentation française), 1996. Reliable source of indispensable information.

Les Chiffres clés de la télévision et du cinéma. Paris, La Documentation française, 1995. Regularly updated, reliable source of indispensable data.

Cojean, A., and Eskenazi, F., *FM, la folle histoire des radios libres*. Paris, Grasset, 1986. Two specialist journalists trace a lively history of early independent (and pirate) radio from 1977 to 1985.

Cortade, J.-E., *La Télévision française 1986–1992*. Que sais-je? vol. 2767. Paris, PUF, 1993. On the creation of the competitive model of television.

Coulomb-Gully, M., *Les Informations télévisées*. Que sais-je? vol. 2922. Paris, PUF, 1995. A historical analysis of French television news broadcasting.

Hare, G., 'The law of the jingle, or a decade of change in French radio'. In Chapman, R., and Hewitt, N. (eds), *Popular Culture and Mass Communication in Twentieth-Century France*. Lampeter, Edwin Mellen Press, 1992. Details the major changes in the 1980s.

Kuhn, R., *The Media in France*. London, Routledge, 1995. Very good, up-to-date overview, especially in relation to the state and policy making.

Lochard, G., and Boyer, H., *Notre écran quotidien. Une radiographie du télévisuel*. Paris, Dunod, 1995. Wide-ranging, up-to-date study.

Lunven, R., and Vedel, T., *La Télévision de demain: câble, satellite et TVHD en*

France et dans le monde. Communication médias. Paris, A. Colin, 1993. Reliable overview of new developments.

Mauriat, C., *La Presse audiovisuelle: 1993/1994*. Connaissance des médias. Paris, CNPJ, 1993. A short descriptive introduction to the institutions of radio and TV.

Mehl, D., *La Fenêtre et le miroir: la télévision et ses programmes*. Paris, Payot, 1992. Excellent study.

A well-stocked, specialist bookshop is La Librairie Tekhne, 7 rue des Carmes, 75005 Paris, tel. 01.43.54.70.84.

The author would like to acknowledge the support of the British Academy and Newcastle University Small Grants Schemes in the preparation of this chapter.

Index

With the improved layout of the text and highlighted subheadings this index is only selective.